Sino–Latin American
Economic Relations

SINO–LATIN AMERICAN ECONOMIC RELATIONS

He Li

New York
Westport, Connecticut
London

Copyright Acknowledgments

The author and publisher gratefully acknowledge permission to reprint extracts from the following:

Li, He, *Sino-Latin American Economic Relations: Recent Trends and Future Prospects*, Latin American Occasional Papers Series at the University of Massachusetts, no. 25 (Amherst: University of Massachusetts, 1990).

Li, He, ''China Tightens Relations with Cuba,'' *Cuba Update*, 12, no. 1-2 (Winter-Spring 1991), pp. 33, 56-57.

Latin America's New Internationalism: The End of Hemispheric Isolation, Roger Fontaine and James D. Theberge, eds. (Praeger Publishers, New York, 1976), pp. 160-61. Copyright © 1976 by Center for Strategic International Studies, Georgetown University. Reprinted with permission of the publisher.

Library of Congress Cataloging-in-Publication Data

Li, He.
    Sino-Latin American economic relations / He Li.
       p.   cm.
    Includes bibliographical references and index.
    ISBN 0-275-93759-3 (alk. paper)
    1. China—Foreign economic relations—Latin America. 2. Latin America—Foreign economic relations—China. I. Title.
HF1604.Z4L295   1991
337.5108—dc20   91-19434

British Library Cataloguing in Publication Data is available.

Library of Congress Catalog Card Number: 91-19434
ISBN: 0-275-93759-3

First published in 1991

Praeger Publishers, One Madison Avenue, New York, NY 10010
An imprint of Greenwood Publishing Group, Inc.

Printed in the United States of America

The paper used in this book complies with the Permanent Paper Standard issued by the National Information Standards Organization (Z39.48-1984).

10 9 8 7 6 5 4 3 2 1

Contents

Contents

Tables and Figures

TABLES

vii

FIGURES

Abbreviations

APRA	*Alianza Popular Revolucionario Americana* (Peru)
BOC	Bank of China
CCP	Chinese Communist Party
CCPIT	China Council for the Promotion of International Trade
CEPAL	*Comisión Económica para América Latina*
FBIS	Foreign Broadcast Information Service (U.S.)
FMLN	Farabundo Martí National Liberation Front (El Salvador)
GATT	General Agreement on Tariffs and Trade
GDP	Gross Domestic Product
GNP	Gross National Product
IDB	Inter-American Development Bank
IMF	International Monetary Fund
LDCs	Less-Developed Countries
MFA	Multi-Fibre Arrangement
MOFERT	The Ministry of Foreign Economic Relations and Trade (China)
NCNA	Xinhua (New China) News Agency
NIEO	New International Economic Order
NICs	Newly Industrializing Countries
OAS	Organization of American States
OECD	Organization for Economic Cooperation and Development
PCCh	Communist Party of Chile
PRC	People's Republic of China

PRI	*Partido Revolucionario Institucional* (Mexico)
SELA	*Sistema Económico Latinoamericano*
SITC	Standard International Trade Classification
UN	United Nations
UNCTAD	United Nations Conference on Trade and Development
UNDP	United Nations Development Program

Acknowledgments

This study is the outcome of several years of research in China, Latin America, and the United States, especially at the University of Texas at Austin. I wish to express my gratitude to Dr. Frank Tomasson Jannuzi for his guidance and valuable suggestions in this study. Further thanks go to Dr. Henry A. Dietz, Dr. Lawrence S. Graham, Dr. Henry Selby, and Dr. Jonathan C. Brown for their helpful comments and sincere suggestions. I would like, in particular, to express my deep appreciation to Dr. William P. Glade for his support and encouragement. With his help, I was able to surmount numerous difficulties and avoid many pitfalls. Thanks also go to Professor G. Pope Atkins for his comments on the draft of this book.

I am very grateful to the Ford Foundation for generous individual grants for three years in support of my graduate study at the University of Texas at Austin and the Tinker Foundation for a field research grant for work in Latin America, which enabled me to visit Mexico City, Lima, and Santiago and collect materials for this book. China's State Education Commission and the Chinese Academy of Social Sciences provided me with the necessary assistance to conduct field studies in Beijing. Most of all, I would like to express thanks to the many authorities in China, Chile, Mexico, and Peru who generously shared their information and insights with me. Interviews with Chinese officials and scholars, who must remain anonymous, were especially useful.

Many friends in Latin America, China, and the United States, through their interest and encouragement, cemented my commitment to this project; I thank them for their kindness over the years. And finally I also offer special thanks to my wife, Naifang, and my son, Bowen, for their patience and affection, which made the preparation of this study possible.

Despite all the help I have received from many sources, I alone am responsible for the contents and any errors this study might contain.

1

Introduction

Sino–Latin American relations date back to ancient times. Historical records suggest that the Chinese and Indians are cognate races, sharing a common origin long before the discovery of the Americas.[1] Historically, trade relations between China and Latin America have been weak and sporadic. Except for the period of the *Manila Galleon* trade,[2] the movement of people from China to Latin America far outweighed the importance of the shipment of goods. In contrast, well-established trade relations between Latin America and the West date to the colonial period.

With the formation of the People's Republic of China (PRC) in 1949, trade relations between China[3] and Latin America were further constrained by complex ideological and political factors. During the pre-Cuban Revolution period, Beijing (Peking) had neither the opportunity nor the incentive for involvement in Latin America. Only in 1960 did China establish diplomatic relations with Cuba, the first such PRC connection with Latin America. Ten years later, Chile under Salvador Allende became the second Latin American state to establish diplomatic ties with China. After the PRC's entry into the United Nations (UN) in late 1971, Chinese diplomatic representation in Latin America increased, and by 1978 China had embassies in twelve Latin American countries. This paralleled the growth of Chinese economic activities in Latin America. Until the Chinese "open-door policy" in 1978, however, the political and economic ties between the two regions were very limited.

Since the late 1970s, Sino–Latin American economic relations have undergone a radical change. Economic interactions have intensified; and financial, commercial, investment, and technical ties have been established

1

where, in general, little existed before. In recent years, economic relations between Latin American countries and China have developed steadily, concurrently exhibiting marked tendencies toward greater diversification. By the end of 1990, China had exchanged diplomatic relations with
seventeen governments in Latin America. These nations account for 90
percent of the total population and 96 percent of the total area of Latin
America. China now has trade relations with all the countries and regions

Figure 1.1
PRC Trade with Latin America, 1950–1989

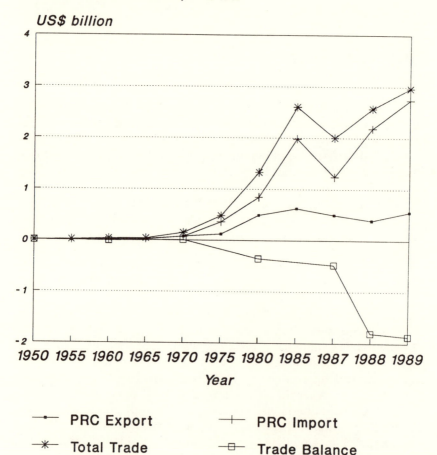

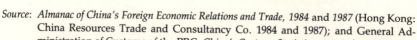

Source: *Almanac of China's Foreign Economic Relations and Trade, 1984* and *1987* (Hong Kong:
China Resources Trade and Consultancy Co. 1984 and 1987); and General Administration of Customs of the PRC, *China's Customs Statistics*, part 1, for *1988, 1989*,
and *1990* (Hong Kong: Economic Information Agency, 1988, 1989, and 1990).

in Latin America. As shown in Figure 1.1, the trade volume between China and Latin America jumped to $3 billion in 1989, an all-time high, compared with only $2 million in 1950.[4] This book focuses primarily on China's relations with Brazil, Argentina, Cuba, Chile, Mexico, and Peru because the volume of trade between these six countries and China usually makes up 85 percent—and in some years even more than 90 percent—of the total trade volume between the PRC and Latin America (see figure 1.2).

PURPOSE AND SCOPE OF WORK

Although the literature on China's and Latin America's external relations is extensive, very little scholarly research on Sino–Latin American economic ties has been undertaken. The recent expansion in economic exchange between China and Latin America has not received adequate attention in academic institutions or research centers and remains largely unexplored, probably because of the lack of available data, the little contact between China and Latin America until recent years, and the low priority given to the region by Beijing in the past.[5]

This study endeavors to compensate for the above-mentioned deficiency by providing a systematic assessment of the basic aspects of these changes in economic connections, and to analyze main causes of such changes

Figure 1.2
PRC Major Trading Partners in Latin America, 1989

Source: General Administration of Customs of the PRC, *China's Customs Statistics, 1990*, part 1 (Hong Kong: Economic Information Agency, 1990).

as well as to discuss problems and prospects of the emerging relations. Admittedly, this study does not explore all aspects of these links; rather, it focuses on major areas in which Sino–Latin American relations have experienced a significant expansion.

Four areas of Sino–Latin American economic relations are examined here: trade, aid, technology transfer, and investment. Strictly speaking, the main focus of this study is on Latin American trade relations with China, as their economic interactions in other areas, such as financial and technical cooperation, have not yet developed to a significant level, although they are on the rise.

This study is an integrated analysis of economic and political factors that together determine Sino–Latin American economic ties. Politics and economics are interwoven strands in the fabric of contemporary international economic relations. Economic relations among states, even for those functioning on liberal market forces, are seldom confined to the simple exchange of goods and services. In particular, the primary role of politics cannot be ruled out of any discussion of economic relations between a socialist economy and a market economy, as both sides tend to mix politics with trade. Indeed, in China's contacts with Latin America, political and economic motives are closely linked. Neither economic nor political determinants alone can explain events successfully. Therefore, an integrated approach forms the basis for this study. In this study, I will attempt to answer the following questions:

1. What reasons account for the recent rapid development of Sino–Latin American economic interaction? To what extent do political considerations drive relations between China and its major trading partners in the region? And in what measure are these relations shaped by economic factors? What is the role of the international context—the structure of the world economy—in shaping relations between China and Latin America?

2. Has the mix or combination of factors, both internal and international as well as economic and political, varied from period to period? Does the recent period of "normalization" following the dislocation of the Cultural Revolution differ significantly from relations prior to the Cultural Revolution?

3. What are the complementarities and conflicts in the economic relations between China and Latin America? Will China increasingly become a competitor vis-à-vis Latin American states in the world market?

4. What is the likelihood of growth in direct investment between the two regions? What are the prospects for technology transfer between the two? Why has appropriate technology become a driving force behind the growth of Sino–Latin American business relations?

5. What other factors stand in the way of a greater expansion of economic interaction? How do Latin American policymakers view the

potential for economic change with China? What is the Chinese government's intention with respect to deepening and broadening relations with Latin American nations?

6. What has been the impact of other countries on the relations between China and Latin America? How does the new relationship between China and Latin America affect the United States?

This study breaks new ground in several respects. First, it contributes to the literature of South-South cooperation (or collective self-reliance). It brings South-South cooperation into a sharper focus in a case study that investigates the burgeoning relationship between China and Latin America. Second, the data used in this study have not been systematically analyzed in previous works. Few authors have tried to examine the economic and political ideas underlying the recent boom in Beijing–Latin American relations. This study is one of the first attempts to utilize the Chinese government's newly published economic data. More importantly, this work derives from the author's extensive series of interviews carried out in the PRC between December 1988 and January 1989, as well as in Mexico, Peru and Chile during the summer of 1989. Finally, the study enriches our understanding of the implications of emerging Sino–Latin American relations for long-term U.S. interests in the region and explores the prospects and implications of such relations in the 1990s.

To understand the role of Chinese relations with Latin American countries, it is better to know the rationale behind them. In 1990, Chinese president Yang laid down four principles for Sino–Latin American relations:

First, China will establish and develop friendly cooperative relations with all Latin American countries on the basis of the Five Principles of Peaceful Coexistence. Second, bilateral trade and economic and technological cooperation should be expanded on the basis of equality and mutual benefit, for the purpose of meeting each other's needs, and by way of learning from each other's strong points to offset weakness. Third, both China and Latin American countries should respect each other's tradition and concepts of values, learn and draw on each other's experience, strengthen people-people contacts, promote understanding and friendship and develop various forms of cultural exchanges on a broad basis. Fourth, China and Latin American countries should make joint efforts for establishing new international political and economic orders through mutual support, earnest consultation and closer cooperation in world affairs.[6]

Sino–Latin American economic relations are analyzed in the light of China's declared principles. In this context, the nature of China's aid to Latin America is examined. The question examined here is: In what way has Chinese aid differed from that of the West and of the Soviet Union? An attempt has been made to assess whether Chinese-Latin American trade is different from colonial and subsequently neocolonial patterns of trade. This study also identifies theoretical approaches behind Chinese policy toward Latin America, such as the theory of South-South coopera-tion. In particular, interactions between China and Latin America are analyzed from an international economic and a political perspective.

To keep the study within manageable proportions, the author has deliberately eliminated all but the most cursory treatment of Sino–Latin American relations prior to 1949, when the Chinese Communists came to power. This study focuses only on a few strands of that history, those that have especially influenced China's economic relations with Latin America.

This book consists of nine chapters, beginning with the introduction. To facilitate tracing and analyzing Sino–Latin American trade relations, Chapters 2 through 5 break trade relations into four major eras (1949–1958; 1959–1969; 1970–1977; 1978–1990). Within each epoch, trade trends, geographic patterns, and commodity composition receive special atten-tion. Within each time frame, there is an analysis of both international (global and subregional) and domestic factors that have shaped economic relations between China and Latin America. For example, a significant expansion in the relationship after 1978 is attributed to such factors as China's dynamic economic growth and the open-door policy, a growing Latin American desire to diversify external relations, and Beijing's rap-prochement with Washington and Moscow in recent years.

Chapter 2 focuses on the period from the founding of the PRC in 1949 up to 1959. These years marked anniversaries of two events of major im-portance in the developing world: 1949, the birth of the PRC; and 1958, the end of Castro's successful "armed struggle" against the Batista regime. Chapter 3 covers the years 1959–1969. After Castro took over the state power in Cuba, Sino–Cuban relations developed rapidly; however, after an open rift between Beijing and Havana in 1966, bilateral trade rela-tions diminished. During this period, China had strictly limited trade with other Latin American countries. Latin American states viewed China as a distant power of little direct consequence to the region.[7]

Chapter 4 begins at the end of Beijing self-imposed isolation in 1970 until the initiation of an open-door policy in 1978. The 1970s witnessed a flourishing of diplomatic relations and economic exchange between China and Latin America. By the end of 1977 China had full diplomatic relations with twelve Latin American nations. The move to establish for-mal state-to-state relations, accompanied by a growth in bilateral trade and economic cooperation, was an indication of fundamental change in PRC foreign policy, not only in Latin America but on a world scale. This was a period of transition in China's international relations from the radical "revolutionary" line of 1960 to 1970, and the more practical "modernization and opening to the outside world" line that began in 1978.

Chapter 5 covers the period from the beginning of the open-door policy in 1978 until 1990, during which time Sino–Latin American relations grew to an unprecedented level. Trade between China and Latin America rose at an extraordinary rate, to billions of dollars annually. In addition, China increased its economic activities in Latin America by supplying fuels and manufactured goods and in return importing grain and mineral products. Thus, China has emerged as an increasingly important trading partner within the region.

Chapter 6 explores how joint ventures have become a critical dimension in China's relations with Latin America. The chapter also evaluates the Chinese aid program, elaborating on the pattern of aid utilization as well as the nature of Chinese aid. The focus of Chapter 7 is on technology transfer between China and Latin America. Along with an analysis of factors contributing to these developments, the chapter includes a discussion on the potential and prospects of such cooperation. Chapter 8 reviews the major issues and constraints in Beijing–Latin American relations and also discusses their causes.

Chapter 9, forecasts future trends and developments and evaluates their implications. Some see China as a newly industrializing country (NIC) that is rapidly upgrading its production technology and aggressively seeking international markets, becoming another, potentially more powerful Japan.[8] The Chinese presence has been growing significantly in Latin America, especially in the past decade. Yet China is a regional power with global strategic significance and political influence. Its basic security and economic interests are largely concentrated in the Asian-Pacific region. The most likely scenario is that if China persists on its open-door and reform policy course and is successful, it will become an important trading partner of Latin America in the next two or three decades.

Finally, Chapter 10 summarizes the findings and draws general conclusions. This chapter examines three external actors that influenced emerging Sino–Latin American relations, namely, the United States, the Soviet Union, and Taiwan. It has been found that China's present involvement in Latin America has been largely compatible with Western interests and is likely to remain so for the immediate future, provided that Beijing continues its current policy in support of economic development and regional stability. The chapter concludes that because Beijing's influence in Latin America is limited and its economic resources are in short supply, China's impacts on U.S. relations with Latin America should not be overestimated. China's present role in Latin America will continue to grow, but China will not be in a position to challenge the U.S. role in the region very soon.

This study shows that mutually beneficial economic ties have served as the engine pulling Sino–Latin American relations forward. Given the potential of both sides, one might reasonably expect China to become an important trading partner of Latin America in the years to come. However, the prospects for greater economic interaction will largely depend on how China's economic reforms continue to unfold and how Latin America copes with its recession.

Throughout this work, I rely mainly on official data from China's statistical authorities, since data from other sources are fragmented. This work also leans heavily on the specialized data and articles on Latin American trade appearing in such periodicals as *Direction of International Trade, Economic Survey of Latin America, CEPAL Review, World Development Report*, and other studies published by the Economic Commission for Latin America and the Caribbean (ECLAC), the United Nations Conference on Trade and Development (UNCTAD), along with many monographs and articles on Latin America, and press dispatches. The author has made full use of the material available in the Spanish and Chinese languages. The translations of both languages are mine.

There are two appendices. Appendix A contains a list of Sino–Latin American trade treaties and agreements. Appendix B is a list of major Sino–Latin American joint ventures in Latin America. The pinyin romanization system (Chinese phonetic alphabet) is used for Chinese names throughout this work.[9] Occasionally, the Wade-Giles transliteration is shown in parentheses when the older proper name may be more familiar to the reader. Throughout this study Chinese names are presented with the surname first. This is also the case for Chinese authors of English-language works. Purely as a literary convenience, I employ such terms as *the People's Republic of China, PRC*, or *Beijing* as interchangeable designations for the regime in mainland China. It should be noted that all monetary figures used in this study refer to U.S. dollar values (except where otherwise stated).

NOTES

1. For a detailed discussion on the early contacts between the Chinese and the indigenous peoples of Latin America, see Henriette Mertz, *Pale Ink: Two Ancient Records of Chinese Exploration in America*, 2d ed. (Chicago: Swallow Press, 1972) and Francisco A. Loayza, *Chinos llegaron antes que Colón* (Lima, Peru: D. Miranda, 1948).

2. In 1579, the Spanish government officially sanctioned Sino–Philippine trade with New Spain, Peru, Guatemala, and Tierra Firme. The *Manila Galleons* began their movement across the Pacific, flooding the Spanish colonies with goods from China and other oriental lands. The trade between Manila and Acapulco, Mexico, continued for more than 250 years.

3. The terms *China* and *Chinese* throughout this study refers to the People's Republic of China, unless otherwise specified.

4. *Beijing Review*, 33, no. 22 (May 28–June 3, 1990), p. 34.

5. Until the early 1980s most information on Chinese foreign trade was classified.

Traditionally, only a few selected data series have been published by the Chinese authorities. The situation is changing, however, and more data are being released year by year. Despite China's increased openness, available official information is still inadequate for the task at hand.

6. *Beijing Review*, 33, no. 22 (May 28–June 3, 1990), pp. 8–9.

7. Robert A. Manning, "The Third World Looks at China," in *China and the Third World: Champion or Challenger?* ed. Lillian Craig Harris and Robert L. Worden (Dover, Mass.: Auburn House, 1986), p. 151.

8. The *Economist* noted that if the respective growth rates of the major powers during the 1980s were sustained for four decades, by 2030 China would be the world's biggest economy. For details, see the *Economist*, March 12, 1988, p. 61.

9. The system of romanization of Chinese characters used in this book is the pinyin system, which is used by the People's Republic of China and, increasingly, by scholars in the West.

2

Early Development of Sino–Latin American Economic Relations: 1949–1958

Although there had been recorded contacts between China and Latin America long before, they were intermittent and casual until the founding of the PRC.[1] Before the establishment of the new China in 1949, relations between China and Latin America were solely a matter of emigration. Even then, relations were very limited. Until the Cuban Revolution in 1959 Latin America was virtually terra incognita as far as China's initial political and economic interests were concerned. During these years, the Beijing's alliance with Moscow was the centerpiece of China's foreign policy. At the same time, the United States pursued a "containment" policy toward both the USSR and the PRC. This policy sought to take maximum advantage of U.S. air and sea power, and also of U.S. economic strength, to defend what was called the free world. Under such a situation, Latin America watched the rising tide of Communist revolution in China initially with disinterest and then with concern. After China's entry into the Korean War, Latin America decided to adopt a cautious but passive policy of nonrecognition toward the new government in Beijing.

With official diplomacy so circumscribed, China concentrated on so-called cultural diplomacy and tried to build up nongovernmental trade relations with various Latin American countries. China expected that separation of politics and economics, and nonofficial trade, would lead to closer state-to-state relations. In this endeavor, China had some success during this period. Nongovernmental trade was established with the region, and trade delegations were exchanged. Although the trade missions had no "official capacity," it had government blessing and support. Apart from on-the-spot trade deals, missions paved the way for a rapid increase of two-way trade during the following years.

This chapter examines the early linkage between China and Latin America from 1949, the birth of the PRC, to 1958, the year before Castro and his guerrillas marched triumphantly into Havana. It explores some changes in international and domestic systems that affected the relationship. In doing this, it is necessary to outline the international environment Latin America faced in the early postwar period. It is also necessary to look at economic conditions and political circumstances of the PRC during its early years. Thus, this chapter falls into three parts. Part 1 deals with the situation in Latin America during the early postwar period. Part 2 looks at China during the same period. Part 3 discusses the economic ties between the two regions. The last part also explains why initial Chinese efforts to establish close economic ties with Latin America failed.

LATIN AMERICA IN THE POSTWAR POLITICAL AND ECONOMIC SYSTEM

In the 1950s, Latin American countries were agrarian economies, with agricultural products being their major commodities. Sugar, coffee, cocoa, wheat, coconuts, rubber, bananas and palms were their main crops. The exception is Venezuela and Mexico, both famous for their petroleum resources. Foreign capital controlled most of the export commodities of these countries but contributed little to the national economies of the host countries. Most Latin American countries lacked necessary capital and technology to explore their rich resources. Further, their economic growth was very slow, with per capita income of about $300. In some nations, such as in Bolivia, the average per capita income was only $100. In terms of foreign trade, Latin America was sucked into the U.S. commercial system, for the main destination of their exports was the United States.

For two decades after China became a People's Republic, in 1949, twenty formally independent Latin American countries refused to recognize it. Anti-communist governments were suspicious of Chinese activities in the region and kept their distance from China because of several factors, including the considerable geographical distance separating the two regions, compulsions of national interest, consideration of expediency, and ideological hostility, in addition to concern for regime security and the international environment.

The limitations imposed upon Beijing–Latin American relations can be analyzed systematically in terms of two external sources of pressure. The first source was the United States, which determined the destiny of Latin America until recent years. Under the charter of the Organization of American States (OAS) in 1948, Latin American relations with Washington shifted to what Celso Furtado calls "the Doctrine of Limited Sovereignty."[2] The hegemony of the United States placed Latin America in a special position, compared to other developing areas. This hegemony seems inescapable, and Latin America could do little except carry out national policies most advantageous to the United States. In 1951 Stalin, denouncing the exclusion of the PRC from the United Nations, berated the twenty Latin American republics for being the "most solid and obedient army of the United States.[3] Throughout the 1950s, Latin American policy toward China was a simple extension of Secretary of State John Foster Dulles's anti-China containment policy. The United States-inspired trade boycott against China during and after the Korean War was accepted in principle by most Latin American countries. When the United States and China were at war in Korea, Latin American countries stood side by side with the United States, and 3,200 Colombian soldiers participated in the Korean War.[4] Latin American countries assumed a pro–United States and anticommunism stance in their foreign policy. As a result, China and the Latin American countries found themselves in two opposing camps.

The second source of pressure was Taiwan. The United States is the only Western power that has consistently supported Taiwan for over four decades since 1949. During this prolonged period of U.S. assistance and protection Taiwan has been able to construct and consolidate its national and international development. Under the auspices of the United States, Taiwan has developed close ties with Latin American countries bilaterally.[5] Since losing mainland China, Taiwan sought to win the support of the Latin American countries because these twenty countries represented a powerful bloc at the United Nations, constituting half of the forty votes cast in support of Taiwan.[6]

United States hegemony over Latin American countries ensured their continued support for its hostile policy toward China. Latin American voting patterns on the UN question concerning the PRC between 1950 and 1971 verify this phenomenon. Except Cuba (since 1960), Latin American governments followed the U.S. line of anti-PRC votes until 1970, when for the first time Chile sided with Cuba. Until this time, the Latin American nations voted in a nearly uniform bloc against resolutions favoring the seating of the PRC. Other than Cuba and Chile in 1970, the uniformity had been broken only by a few abstentions over the twenty-one-year period of attempts to seat the PRC in the United Nations.[7]

In general, the political atmosphere of the 1950s made impossible any big development of Sino–Latin American links. The situation deteriorated even further with the outbreak of the Korean War.

THE PRC IN THE POSTWAR INTERNATIONAL POLITICAL AND ECONOMIC SYSTEM

The Chinese economy presented a sharp contrast to the economies of Latin America. China is a continent-sized country with a large population. Before the 1980s the Chinese economy was inward-looking in its orientation, a feature due partly to its physical size, partly to its economic policy. Its economy is inherently less dependent on external economic operations and tends to have a higher degree of self-sufficiency. During the 1950s and 1960s, the total value of foreign trade was only about 2 percent of the gross national product (GNP).[8] The figure was among the lowest in the Third World and certainly well below the figures of Latin America. This does not imply that foreign trade is not important to the economic planning of China. On the contrary, as one China expert has pointed out, foreign trade has played a "very significant role both in maintaining stability and in contributing to growth" in China even at a time when trade was quantitatively small.[9]

The China of 1949 was impoverished and in economic disarray after years of foreign invasion and civil war, and it was known as a backward, agrarian society with very little industry. After the founding of the PRC, the Chinese leadership was concerned above all with ensuring national security, consolidating power, and developing the economy. In the late 1940s, Mao Zedong (Mao Tse-tung) theorized that the world consisted of a capitalist system, led by Washington, and a socialist system, led by Moscow. Between them there was an intermediate zone of conflict that China wanted to avoid for the time being. Thus the PRC would "lean to one side"—the socialist side.

On the other hand, during the early years of the new regime, China was too busy with other matters to think much about Latin America. China showed little interest in Latin America and the Caribbean, the part of the world that is most distant from China, and thus most remote from China's security concerns. As far as China's trade was concerned, Latin America was not regarded as a primary target for intensive attention. In fact, the Ministry of Foreign Trade[10] did not have a subdivision for trade with the Latin American region until the 1960s.[11] Beijing generally assumed a low profile in this region, although it did try to establish friendly ties with established governments to counter the White House's efforts to isolate China.

In sum, relations between China and Latin America from the establishment of the PRC to the early 1970s were doomed to be weak, even virtually nonexistent. The hegemony of the United States in Latin America during this period was supreme. At the same time, Western embargoes were disrupting China's trade links with the West and Latin America, compelling it willy-nilly to rely more on the Soviet bloc.[12]

NONGOVERNMENTAL TRADE

The leaders who governed China during the early years of the PRC were revolutionaries, but they were also pragmatic. They did not reject relations with Latin America on ideological grounds. On the contrary, they sought relations that would promote Chinese national interests. The principal PRC objectives toward Latin America during the 1950s were to weaken their ties with the United States, to gain greater influence on their governments, and ultimately to establish official relations with them. Trade was used as a means toward these ends. Such trade relations were characterized as nongovernmental trade, for trade negotiations between the interested parties usually took place in the absence of formal diplomatic framework. Sometimes, as in the case of China and Chile, the method used was like an agreement between two central banks, which did not vary substantially from an agreement signed between governments. In other cases—such as those of China and Argentina—intercompany agreements were made. In the 1950s, China's trade with all Latin American countries totaled only $38.8 million. And of that total, China's imports accounted for $37.5 million.[13] Officially, most Latin American countries had no record of trade with Communist China until 1970. Not surprisingly, a survey by the UN Economic Commission for Latin America (ECLA) considered that, practically, China had no trade relations with Latin America.[14] Although many Latin American governments viewed trade as a vehicle for "Communist subversion" and imposed a strict ban on the imports of Chinese products, there was no lack of sale of Chinese-made products in Latin America even in the early 1950s.

The Latin American countries that carried on the greater part of the trade with China were Uruguay, Argentina, and Chile. From 1950 through 1959, almost 70 percent of China's trade with Latin America was conducted with these three countries. Latin America's most important exports to China were primary products, with a heavy concentration in just a few categories such as cotton, wool, and meat. The annual average import value was $3 million. The export value was only $1 million for the whole decade.[15] In 1959, when Sino–Latin American trade had not yet reached the governmental level, the trade value stood at $7.69 million, nearly four times that of 1950.[16]

Uruguay

Uruguay was China's most important trading partner in Latin America during this period. In the 1950s, Uruguay exported $14.89 million to China. This represented 40 percent of total Latin American exports to China during that period. Sino-Uruguayan trade officially began in 1955 when the then Uruguayan consul in Hong Kong went to Beijing, met with leading Chinese foreign trade officials, and signed a trade accord with the China National Animal Products Corporation.[17] Uruguay's trade was increasing, while that of Argentina was decreasing after the fall of Perón in 1955. Uruguayan exports to China rose from $1.35 million in 1955 to $6.15 million in 1959. Nonetheless, very few imports were bought by Uruguay from China. The large increase of trade was all almost entirely accounted for by Uruguay's sales of wool to China. Although exports reached a high level in the 1950s, during the following two decades there was very little trade between the two countries.

Argentina

Argentina was an important trading partner for China in the early 1950s. As early as 1950, two-way trade with China reached $2 million, accounted for virtually all of the Latin American trade with China in that year. Argentina was the first Latin American country to establish direct nongovernmental trade relations with China when, in 1953, the Melati S.A. began contacting officials of the China import and export corporation in Berlin about wheat export.[18] In 1954, a group of seventeen representatives of Argentine industrial and business circles visited China and had talks with Chinese counterparts. Before they left, they issued a joint statement with the China Council for the Promotion of International Trade (CCPIT), expressing the sincere wish of both parties to expand trade. With the visit to Beijing by an Argentine "industrial and commercial delegation" at the invitation of the CCPIT, a "good basis had been laid for future development of trade between China and Argentina," according to the New China News Agency (NCNA). The visit of the Argentine delegation semiofficially marked the first contact between Beijing and a South American country.

In June 1955, at Argentina's invitation, representatives of the CCPIT attended the second annual meeting of its Argentine counterpart in Buenos Aires and made valuable contacts with representatives of Argentine financial, industrial, and commercial worlds. In 1957, a group of officials of the People's Bank of China visited Argentina and held talks with officials of the Argentine Ministry of Industry and Commerce and the director and general manager of the Central Bank.[19]

From year to year, the absolute amount of trade between Argentina and China fluctuated. In 1950 Argentina's two-way trade with China reached about $2 million, falling to almost nothing in 1952. In 1954 and 1955 Argentina was under the leadership of Perón. Therefore, in these two years, Argentine trade with China rose perceptibly. The rapid decrease in trade relations in 1956 continued to the 1957 low. This was due in large part to the fact the Argentine Trade Promotion Institute (*Instituto Argentino de Promoción de Intercambio*) was abolished right after Perón was disposed. With that, no direct means then existed by which private importers could be induced to purchase goods from the Soviet bloc (including China).[20]

Chile

China did not have diplomatic ties with Chile until 1970. However, lack of diplomatic relations did not prevent commercial ties from developing. The Chinese interest in obtaining Chilean copper and Chile's desire to sell its products sometimes outweighed political aversion. In June 1959, Guillermo del Pedregal, former vice-president of Chile, visited China to foster the trade relations between two countries. In his speech at Beijing University, he pointed out that

the purpose of my China visit is to try to sell copper to China directly. Chile also produces saltpetre and nitrogenous fertilizer. China needs fertilizer and we want to sell these fertilizers to China. These fertilizers are very suitable to China. We can trade saltpetre for China's tea. . . . I hope the trade between our two countries could be further developed, it is because without closer trade ties, the friendship between our two peoples cannot be consolidated.[21]

Although the PRC and Chile did not have state-to-state relations, they concluded a trade agreement on October 27, 1952, the PRC's first with a Latin American country. The only information available is that it was signed by a "representative of the Chinese National Import and Export Company, and a Chilean delegate to the Peace Conference of the Asian and Pacific region, a representative of a Sino-Chilean Trade Corporation."[22] A formal link was not made until 1957, when a delegate from the People's Bank of China visited Chile in the course of a tour of Latin American states and thus paved the way for future contacts. It is believed the mission also negotiated a contract for a Chilean export of goods valued at $2 million to China during 1957–1958.[23]

Besides these two agreements, China made a third commercial contact with Chile at a trade fair held in Guanzhou (Canton) in November 1958. The Canton Fair,[24] which the Chinese government claimed to be the largest of its kind ever held in China, invited about forty countries, including Chile.[25] Overall, Sino-Chilean commercial relations developed sporadically with minor trade in the 1950s.

SUMMARY

From the materials covered in this chapter, one can draw certain conclusions. First, political factors dominated Sino–Latin American relations during the 1949–1958 period. Under the cold war climate, for ten years (from 1949 to 1958) the PRC was not recognized by any country in Latin America. Beijing perceived of Latin America as within the U.S. economic and political "sphere of influence." United States policy toward Latin America determined in part the course of Sino–Latin American economic relations.

Second, the PRC in its earlier years was preoccupied with internal political and economic affairs and was unwilling to confront the United States in its "backyard." Until well into the 1960s, Chinese leaders did not feel they had to pay much attention to Latin America. Except for the Cuban Revolution, in 1959, nothing much happened there that was considered of international importance. In the absence of significant political and economic relations with most countries, the Chinese long relied heavily on cultural (or people-to-people) diplomacy in their efforts to become known in Latin America.[26]

Third, from 1950 through 1958, the Sino–Latin American economical relations were sporadic rather than consistent and confined to only a few countries. Latin America played only a marginal role in China's foreign trade. In addition to the adverse political atmosphere, this was also a result of a low level of complementarity between the economies of China and the Latin American countries. During the immediate postwar period, both regions were largely agricultural societies, and therefore they had little to exchange.

Fourth, although Latin American governments imposed strict control over sales of strategic materials, the PRC managed to have nongovernmental trade relations with several Latin American countries. Nevertheless, trade relations with most Latin American countries were not established until two decades later. The trade was overwhelmingly in Latin American favor, owing to massive Chinese demands for cotton, wool, and meat. Chinese exports to the regions were statistically naught.

In brief, the low level of bilateral trade reflects not only the backward state of economy of both regions but also the Chinese alliance with the Soviet bloc, Latin America's extremely close ties with the United States, and Latin American fears of Communist penetration in the region. During the 1949–1958 period, trade relations were low key. A move in the direction of greater bilateral trade was just beginning.

NOTES

1. A more in-depth analysis of this process may be found in Felipe Pardinas, *Relaciones diplomáticas entre México y China: 1898–1948* (México: Secretaria de Relaciones Exteriores, 1982).

2. Celso Furtado, *Obstacles to Development in Latin America* (Garden City, N.Y.: Anchor Books, 1970), chap. 1.

3. Quoted in Nicola Miller, *Soviet Relations with Latin America, 1959–1987* (Cambridge: Cambridge University Press, 1989), p. 6.

4. Russell W. Ramsey, "The Colombian Battalion in Korea and Suez," *Journal of Inter-American Studies*, 9, no. 4, (July 1967), pp. 541–60, and Man-Shik Min, "Korean–Latin American Relationships," *Korea and World Affairs*, 4, no. 2 (Summer 1980), pp. 323–24.

5. From 1951 to 1965, the Nationalist regime received a total of almost $1.5 billion in U.S. economic aid (in addition to $2.5 billion in U.S. military assistance). Annual obligations average almost $100 million, about $80 million over the eighteen-year period 1951–1968. On a yearly average, U.S. aid amounted to $10 per capita, 6.4 percent of Taiwan's GNP, 34 percent of its gross investment, and covered 91 percent of its aggregate net import surplus of goods and services. For details, see Lung-chu Chen and Harold D. Lasswell, *Formosa, China and the United Nations: Formosa in the World Community* (New York: St. Martin's Press, 1967), p. 301.

6. For a fuller account of the PRC-Taiwan rivalry in Latin America, see Ming Chen-hua, *Penetration of Latin America by the Chinese Communists*, Joint Publications Research Service, publication no. 3498 (New York: PRS, 1959), and Wang Yu San, "The Republic of China's Relations with Latin America" in *Foreign Policy of the Republic of China on Taiwan: An Unorthodox Approach*, ed. Wang Yu San (New York: Praeger, 1990).

7. Robert L. Worden, "China's Foreign Relations with Latin America," in *Dimensions of China's Foreign Relations*, ed. Chün-tu Hsüeh (New York: Praeger, 1977), pp. 193–94.

8. Robert L. Worden, et al., eds., *China: A Country Study*, 4th ed. (Washington, D.C.: U.S., 1988), p. 345.

9. Alexander Eckstein, *China's Economic Revolution* (Cambridge: Cambridge University Press, 1977), p. 233.

10. In 1982, the Ministry of Foreign Trade, the State Council's Import-Export Control Commission, the Foreign Investment and Control Commission, and the Ministry of Foreign Economic Relations were merged to form the Ministry of Foreign Economic Relations and Trade (MOFERT).

11. Interview with a scholar in the Institute of International Trade in Beijing in January 1989.

12. Whereas in 1950 only four Communist countries traded with China, their number increased to eleven in 1954. China's trade with the Soviet bloc constituted 26 percent of the total value of its trade in 1950, 61 percent in 1951, 70 percent in 1952, 75 percent in 1953, and 81 percent in 1954. C. F. Remer, ed., *Three Essays on the International Economics of Communist China*, (Ann Arbor: University of Michigan Press, 1959), pp. 210–11.

13. *Almanac of China's Foreign Economic Relations and Trade*, 1984 (Hong Kong: China Resources Trade Consultancy Co., 1984).

14. United Nations Economic Commission for Latin America, "Preliminary Notes on Latin American Trade with the Countries with Centrally Planned Economies," *Economic Survey of Latin America, 1958* (Mexico City: UN Department of Economic and Social Affairs, 1958), p. 61.

15. Cheng Fei, "China's Trade with Latin America," *China's Foreign Trade* (China), January-February 1981, no. 1, p. 62.

16. Luo Liecheng, "Development of Economic and Trade Relations between China and Latin American Countries," *Latin American Review* (China), no. 3 (1985), p. 48.

17. Daniel Tretiak, "China's Latin American Trade," *Far Eastern Economic Review*, 41, no. 4 (July 25, 1963), p. 224.

18. Luo, "Development of Economic and Trade Relations between China and Latin American Countries," p. 48.

19. *Peking Review*, 1, no. 38 (November 18, 1958), p. 21.

20. "Preliminary Notes on Latin American Trade with the Countries with Centrally Planned Economies," *Economic Survey of Latin America, 1958,* pp. 63–64.

21. *Renmin Ribao,* July 7, 1959.

22. Peter Cheng, ed., *A Chronology of the People's Republic of China from October 1, 1949* (Totowa, N. J.: Littlefield, Adams, 1972), p. 18.

23. George Ginsburgs and Arthur Stahnke, "Communist China Trade Relations with Latin America," *Asian Survey* 10, no. 9 (September 1970), p. 809.

24. The Canton Fair is one of the important ways by which China advertises to the world. However, its significance declined since the great expansion of other forms of economic contact between China and the outside world following the fall of the Gang of Four.

25. "Autumn Export Fair Ends," *Peking Review,* 1, no. 41 (December 9, 1958), p. 17.

26. For more details on Chinese cultural diplomacy during this period in Latin America, see William E. Ratliff, "Chinese Communist Cultural Diplomacy toward Latin America, 1949–1960," *Hispanic American Historical Review,* 49, no. 1 (1969), pp. 53–79.

3

The Years after the Cuban
Revolution: 1959–1969

Prior to the Cuban Revolution, Beijing showed little interest in Latin America. Latin America was considered a U.S. sphere of interest. Despite the long-range interest of China in the sphere of economic relations with Latin America, it was not until Castro's victory in 1959 that China was willing to increase its economic relations with the Latin American region on a substantial as well as sustained basis. The Cuban Revolution of 1959 gave the PRC an opportunity to gain a foothold in the Caribbean region and establish relations with Latin American countries. Besides its geopolitical interests in Cuba as well as in Latin America, China also developed some economic interest. Trade between the two regions expanded in the first half of the 1960s.

The central theme of this chapter is that in the 1960s, China's economic relations with Latin America were carried on primarily for political purposes and that economic policies were just a part of foreign policy to Latin America.[1] For instance, Beijing-Havana economic ties were the most politicized, with a close correlation between trade and political developments. In this period, Beijing's policies toward Latin America had two dimensions: (1) to attain recognition from Latin American countries as the sole legitimate government of China and take over the seat held by Taipei in the United Nations and (2) to break out of the isolation imposed upon it by the U.S. "containment" policy.

Yet Beijing's goals remained to be achieved. In spite of its efforts, from 1961 to 1969 not a single Latin American nation recognized the PRC. It should be noted that until the 1970s, most of the Chinese trade with Latin America had been concentrated on Cuba. Before the late 1970s, China had never been an important trading partner with any Latin American country except Cuba. This is no surprise, since direct trade with others was either banned or restricted by political factors. Aside from the Sino-Cuban rift, there were other Chinese setbacks in the region. In the 1960s, the offices of the NCNA, which as the official Chinese press agency often functions as the Chinese embassy in countries with no diplomatic ties to the PRC, were closed in Panama, Argentina, Venezuela, Brazil, Mexico, and Ecuador and all Chinese representatives were expelled because China seemed to support Fidel Castro.[2]

In spite of the absence of diplomatic relations and economic difficulties at home, the PRC managed to have nongovernmental trade and people-to-people contacts with Latin America, and it arranged several agreements with Latin American countries during this period (see Appendix B). The number of countries having trade relations with China increased from five in 1952 to seventeen in 1963, and trade turnover increased by many times.[3] While trade relations did expand somewhat, China's trade with Latin America throughout the 1960s showed a consistently positive balance for Latin America.

This chapter examines the nature and extent of Sino–Latin American trade in the 1960s. The first two sections discuss the changing situation in both China and Latin America. The third section provides an overview of trade between the two regions in the 1960s. The chapter ends with an assessment of trade relations in the 1960s.

CHANGING SITUATION IN CHINA

The late 1950s witnessed a major period of change in Chinese foreign policy. The PRC broke away from its alliance with the Soviet Union and charted a more independent course in world affairs in staunch opposition to both superpowers, the Soviet Union and the United States. In its economic relations with the outside world, China adopted a "self-reliance" approach. Although such policy did not signify complete economic independence or isolation, foreign trade constituted a very low proportion of national economy. Despite this strategic shift, throughout the 1960s China retained its radical perspectives on international issues as well as its insistence on revolutionary change in the global system. During the post-1959 period, the Chinese were convinced that the Cuban Revolution would herald a spread of other revolutions in Latin America. Constant attempts were made to encourage Latin American Communists and non-Communist leftists to carry out protracted armed struggle to overthrow existing governments.

Besides, the Chinese perceived that armed struggle was the only route to national liberation in the Third World. From time to time, the Chinese government haughtily dismissed Latin American countries for not being independent countries but merely "lackeys" of American imperialism.

In a sense, the Chinese faced the fact that its main enemy, the United States, was firmly committed to a policy of combating Chinese influence in Latin America.

The Chinese paid scant attention to Latin America until the 1960s. Since 1959 when Fidel Castro came into power in Cuba, Chinese interest in Latin America has grown. Cecil Johnson's valuable work *Communist China and Latin America, 1959–1967* suggests six reasons for this increasing interest:

First, the Chinese were convinced that the main "contradiction" in the contemporary world was that between the "oppressed" peoples of the Third World on the one hand and the "imperialists" led by the United States, on the other. In more concrete terms, they believed that the scene from the sharpest fighting between the two groups would be the countries of Asia, Africa, and Latin America. In fact, they contended that the entire course of history would be determined by the outcome of the fighting in the continents constituting the so-called Third World. The Chinese, then, regard Latin America as an integral part of that region of the world that most interests them.

Second, the Chinese maintained that revolution in Latin America would follow the Chinese model. They assumed that conditions in Latin America were essentially the same as those in China before 1949—conditions such as warlordism, "unequal treaties," "semicolonial and semifeudal" system. And thus, the best way to win the war over imperialism and reactionary regimes in Latin America was to follow the Chinese experiences.

Third, the fact that Marxist ideas are quite respectable in Latin American intellectual circles also stimulated Chinese interest in the area. Fourth, Chinese interest in Latin America also increased as a result of Fidel Castro's advent to power in January 1959. Fifth, the Sino-Soviet dispute was yet another reason for arousing Chinese interest in this part of the world. Sixth, the Chinese have interests that are not necessarily related to their revolutionary interest. For example, China's efforts to expand trade and cultural relations with Latin American countries were designed to achieve an economic and cultural objective, as well as to make these nations less dependent on the main enemy; in this case, the United States.[4]

Under the influence of the radicals, Chinese foreign policy became increasingly militant. From late 1967 to early 1968, Beijing repeatedly condemned some Latin American governments for collaborating with the United States in oppressing and exploiting their people and called on the Communist parties in these countries to step up armed struggle to overthrow the "reactionary governments." In the late 1960s, Chinese decisionmakers were preoccupied with the Cultural Revolution,[5] which wrought both political and economic dislocation. The only Chinese ambassador in the hemisphere (in Cuba) was called back for three years, from 1967 to 1970. Sino-Latin American relations toward the end of the 1960s appeared to have come to an impasse.

LATIN AMERICA IN THE 1960s

In the 1960s, the Alliance for Progress gave a new impetus to Latin American development and, at least temporarily, to inter-American solidarity.[6] Latin American military leaders, many of whom have close ties with the United States, also quite frequently adopted a militarily anti-Communist posture. Nevertheless, leading Latin American countries like Brazil (during the presidencies of Quadros and Goulart) and Mexico under López Mateos (1958–1964) sought a somewhat broader range of international relations and adopted a stance of moderate economic nationalism on key issues such as aid and trade in an attempt to support a domestic economic policy of import-substitution industrialization (ISI).

In many Latin American countries, "traditional" dictatorships gave way to new popular-democratic governments and "technocratic" military regimes. However, during the 1960s, Cuba was the only country that recognized the PRC. With official diplomacy so circumscribed, Beijing aimed to develop trade relations with various Latin American countries in order to gain diplomatic recognition.

TRADE RELATIONS IN THE 1960s

From a low point in the early 1950s, trade between China and Latin America developed rapidly after Castro took power in 1959. In October 1960, the Chinese government announced that China desired Latin America's "rich industrial raw materials and mineral products, particularly nitrate and copper from Chile." In exchange, China would export tea, resin, medicinal herbs, animal products, textiles, medical supplies, radio equipment, and laboratory instruments. Although the Chinese government claimed its products were of "high quality," one writer felt "these brave words presaged little" and "trade has not expanded markedly except with Cuba."[7] The 1960s saw modest developments of overall trade. Average annual two-way trade figures reached $200 million in that decade.

Chiefly because of economic difficulties during 1960–1963, China's external trade dropped sharply. Serious disruption of the economy during the Cultural Revolution led to the stagnation of China's foreign trade. Chinese exports to Latin America suffered a continuous decline between 1966 and 1969. In 1969, Beijing somewhat increased its imports from Latin America, with its unfavorable balance of trade reaching $63 million, the highest in the period 1966–1969. During this time, China's trade with Latin America did not exceed 0.3 percent of its total trade; excluding Cuba, the proportion was only 0.1 percent.

Latin American exports consisted mainly of typical primary products, such as grain from Argentina and sugar from Cuba. Other significant Chinese imports were cotton and wool. Three goods comprised 99 percent of the PRC's imports from Latin America in 1965: wheat (90 percent), maize (3.9 percent) and cotton (5.4 percent).[8] Until 1960, as a result of a number of good harvests, China had not imported any sizable amount of grain since 1949. However, agriculture was severely damaged by the disruptions of the Great Leap Forward from 1958 to 1961, coupled with famines and floods from 1959 to 1962. Between 1960 and 1961, wheat imports jumped from nothing to 3.9 million tons. They remained at or around this level, as China actively exported rice to take advantage of the higher international price and maintained a balanced foreign exchange account.

MAJOR TRADING PARTNERS

China's trade with Latin America between 1960 and 1969 was greatest with Cuba, Argentina, Mexico, and Chile. A more detailed review of economic relations with major Chinese trading partners in the Latin American region is as follows.

Cuba

On January 1, 1959, Fidel Castro and his guerrillas marched into Havana. Considering Cuba as a forward base for Chinese activities in Latin America, Beijing initially supported Castro with much enthusiasm. For the Chinese, this was a political breakthrough in the Western Hemisphere, especially in view of China's isolation at the beginning of the 1960s. On September 28, 1960, Cuba became the first Latin American country to establish diplomatic relations with the PRC. Disaffection with the Soviet Union over the withdrawal of missiles, an issue over which Castro was not consulted, led to Castro's serious attempts to cement links with the PRC. On the other hand, Castro desperately needed to sell Cuban sugar to China and receive in return Chinese rice and light manufactured goods.

In 1960, Cuba asked the leading Communist states to pledge support for its industrialization program. The Soviet Union, however, was unwilling to provide economic aid without assurance as to its proper use. As for the Chinese, they simply lacked the economic resources to meet their commitment. Soviet trade, much of it really in aid, accounted for about 45 percent of Cuba's total trade turnover from 1961 through 1964. China's share amounted to a negligible 10 percent in the same period. During the 1961–1964 period, Cuba's trading activities with the Soviets were consistently more intensive than its dealing with the Chinese and their adherents.[9]

Sino-Cuban relations reached a peak in 1961 when Ché Guevara visited Beijing. Arriving in Beijing empty-handed from Moscow, Mao offered Guevara a trade agreement that would provide the Chinese with 1 million tons of Cuban sugar per annum and give Havana a credit of $60,000,000.[10] With growing Chinese economic aid to Cuba, Sino-Cuban relations developed rapidly, building up the major part of Sino–Latin American trade. Following are the principal forms of Sino-Cuban cooperation from 1960 to 1965.

Trade

In 1965, China accounted for more than 14 percent of Cuba's imports and exports, ranking second to the Soviet Union in importance for Cuban trade. Indeed, China alone was more important than all Eastern Europe (not including the Soviet Union) for Cuban trade. China also approved a loan to Cuba to finance its bilateral trade deficit of 22.8 million pesos in 1965. Notwithstanding their poor political relations after 1965, China still bought almost 8 percent of Cuban exports and supplied nearly 6 percent of Cuban imports in 1970.[11] From 1960 to 1969, the two-way trade between China and Latin America was $2 billion. Of this, Sino-Cuban trade amounted to $1.5 billion, accounting for 77 percent of China's total with all the countries in the region. This continued to be the case even though their political relations deteriorated after 1966.[12]

Signing of Various Cooperation Agreements

In July 1960, China and Cuba signed a trade payment agreement as well as a scientific and technical cooperation agreement. In September of the same year, they reached an economic cooperation agreement, whereby China would give a loan of $60 million to Cuba without interest for five years. In March 1963, the two countries signed another loan agreement, under which China agreed to extend an additional interest-free loan of $40 million to Cuba. In December 1964, a five-year trade and payment agreement was signed. This agreement stipulated that China should supply rice, soybean, cotton cloth, tools, and medicine to Cuba on a long-term basis in exchange for Cuba's brown sugar and mineral ores.[13] According to the Chinese source, during much of the 1960s China not only bought Cuban sugar at the fixed price, which was above the world market price for most of the years, but also provided substantial economic aid to Cuba.[14]

Donations

After establishing diplomatic relations with Cuba, Beijing in 1963 also donated to Cuba 20,000 tons of rice, 30,000 tons of wheat and corn, 3.6 million meters of cotton cloth, 20,000 bags of cement, and 10,000 tons of steel materials.[15] However, Castro needed more aid than the Chinese could or would provide, and China did not have the resources to approach Soviet largess; thus, Cuba had to turn to the Soviet Union.[16]

When political differences developed after 1965, Chinese-Cuban relations deteriorated as well. In February 1966, at exactly the same time another Soviet loan to Cuba was announced, and just one month after the first Chinese credit expired, Castro assailed Beijing for not accepting 800,000 tons of sugar it had agreed to purchase and for not delivering 250,000 tons of rice, a staple of the Cuban diet. Furthermore, Castro accused the Chinese of breaking a protocol agreement and of "brutal reprisals" of an economic nature for purely political reasons. He also denounced the PRC for committing a "criminal act of economic aggression." Consequently, an almost complete break followed and trade decreased rapidly.[17] Two-way trade fell from $216 million in 1965 to $120 million in 1969. Needless to say, Beijing offered no more aid.[18] By the mid-1960s, Cuba had clearly sided with Moscow in its ideological conflict with Beijing, and relations between Cuba and the PRC reached their lowest point. In 1967, the Chinese ambassador to Cuba was withdrawn to China; the new Chinese ambassador did not arrive to Havana until 1971. Meanwhile, Cuba has been increasingly integrated, politically and economically, into the Soviet system. Sino-Soviet competition in Cuba demonstrated that China's capability of providing economic aid to distant Latin American countries was quite limited. In terms of trade, their relations with Moscow played a key role in Sino-Cuban relations; and with the deterioration of Beijing's relations with Moscow, China's trade with Cuba began to decline significantly after reaching its height in 1965. The causes of the Sino-Cuban rift in the mid-1960s are several. Yet the growing awareness that Beijing was not in a position to compete with Moscow in terms of economic aid and exchange of trade was one of the most important ones.

In the 1960s, Cuba accounted for roughly 80 percent of Chinese trade with Latin America, a pattern reflecting the political basis of trade in this period. During the late 1960s, relations between Beijing and Havana deteriorated, but Cuba continued to be China's biggest trading partner, accounting for 63 percent of the total Sino–Latin American trade in 1965 and 92 percent in 1969.[19] Thus, Cuba's share of Chinese–Latin American trade was more a product of low overall volume of Chinese trade in the region than a reflection of large absolute trade volume between China and Cuba. Annual trade protocols were regularly renewed despite the rift (see Appendix B) largely because Cuba offered China a market for its consumer manufactures, which averaged about $79 million annually between 1960 and 1973.[20] China exported mainly rice, soybeans, textiles, paper, rolled steel, machinery, chemical products, and medical supplies. Chinese imports primarily consisted of such raw materials as sugar, nickel, copper, tobacco, and canned food. Moreover, unlike China's trade with other Latin American countries that encountered large deficits on the Chinese side, Sino-Cuban trade was fairly balanced, since the bulk of the bilateral trade was made through barter.

Argentina

China attached great importance to Argentina because in Argentina it found an important source of wheat, particularly in the case of bad harvests. In 1962, China turned to Argentina for grain imports hoping to alleviate its shortage of foodstuffs; imports from Argentina totaled $9.7 million. During 1960–1969 trade between the two countries remained a one-sided affair, dominated by China's imports of Argentina's grain—varying from a high of $108 million in 1966, at the outbreak of the Cultural Revolution, to nothing in 1968 and $70,000 in 1969. Regarding exports, China sold Argentina only a small quantity of textiles and light industrial products.[21]

The Chinese manifested an interest in Argentine millet, meat, and wheat. According to the Brazilian radio station Radio Tupi, in 1962 the Chinese purchased 50,000 tons of millet and 28,000 tons of wheat. In 1963 they attempted to purchase 100,000 tons of meat. And again in 1964, they asked to purchase 300,000 tons of meat, a request with which the Argentine authorities could not comply. In the latter year, the Chinese stepped up their efforts to purchase wheat, asking on January 23 to buy 700,000 tons from Argentina's National Grain Committee. The Argentines, after long negotiations, agreed to sell half that amount. A second agreement was signed shortly thereafter, however, covering 400,000 tons of "agricultural products," and on September 20, a three-year agreement to buy wheat was signed. The delivery terms stipulated 400,000 tons in 1964, 300,000 tons in 1965, and the same quantity in 1966. In April 1965, a Chinese mission met a delegation from the Argentine National Grain Committee to consider the purchase of 300,000 tons of wheat. Later in the year the Chinese requested a similar amount. Finally, 1 million tons were sold to the Chinese in a cash transaction. During the same year, the Argentineans delivered an additional 500,000 tons of wheat to the Chinese.[22]

In brief, in the decade of the 1960s, despite periodic exchanges of delegations between the two countries, trade developed at a slow pace. In addition, Argentina was extremely cautious in its dealing with the Chinese. For example, although the PRC trade exhibitions were staged in Chile and Mexico in 1963, none was allowed in Argentina. This was due, among other reasons, to the coup of June 1966. Soon after the coup, General Onganía announced that his foreign policy was to be based on "ideological frontier," an extension of national security policy.[23]

Mexico

Mexico has been one the Latin American countries with which the Chinese have been most active commercially. On November 24, 1963, a

Chinese trade mission, led by Zhang Guangdou (Chang Kuang-tou), manager of the China National Chemicals Import & Export Corporation, arrived in Mexico to prepare for the first Chinese trade exhibition in Latin America. In his speech at the airport, he said the display would promote friendship and trade ties between the two countries, despite geographical distance. Zhang also stressed friendship and the need for trade relations based on mutual respect and benefit.[24] As in the case of the trade fair held in Chile, China used this opportunity for both trade promotion and political advertisement. The exhibition opened on December 7 with over 5,000 Mexicans visiting the first day, including President López Mateos and former president Cárdenas. The exhibition closed on January 6, 1964, having drawn a total of 230,000 excited Mexicans.[25] In January 1964, the NCNA announced that the delegation had purchased 26,000 bales of Mexican cotton, 20,000 bales of which were already en route to China. It also announced that new cotton purchases were being negotiated under an agreement signed between the delegation and the Mexican International Compensation Stock Company. In late February 1964, the Chinese also bought from Mexico 450,000 tons of wheat worth approximately $30 million.[26]

An eleven-member Mexican trade delegation, led by Gustavo Solórzano, a high official in the National Bank of Foreign Trade (*Banco Nacional de Comercio Exterior*), arrived in Beijing on April 20, 1964, to promote the sale of grain and cotton. Xiao Fangzhou (Hsiao Fangchou), vice-chairman of the China Council for the Promotion of International Trade (CCPIT), thanked the commission for the promotion of economic relations between Mexico and China, as well as other "Mexican friends" for promoting Sino-Mexican trade, and for making arrangements for the trade exhibition. The importance the Chinese attached to the mission is indicated by the fact that Premier Zhou Enlai received the Mexican guests. Solórzando Hernández released a written statement to the NCNA in which he asserted that there were wide prospects for further expansion of trade between the two countries.[27]

In the political arena, despite Chinese efforts, Mexican attitudes toward the PRC remained unchanged. Mexico still maintained diplomatic relations with Taiwan, and there was a Nationalist embassy in Mexico City as well as a consulate in Mexicali on the U.S.-Mexico border. In general, in the 1960s, trade volume was still very low but continued to grow.

Chile

In the 1960s economic relations between China and Chile grew very much on the foundations created in the earlier period. Chile continued to be one of China's largest trading partners in Latin America. From the Chinese standpoint, a key motive for trade with Chile was the need to obtain such essential raw materials as copper. The Chinese were thought to have purchased 10,000 tons in 1966, and at the time there were reports that they would probably buy twice that amount in 1967. The Chileans, according to these reports, required payment in full in U.S. dollars before the shipping date. The price paid was believed to be equal to the best London price. It was also reported that the Chinese purchase of copper in Europe doubled its average annual purchase for the preceding five years. The increased Chinese buying of copper in Chile and Europe was thought to be related to the Chinese war effort in Vietnam.[28]

The Chilean side was also interested in expanding trade with the PRC. Javier Lagarrique, vice-president of the Copper Department, said that China's economic construction was developing rapidly. Chile, therefore, took "a great interest in selling its copper to this great power." Edward Simian, minister of mining, added that Chile's plans for developing its national copper industry "should take into account the People's Republic of China as a market."[29]

The Chinese held an economic and commercial exhibition in Chile just as they had done in Mexico and attempted to do in Brazil. It opened on May 16, 1964, and lasted until June 7. In all, the Chinese displayed over 4,000 items, including the products of heavy and light industries (but primarily textiles), farm products, and handicrafts.[30] There were several obvious benefits from the trade fair. First, Beijing used the occasion to sharpen the average Chilean's awareness of China's economic achievements and to foster a sympathetic impression of the political system that stimulated such rapid advances. Of course, the trade fair also served a definite economic purpose. That forum did encourage and facilitate the establishment of commercial links. While preparations for the exhibit were nearing completion, China signed a contract to purchase 5,000 tons of copper ingots and soon after entered into an agreement for the delivery by local companies of 20,000 tons of nitre. Moreover, such Chinese purchases continued into 1965, with an order for 58 tons of iodine and 40,000 tons of nitrate placed in April and for 6,000 tons of electrolyzed copper and 1,500 tons of refined copper in May.[31] Finally, a trade mission was opened to promote further business contacts. The next year, trade volume between the two countries reached $17.56 million. During this period, China exported textiles and light industrial products in limited quantities to Chile while Chile exported copper and nitrite in return. The most remarkable feature about Sino-Chilean trade was its tenacious and persistent character. For over two decades trade activities between the two countries were conducted in the absence of a formal diplomatic framework. Each side was apparently contented with pragmatic arrangements, which proved to be quite effective in overcoming the ideological antipathy that often cropped up in the heyday of the cold war.

Two-way trade volume jumped to $13.6 million in 1965 and $17.6 million in 1966, compared with only $1.25 million in 1964. The Cultural Revolution interrupted this trend, and Sino-Chilean trade fell drastically at the end of the decade, dropping below $1 million in volume in 1969. During the years 1959–1969, China's two-way trade with Chile reached $40 million. Of that total, Chinese exports accounted for less than $2 million. Yet when China returned to the world scene in the early 1970s, it was able to build upon an established economic relationship with Chile, finding a newly elected president (Salvador Allende) who was anxious to expand commercial and diplomatic ties with the PRC.

Overall, trade between China and Chile was small in value and sporadic, averaging less than $3 million annually between 1957 and 1970. Professor Chin Ha concluded that Chinese relations with Chile were hindered by three factors. First, Beijing was not recognized by the Chilean government because of the growing tension of the cold war. Second, the banning of the Chilean Communist Party (PCCh) from 1947 to 1958 presumably forced the Chinese Communist Party (CCP) to be very timid in its approach to its Chilean counterpart. And finally, in the 1950s, China's foreign policy dealt with "armed struggle," including the Korean War, and "peaceful coexistence" in Asia, not Latin America.[32]

Brazil

Under the administrations of Jânio Quadros and João Goulart, strong nationalistic sentiment moved to the forefront of Brazilian decision making. At the same time, Brazil began shifting toward the pursuit of links with African countries, China, and other socialist nations. When Goulart became president of Brazil in August, 1961, the Chinese were quite optimistic regarding the prospects for expanding trade with Brazil, as well as for gaining diplomatic recognition. Their optimism was based on the fact that Goulart was visiting China at the very time that he became president after the unexpected resignation of President Jânio Quadros (1961–1962). While in China, Goulart made statements that were most encouraging to the Chinese, and he signed a trade and payment agreement with his Chinese counterpart.

In June 1963, the Chinese dispatched a preparatory working team to make arrangements for an economic trade exhibition in Brazil. In November 1963, the Brazilian Foreign Ministry denied them permission to hold the exhibition, and it was not until February 1964, when the Goulart administration moved sharply to the left, that approval was granted. Goulart's downfall was one of the most serious setbacks suffered by the PRC in Latin America, since he had been a staunch supporter of Sino-Brazilian relations.

The administration of Castelo Branco (1964–1967) represented one of the lowest points in the history of China-Brazil relations. In the wake of a coup in 1964, nine PRC trade exhibition officials and NCNA journalists were arrested. The nine were charged with sedition and espionage by the Brazilian junta, put on trial after six months' detention, and sentenced to ten years' imprisonment by a military tribunal. Shortly after the first anniversary of their arrest, the nine were expelled from Brazil. In the United Nations, Brazil voted against the seating of the People's Republic of China. After the military coup, Beijing maintained a wide distance from Brazil's military regime, which the Chinese criticized for its dependence on Washington and "anti-China attitude." Needless to say, trade with Brazil entered the doldrums, the volume of trade decreased from $2 million in 1964 to $0.3 million in 1969.[33] In short, after the military took power, relations between the two countries were almost severed—up until to 1974, the year two countries established full diplomatic relations.

SUMMARY

For a decade China made no diplomatic breakthrough in the Western Hemisphere, except in Cuba; Beijing-Latin American relations remained at a very modest level. In the absence of political ties between Beijing and most nations in the region, China's bilateral trade with these countries was diminutive. Many reasons could account for this development. Very briefly, first of all, the Cultural Revolution had severe adverse consequences for Sino–Latin American ties. Chinese foreign policy was fundamentally an extension of its domestic confrontation between radicals and moderates with the radicals dominating the leadership. In spite of China's economic and political isolation during the period of Cultural Revolution, it actively promoted the revolutionary struggle in Latin America, which further worsened its relations with the regimes in the region. Second, largely because the radicals were ignorant of and lacked experience of the outside world, they tended to be inflexible. Third, during much of the 1960s China attempted to oppose both superpowers simultaneously, aligning itself with what it regarded as "progressive forces" in the Third World. Under such circumstance, it is understandable that Beijing firmly supported an armed struggle in the backyard of the United States. Fourth, until the late 1970s, China pursued a self-sufficient economic strategy; foreign trade did not play an important role in its external relations. These factors prevented trade and economic relations. Yet even during this period, the grounds were laid for further development of trade and economic cooperation between China and the countries of Latin America.

NOTES

1. During this period, China openly acknowledged foreign trade as a tool of class struggle.

2. Wolfgang Deckers, "Latin America: How the Chinese See the Region," *The Pacific Review*, 2, no. 3 (1989), p. 246.

3. Lin Min, "Development of Economic and Trade Relations between China and Latin America," *Foreign Trade of the People's Republic of China*, March 1964, p. 7.

4. Cecil Johnson, *Communist China & Latin America, 1959–1967* (New York: Columbia University Press, 1970), pp. 1–5.

5. The Cultural Revolution began with the rise of the Gang of Four (headed by Mao's wife) and ended with the fall of this group right after Mao's death in September 1976. It lasted for ten years. However, its peak occurred from 1966 to 1969.

6. In this context, I am not including Cuba when I speak about Latin America as a whole. The reason is that Castro's Cuba differs fundamentally from all other countries in this region.

7. Pauline Lewin, *The Foreign Trade of Communist China: Its Impact on the Free World* (New York: Praeger, 1964), p. 73.

8. Michael A. Weininger, "People's Republic of China Latin American Trade Composition and Direction of Trade, 1965–1977," in *Change and Perspective in Latin America: Proceedings of the 1982 Meeting of the Rocky Mountain Council in Latin American Studies 1982*, ed. Richard Bath, El Paso: University of Texas at El Paso, Center for Inter-American and Border Studies, 1982), p. 55.

9. See Daniel Tretiak's "Cuba and the Soviet Union: The Growing Accommodation," *Rand Memoranda*, RM-4935-PR (July 1966), for detailed analysis of Sino-Cuban relations.

10. Andrés Suárez, "Castro between Moscow and Peking," *Problems of Communism*, 12, no. 5 (September-October, 1963), p. 21.

11. Jorge Domínguez, *To Make a World Safe for Revolution: Cuba's Foreign Policy* (Cambridge, Mass.: Harvard University Press, 1989), p. 69.

12. Ibid., p. 48.

13. Wang Chien-hsun, *Changes in Relations between Peiping and Latin American Countries* (Taipei: World Anti-Communist League, China Chapter, 1973), pp. 1–2.

14. Luo Liecheng, "Development of Economic and Trade Relations between China and Latin American Countries," *Latin American Review* (China), no. 3 (1985), p. 48.

15. Wang Chien-hsun, *Changes in Relations between Peiping and Latin American Countries*, pp. 1–2.

16. John Franklin Copper, *China's Foreign Aid: An Instrument of Peking's Foreign Policy* (Lexington, Mass.: Lexington Books, 1976), p. 34.

17. Ibid., pp. 34–35.

18. Only one of the twenty-four factories which China had promised to construct for Cuba was actually completed. For details, see Wolfgang Barkte, *The Economic Aid of the PR China to Developing and Socialist Countries*, 2d ed. (London: K. G. Saur, 1989), p. 153.

19. *Almanac of China's Foreign Economic Relations and Trade, 1987* (Hong Kong: China Resources Trade Consultancy Co., 1987), pp. 890–94.

20. Ibid.

21. Luo, "Development of Economic and Trade Relations between China and Latin American Countries," p. 48.

22. "Communist China in Latin America," *Este & Oeste*, December, 1966, as translated in Joint Publication Research Service, *Translations on International Communist Development*, no. 940 (New York: JPS, n.d), p. 74.

23. The national security doctrine (NSD) is an interrelated set of concepts about the state, development, counterinsurgency warfare, and, above all, security. All states are security-conscious. But within the NSD, national security assumes overwhelming proportions; it is the yardstick by which all policies are measured, and the beginning and the end of policies.

24. *Survey of China Mainland Press* (hereafter cited as SCMP), no. 3110, p. 37.

25. *Peking Review*, 7, no. 3 (January 17, 1964), p. 3.

26. Daniel Tretiak, "Mexican Traders,"*Far Eastern Economic Review*, 44, no. 9 (May 28, 1964), p. 415.

27. SCMP, no. 3205, p. 32.

28. John Gettings, "Chinese Copper," *Far Eastern Economic Review*, 55, no. 3 (January 19, 1967), pp. 101–102.

29. SCMP, no. 3472, p. 26.

30. *Peking Review*, 7, no. 22 (May 29, 1964), p. 4 and p. 21.

31. George Ginsburgs and Arthur Stahnke, "Communist China Trade Relations with Latin America," *Asian Survey*, 10, no. 9 (1970), p. 810.

32. Suk Chin-ha, "The PRC's Influence in Latin America (1949–1973): A Reassessment," *Political Studies Review: The Journal of the Association of Korean Political Scientists in North America*, 1 (1985), pp. 107–22.

33. *Almanac of China's Foreign Economic Relations and Trade, 1984* (Hong Kong: China Resources Trade Consultancy Co., 1984), p. 892.

4

The Period of Normalization
of Relations: 1970–1977

The year 1970 marked a turning point in Chinese relations with Latin America. With Chile's diplomatic recognition of the PRC on December 15, 1970, Beijing entered the third phase of its relations with Latin America. Membership in the United Nations and the U.S.-China rapprochement set the stage for rapidly increasing Sino–Latin American interactions. With the thaw in the cold war, a new trend was set for Latin American countries to review their existing political and economic relations with the PRC on a basis free of ideological biases and cold war assumptions. By the end of 1977, twelve Latin American countries had established diplomatic ties with China. There was a similar increase in economic links between the two regions. In a major policy change, economic and strategic considerations China during this phase maintained good relations with several military authoritarian regimes, such as Chile under Pinochet, Argentina, and Brazil. A decade ago, it had been impossible even to contact these anti-Communist regimes.

With the establishment of diplomatic relations, the trade between China and Latin America developed quickly. This development is not too difficult to account for. On the Latin American side, there was an eagerness to find new customers for commodities whose international market was weakening. This eagerness was limited by two factors: the difficulty of finding suitable articles to import in exchange for exports and the shortage of hard currency. On the Chinese side, political and economic motives are evident. The grain purchases from Argentina must be traced to economic necessity rather than to any political factors. Relations with Chile under Pinochet, on the other hand, have had some political overtones.[1]

Regarding the aid program, although China's aid program could not match that of the United States or the Soviet Union in the region, economic aid is recognized as an effective weapon in establishing state-to-state relations in the Third World. A little aid often paved the way for better relations, including eventually diplomatic recognition.[2] The aim of this chapter is to examine briefly the scope and trends of Beijing's trade and aid relations with Latin America from 1970 to 1977 and review several positive, essential factors facilitating the linkage between China and Latin America. The first section studies the political and economic situation in China and analyzes the impact of domestic affairs on the country's foreign policy. The second section discusses the changing situation in Latin America and reasons why the Latin American countries were trying to diversify their external economic relations in the 1970s. The third section reviews the overall picture of trade relations between two regions. The principle characteristics of Chinese trade with Latin American countries included (1) low volume, (2) a tendency toward a Latin American export surplus, (3) concentration of most trade among a few trading partners, and (4) continued heavy concentration in relatively few products. The fourth section examines the Chinese aid program in the region during the 1970s.

CHANGING SITUATION IN CHINA

In the late 1960s, China cooled the political temperature of the past years and attempted to get its economy moving forward again. Foreign policies after 1971 were modified to complement Chinese internal policies. During the decade of the 1970s, the hallmark of Beijing's foreign policy was a united front with the United States, Japan, and Western Europe against Soviet hegemony. China used almost every available occasion to show its strong opposition to any move that might help the Soviet Union gain ground in the Third World. Just as domestic plans accentuated economic development, foreign policies emphasized sound diplomatic relations bolstered by aid and trade. China launched one of its most successful diplomatic campaigns ever. The return of normalcy in China, especially in foreign affairs, coincided with Allende's electoral victory in Chile. The PRC responded favorably to the Allende government, and the Chilean recognition of the PRC created an enormous impact upon the PRC, the Soviet Union, the United States, and Latin America.

Abandonment of Support of Armed Struggle

It is well known that the Chinese considered armed struggle as the only form of revolution possible for developing countries. Since the early 1970s, however, the Chinese line has been that the "masses" in nonsocialist developing countries must make their own revolutions and, meanwhile,

China would support the combined efforts of the governments of these countries in their attempt to establish a New International Economic Order (NIEO).

According to the theory of self-reliance, China "will not export revolution. The choice of political systems in other countries must be decided by the people of those countries." However, China "supports the struggle for independence, liberation, and revolution of peoples in all countries."

Chinese trade delegations again began to visit Latin America in the early 1970s and Latin American delegations from many countries traveled to the People's Republic. The PRC was active at the U.N. Conference on Trade and Development (UNCTAD) that convened during April and May 1972 in Santiago, Chile. On April 20, Zhou Huamin (Chou Hua-min), China's vice-minister of foreign trade, outlined to the UNCTAD delegates the current Chinese attitude toward Latin America and the developing world generally. He declared that all international relations should be based on the principles of equality and mutual benefit, and he emphasized the importance of international trade and aid among developing countries themselves in order to promote their production and self-reliance.[3]

Three-Worlds Theory

The Tenth Chinese Communist Party Congress, held in August 1973, marked a turning point in the development of the Three-Worlds Theory. In his report to the congress, Premier Zhou Enlai (Chou En-lai) depicted the emerging struggle between the poor and developing countries of the Third World and the two super powers—the United States and the Soviet Union—as the main feature of international politics. He saw the "awakening and growth of the Third World" as a major event in contemporary international relations. Zhou declared that the Third World "has strengthened its unity in the struggle against hegemonism and power politics of the superpowers and is playing an even more significant role in international affairs."[4] Zhou placed particular emphasis on the efforts of the Third World countries "to win and defend national independence and safeguard state sovereignty and national resources" against the United States and the Soviet Union.[5]

In 1972, Chinese leader Deng Xiaoping (Teng Hsiao-ping) emphatically stated that the so-called socialist camp no longer existed and that China belonged to the Third World countries. Thus, China looked forward to building a broad united front comprising the Third World countries (the developing countries in Asia, Africa, and Latin America) and the Second World countries (the industrialized, developed societies of Europe and other regions) under its leadership and against the hegemonical policies of the First World—the two superpowers.

Latin America is an integral part of the Chinese concept of the Third World. Under the new, outward-looking foreign policy, during the 1970s China stepped up its activities in this region to complete its network of Third World supporters, hoping to stymie rival efforts from the Soviets and further isolate Taiwan. To gain more friends in Latin America, the PRC addressed itself to the support of various issues of regional political and economic interest to the leadership in Latin America. Among issues supported by the PRC were the 200-nautical-mile economic zone, Panama's demand for sovereign right over the Canal Zone, economic independence, the Latin American nuclear-weapon-free zone, and the NIEO. Beijing's active support of these issues won it important friendship in the region.

LATIN AMERICA IN THE 1970s

Theories of imperialism and dependency gained wide currency in the late 1960s and 1970s. The major lines of radical thought were widely accepted. These ideas emphasized the unbalanced relations between Latin America and the United States, which has retarded the process of proper development in Latin America. For many, this neoimperialist relationship must be destroyed and a NIEO attuned to the needs and realities of development must be established. Diversification of trade relations was considered an effective weapon to solve the problem of overdependence.

The 1970s witnessed a phenomenal increase in diplomatic representatives and economic exchange between China and Latin America. The improved relationship with Washington helped Beijing establish contact with Latin American countries. However, credit should not go to President Richard Nixon alone. The dramatic announcement of his intention to visit Beijing certainly precipitated changes and initiated the trend for Latin American countries to review their relations with China. It is also apparent that even without the U.S. initiative, the time had come for many countries in Latin America to seriously tackle their China question. James Theberge, author of *Latin America's New Internationalism,* mentioned the following six factors that contributed to the region's interest in increasing economic ties with the Soviet Union, Eastern Europe, and China:

1. The widespread desire to diversify export markets and obtain access to new resources of capital and technology so as to reduce what is considered excessive economic dependence on the United States. This long-term aim of the Latin American countries is now encouraged by East-West détente and socialist states' increased interest in widening trade relations with the nonsocialist world.
2. A strong anticapitalist and anti-U.S. trend pushes many Latin American governments toward policies of greater autonomy and more balanced relations with the world community, favoring in particular the establishment of economic relations with the socialist world.

3. The protectionist trend in the United States, which has led to trade restrictions that protect domestic labor-intensive industries (such as textiles and footwear) against import competition, has driven some Latin American countries to redouble their efforts to find markets elsewhere, including socialist countries.
4. Some Latin American governments advertise the establishment of diplomatic and economic relations with the USSR, Cuba, and other socialist states as a sign of "independence" from the United States, which is popular with anti-U.S. nationalist forces at home. In some countries, revolutionary rhetoric and gestures of independence from the United States are convenient substitutes for needed radical reform.
5. More recently, OPEC's (Organization of Petroleum Exporting Countries') ability to raise oil prices fourfold in 1973–1974 has contributed to balance of payments problems that press these countries to seek new export markets and explore trade relations with the socialist states.
6. Ideological sympathy has led some Latin American countries (such as Allende's Chile and Velasco's Peru) to open trade relations and use that in the anti-U.S. struggle.[6]

In addition, there was a need for mutual help and legitimation among the developing countries. Due to the PRC's long exclusion and isolation from the postwar international system and the still unsettled nature of the "two Chinas" issue, its quest for full legitimacy became the most sensitive part of Beijing's foreign policy. Given the Third World's dominance in the global politics in the United Nations, the Chinese search for foreign policy legitimation could not succeed without Third World support. China's quest for foreign policy legitimation thus has been an integral part of its Third World policy. For both psychological and symbolic reasons, the Third World also needs China's moral and political support in its pursuit of more equitable international order. In brief, both Latin America and the PRC need each other in order to improve their international position.

OVERALL PICTURE OF TRADE RELATIONS

As the turmoil of the Cultural Revolution in China subsided, Sino–Latin American trade relations resumed their upward trend. Chinese trade with Latin America was sparse and, until 1972, ranked in last place when compared with other regions of the world. In 1972, China–Latin American two-way trade for the first time surpassed that between China and the Middle East and China and South Asia. It continued to increase almost every subsequent year, competing well with the Middle East trade and far outstripping trade with South Asia by the end of the 1970s. China–Latin America two-way trade figures for 1980—$1.5 billion—represented an increase of ten times that reported for 1970 ($150 million). This placed

China–Latin America trade second only to China–Southeast Asia trade and ahead of that with the Middle East ($1.4 billion) and Sub-Saharan Africa ($1.3 billion).[7] By the end of 1977, the PRC had established a foreign trade network throughout Latin America.

During 1970–1977, China's exports increased from $75 million to $90 million and its imports from $70 million to $392 million. A national breakdown shows that China's trade was valued at $1,239 million with Cuba, $409 million with Chile, $392 million with Peru, $256 million with Argentina, $210 million with Mexico, and $146 million with Brazil.[8] However, between 1975 and 1976, China became embroiled in domestic political turmoil as the secession struggle between radicals and moderates intensified. As a result, PRC foreign trade with Latin America, and in general, declined from 1975 to 1977.

From the beginning of the 1970s, relations between Latin American countries and China took on new momentum. If we analyze the total trade between the two regions, we can see that although the sum was significantly small, the evolution is dynamic. Two observations are necessary to appreciate the significance of these figures. First, it is certain that although they increased, the percentages continue to be small, particularly in the case of Chinese exports. Nevertheless, this increase (from 0.2 percent in 1970 to 0.6 percent in Chinese total exports in 1977)[9] is important if we take into consideration all the political and economic difficulties encountered in attempts to increase trade. Second, although trade figures remained very small in the percentage of both regions' total trade, they were growing dramatically in absolute terms.

Throughout this entire period, China had a yearly trade deficit with Latin American countries. It was only in exceptional cases that some Latin American countries showed a surplus in certain years (e.g., Cuba in 1970 and 1972) or their trade was more or less balanced (e.g., Panama in 1976–1977). The biggest deficit in trade with China was registered by Argentina, from whom China purchased large quantities of agricultural goods. During this period, China developed good relations with leading Latin American countries; with other states, relations were minimal. China's trade relations with these key states is discussed in some detail in this section.

Cuba

After the peak of the Cultural Revolution, Beijing showed renewed interest in foreign affairs; this fact was quickly reflected in China's Latin American policy. The first sign of that was China's efforts to reach reconciliation with Cuba. China took the initiative by sending a delegation to the celebration of the National Day of Cuba in July 1970. In early 1971, after a four-year gap, the PRC dispatched a new ambassador to Cuba, Zhang

Dequn.[10] In March 1972, Beijing extended an interest-free loan of £8.75 million to Havana to finance the bilateral trade deficits on the Cuban side.[11]

In 1975, the PRC and Cuba resumed cordial relations and even apparently developed a modus vivendi regarding their role in the Sino-Soviet split. Although the PRC did not hesitate to criticize "Soviet imperialism" in Eastern Europe, it did not attack the relationship between Havana and Moscow. Playing the role of Moscow defender, Castro consistently rebuked the PRC's charge of Soviet imperialism, but he and his fellow officials refrained from mentioning the PRC specifically. He also managed to avoid attending a Soviet-sponsored international Communist conference called for the purpose of condemning the PRC. Trade relations remained normal throughout the 1970s, and the PRC was Cuba's third or fourth most important trading partner throughout the first half of the 1970s. Yet the total value of trade between China and Cuba remained at a low level. Trade between the two countries consisted primarily of sugar and nickel from Cuba for rice and consumer goods from China. Although Cuba was China's biggest trading partner in Latin America, its share in China's overall trade with Latin America dropped significantly, from 77 percent in the 1960s to 23.4 percent in 1970–1977.

In late 1975, the PRC had a major trade delegation in Havana, its first since 1966. In early 1976, relations with the PRC again began to deteriorate, as Havana supplied troops and assistance to Soviet-backed forces in Angola in opposition to forces supported by Beijing. Cuba was frequently described by China as Moscow's "Trojan horse" in the Third World. China's relations with Cuba cooled considerably for the rest of the 1970s. In short, over the years Cuban-Chinese relations underwent a complete metamorphosis: What began as a love feast of revolutionary comraderie turned into an all-out political and ideological war.[12]

Chile

Salvador Allende, a Marxist, was elected president of Chile in 1969. Shortly after that both Beijing and Santiago made serious endeavors to approach each other. The Chinese were very interested in gaining a foothold in South America. In December 1970, Chile became the second country in Latin America with which the PRC established formal diplomatic relations. Chile under Allende was the first real opportunity for Beijing to gain substantial influence in Latin America since the Cuban Revolution in 1959. As a result, Latin America assumed a higher priority in China's scheme of political aspirations that it had between 1950 and 1970. During the Allende administration (1970–1973), economic relations between China and Chile increased markedly. Chinese exports to this country recorded continuous increases in the early 1970s.

On December 15, 1970, a "Joint Communiqué of the Government of the Republic of Chile and the Government of the PRC on the Establishment of Diplomatic Relations between Chile and China" was announced in Paris. Supplementing this joint communiqué, Chilean foreign minister Clodomiro Almeyda issued a statement on January 5, 1971, indicating the Chilean motives for recognizing China. First, Chile would "establish relation with all countries of the world regardless of their ideological and political position." This implied Chilean independence in foreign affairs. Second, Chile considered Chinese isolation from world affairs an obstacle to the achievement of peace and security. Therefore, Chile would support the admission of China to the United Nations. Finally, Chile hoped to increase its volume of trade with China, which was looked upon as "a potential market of gigantic dimension" for Chile.[13] The establishment of diplomatic relations was soon followed by a number of important economic agreements and a rapid increase in China's purchase of copper.

On April 7, 1971, a five-person Chinese commercial mission headed by Zhou Huamin, vice-minister of foreign trade, arrived in Santiago. On April 20, Zhou Huamin and Pedro Vuskovic, the Chilean acting foreign minister, signed the first formal commercial accord between the government of the PRC and the government of Chile. The agreement consisted of the following provisions: (1) reciprocity (Article 1), (2) most-favored-nation treatment for exports and imports (Article 2), (3) merchant vessels of each country to enter the other's port under favorable conditions granted to third-country vessels (Article 3), (4) establishment of a mixed commission to supervise agreement and export trade (Article 6).[14] Under this agreement, China was to buy 65,000 tons of Chilean copper a year from 1972. The sale included 56,000 tons of electrolytic copper and 9,000 tons of copper wire at London market price. Other sections of the agreement provide for Chile's sale of refined and semiprocessed copper, nitrate, iodine, wood pulp, synthetic fibre, wool, minerals, and other products and the purchase from China of rice, soybeans, preserved food, tea, light industry goods, chemical products, machinery, tools, and other articles.[15]

Sino-Chilean relations reached a peak in 1972 when Allende visited Beijing and Chile became China's second largest trading partner in the region. The volume of trade between the two countries dramatically increased 136 times, from less than $1 million in 1970 to $115 million in 1973.[16] Chile in 1971 and 1972 was a vital source of needed imports. Chilean goods, on average, made up over 30 percent of Chinese imports from Latin America and nearly 10 percent from all less-developed countries; China became the third largest purchaser of Chilean copper.[17]

Compared with previous expressions of outrage over similar events in the past decades, China's reaction to the violent coup that ended in Allende's death in September 1973 was drastically subdued. In the wake of the coup, the PRC remained one of only two Communist nations to continue relations with the military junta.[18] No economic aid was given to Chile after Allende's death. Trade, likewise, experienced a decrease. Within a few years, state-to-state, economic, and cultural relations between China and Chile had returned to pre-coup level.

A variety of political and economic factors help to explain the existing relations. China's foreign policy in the 1970s identified the Soviet Union as the principal threat to world peace. This implied that the PRC would be willing to establish relations with any government that shared its strategic concerns about the Soviet menace. Despite the unsavory circumstance under which it came to power, the rabidly anti-Soviet Chilean junta obviously fitted well with the global posture outlined by Zhou and Deng in 1973–1974.[19] To Beijing's great satisfaction, the Soviet diplomats were expelled and relations unilaterally severed by Santiago on charges of internal interference.

Mutual economic interests also help explain the continuing Sino-Chilean relationship. While Chile accounts for only a tiny fraction of the total of the PRC's greatly expanded global economic activity, it remains a major source of vital copper imports. Similarly, China was an important market for Chilean exports when the military regime in Santiago remained somewhat of an international pariah. Furthermore, despite its highly repressive character, the Chilean junta did not completely reverse some measures the PRC regarded as indicators of steps toward national independence and state sovereignty under Allende. Indeed, the junta showed a willingness to continue the relationship with Beijing, and it decided to honor the nationalization of the Chilean copper industry initiated by the Popular Unity government.[20]

In terms of economic policy, the Pinochet regime (1973–1989) followed a free market economy and did not face a severe foreign exchange problem to the extent its neighbors did. Therefore, it was much easier for Chinese manufactured goods to enter this market. In short, that relations between the two nations were not broken after the coup d'etat was evidence that the relationship was of mutual benefit.

Peru

Until the late 1960s, nonhemispheric relations were in large part limited to the extensive economic ties to Britain and cultural ties to Spain. After the military coup in 1968, the new government headed by Juan Velasco Alvarado (1968–1975) sought economic independence and attempted to establish a new relationship to foreign capital through a readjustment with capitalist centers of power. Between 1968 and 1974, the Peruvian government nationalized over a dozen U.S. corporations in agriculture, banking, automotive, mining, construction, fish meal, industrial, petroleum, and public utility sectors. The United States exerted economic pressure by terminating its aid and loans and discouraging foreign investment. Through the use of its veto power and influence, it caused a cutback of all private, bilateral, and multilateral loans to Peru. Peru resented the position taken by the U.S. government, and relations between the two countries sank to an all-time low. In an effort to achieve a greater degree of sovereignty, Peru increased its trade and economic cooperation with socialist countries.

With this background, China's relations with Peru took a sharp upward turn beginning in the 1970s. A trade agreement was signed in June 1971 in Beijing during the visit of a Peruvian commercial delegation headed by the minister of fishing and under-secretary of economic affairs. The Chinese agreed to buy during the following eighteen months 35,000 tons of copper, 10,000 tons of lead, and 10,000 tons of zinc for a total value of $45 million in cash. The shipments were to begin the following month.[21] In the same year, when Washington decided to reduce Peru's U. S. fish meal import quotas, in support of Velasco's confrontation with Washington, the Chinese government contracted to buy at least 150,000 tons of Peruvian fish meal, about 10 percent of its fish meal exports for that year. However, it was only several years later that fish meal became a favorable import item for Chinese customers.[22] This episode indicates that Beijing was prepared to absorb whatever financial loss this purchase incurred in turn for diplomatic gains.

In October 1971, Peru voted in favor of the Albanian resolution proposing the PRC as a member of the United Nations in place of Taiwan. During the following month, Peru and China decided to establish diplomatic relations. The Chinese government recognized the sovereignty of Peru over the maritime zone adjacent to its coast within the limit of 200 nautical miles. The Peruvian government recognized the government of the PRC as the sole legal government of China. Indeed, Peru was the first Latin American country to recognize China since the international détente following the announcement of Nixon's visit to Beijing, at a time when most Latin American countries were still dragging their feet in their normalization process with China. After the establishment of diplomatic relations, trade increased dramatically. During 1960–1970, overall Sino-Peruvian trade was less than $1 million; however, bilateral trade reached $58 million in 1971.[23]

Argentina

At the beginning of the 1970s, the policy of "ideological frontier"—which in effect amounted to refusals to develop relations with socialist, revolutionary, or reformist governments—was called to an end. The new foreign policy orientation was labeled ideological pluralism and called for the development of normal and mutually profitable relations with all countries, regardless of their ideological or political inclinations.

As was the case with most major countries in Latin America, China's establishment of formal diplomatic relations resulted in a joint communiqué, signed in this instance on February 19, 1972. Following the normalization of diplomatic relations with China, trade prospered. On December 8, 1972, China agreed to buy 3 million tons of wheat and maize from Argentina over the next three years. The agreement was initialed in Beijing.[24] The return of the Peronists to power in 1973 resulted in the further strengthening of bilateral relations. Within the framework of the "Third Position" doctrine—a kind of nonaligned foreign policy orientation promoted by Perón—the Peronist government acted quickly to improve relations with the socialist countries.

Argentina became an important trading partner of China's, especially on the export side. Although the general foreign trade regulations of the various Argentine governments in the 1970s were based on different criteria and approaches, similar external and internal economic imperatives influenced Argentina's attitude toward trading with China. Particular mention should be made in this respect of the growing difficulties Argentina encountered in its economic development, difficulties due to its unfavorable state of trade with its traditional trading partners in North America and Western Europe, following the crisis in those countries during the period in question. The situation was aggravated by the growing protectionism in developed market economy countries that seriously damaged Argentina's traditional exports (e.g., meat) and its exports of manufactured goods. The adverse situation led the authorities to search for new solutions in the external sector. China appeared to offer an important alternative on the basis of long-term trade relations supplemented by the promotion of economic cooperation in areas where China was considered to have comparative advantages. After the military coup in 1976, China maintained close economic ties with Argentina despite that government's anti-leftist and anti-Communist policies, this is perhaps the clearest example of the extent that economic motivation replaced the political and ideological approach.[25] For China, Argentina was seen to be of great importance as a supplier of vital agricultural products such as grains as well as some types of manufactured products.

For Argentina, China has been more important as an export market than as a source of imports. The trade deficit remained very high in the 1970s. Argentina's exports to China were made up entirely of grains. The Chinese exported only small quantities of manufactured goods in return. The 1970s saw a tendency for the commodity concentration to become more diversified, but wheat still accounted for more than half of the trade.

Mexico

Until 1970, Mexico tended to follow the United States, maintaining distant relations with China. Beginning with the Echeverría administration (1970–1976), Mexico's foreign policy became more assertive and more active in world affairs than it had been traditionally. Mexico proposed the Charter of Economic Rights and Duties of States, which authorized the formation of commodity cartels and the expropriation of foreign investment to the UNCTAD in 1972 and was instrumental in the formation of Latin American Economic System (SELA) and the Multinational Caribbean Shipping Fleet. In the fall of 1971, when the United States still proposed recognition of both Chinese governments (the PRC and Taiwan), Mexican president Luis Echeverría made a speech in the United Nations advocating the admission of the Beijing government and the expulsion of Taiwan; Mexico recognized Beijing soon after and began actively promoting trade with China—a sign of increasing independence and self-assertiveness in foreign policy. However, the fundamental motivation behind Mexican desire to have diplomatic and commercial relations with China stemmed from its wish to expand its markets.[26]

Since taking office, President Echeverría endeavored to reduce Mexico's economic dependence and traditional alignment with the West and looked toward the socialist countries for help. He felt that an enhancement of Sino-Mexican bilateral relations would contribute significantly toward the realization of this new eastward-looking policy.

On February 14, 1972, China and Mexico signed a joint communiqué that formally established diplomatic relations between the two countries. Trade between the two has been expanding since then. Invited by Mao in April 1973, Echeverría was the first Latin American president to visit the People's Republic. Premier Zhou Enlai accompanied his visits to Beijing and other Chinese cities. During 1970–1977, Mexican sales to China were concentrated on a limited number of products, including baled cotton, coffee beans, and some materials such as sulphur and lead oxide. Mexican purchases from China were dominated by rice. Other purchases included paraffin, amp gauges, clothing, toys, and asbestos.[27] In 1972 when the United States reduced Mexico's U.S. sulphur import quotas, the Chinese imported fifty tons of sulphur. The Mexicans expressed gratitude for China's timely help.[28] Two-way trade between China and Mexico rose from less than $1 million in 1970 to $52 million in 1977, and Mexico enjoyed a large trade surplus. Over this period, Mexico exported $160 million worth of goods to China and imported only $51 millon worth in return.[29]

Brazil

Brazil and the People's Republic of China had little to do with each other either politically or as trading partners for more than a quarter century after 1949. Ideologically, they were poles apart except for a short period under the presidencies of Quadro and Goulart. In late 1971, the minister of finance, Antônio Delfim Netto, set forth the official position of the regime in stating that economic relations with China (1) were not practical because the Communist Chinese economy is controlled by the state and (2) were not possible because the two countries do not have political relations.[30] During the Garrastazú Médici administration (1969–1973), Brazil's international relations were characterized by orthodox anticommunism with great emphasis on national security. Brazil's conservative governments were more comfortable with Taiwan's regime, with which they maintained diplomatic relations until 1974, three years after China was voted as a member of the United Nations.

However, since the mid-1970s, relations with China improved after they were frozen in the mid-1960s. The Ernesto Geisel administration (1974–1979) launched its famous "independent" policy based on the idea of responsible pragmatism. This policy was centered on the idea that "to diversify dependency was an essential strategy for Brazil to acquire a more relevant international status."[31] This diversification involved the following conditions: reducing dependency on the United States, increasing trade and diversifying the markets for it, and opening relations with other regions of the world.[32] Brazil began to expand its trade throughout the Third World and the socialist camp.

In 1973, the military government initiated serious but limited efforts to establish commercial links with the PRC. It was a departure from the long-standing policy of banning trade with Communist China. On August 15, 1974, Brazil established diplomatic relations with China. Trade between the two remained insignificant during this period, although the potential for long-term Chinese economic relations with Brazil seemed more favorable than with any other Latin American country.

Major Features of Trade

The most conspicuous feature of Sino–Latin American trade during this period was its extreme commodity concentration, though there were signs of commodity diversification in the late 1970s. The PRC's exports to the regions were negligible but existed in commodities where the PRC had a strong advantage in labor-intensive industries of light manufactured goods. On the import side, the Chinese bought mainly primary commodities (90 percent of total trade).[33]

Second, during the first two decades of the PRC, Beijing openly admitted that it regarded foreign trade as ''a weapon for international political struggle.'' Trade was often used as a tool for attaining political objectives such as diplomatic recognition. The establishment of trade relations prior to diplomatic relations has been very common in Sino–Latin American relations since 1970. Trade agreements between a Latin American nation and one of China's state-owned import and export corporations had usually preceded diplomatic exchanges.[34] Actually, a monopoly over foreign trade was not only an instrument of domestic plan but also a powerful diplomatic tool in various international political situations. The Chinese leaders shifted their purchases from one market to another (e.g., Argentine wheat) and for certain goods (e.g., Cuban sugar) offered prices above world market prices. Thus, China used its monopoly over foreign trade as an offensive tool for its foreign policy.

Third, expansion of China's trade with Latin America during this period was mostly on the import side. Excepting their trade with Cuba, the Latin Americans did not purchase much in return. The total cumulative deficit on the Chinese side amounted to $2.5 billion in the 1970s.[35] Fourth, trade was characterized by the comparatively high degree of fluctuation, which was partly attributable to variations in Chinese economic and political conditions during the Cultural Revolution (1966–1976).

Chinese Aid to the Region

To strengthen its links with the Third World, Beijing also employed an active economic assistance program as a part of its Third World policy. In the 1970s, China was a significant Communist donor of economic assistance to developing countries. Although the bulk of its aid went to Tanzania, Zambia, and Pakistan, several South American countries came into the picture (see Table 4.1). The recipients of Chinese aid in the region included Chile, Peru, and Guyana. Peru was the South American country

Table 4.1
PRC Economic Aid to Latin America: 1970–1977 (in millions of U.S. dollars)

	1970	1971	1972	1973	1974	1975	1976	1977	1970–77
Chile			65						65
Guyana			52			10			62
Peru		42							42
Jamaica							1		10
Other									
Total	0	42	117	0	0	10	1	0	179

Source: Directorate of Intelligence, *Handbook of Economic Statistics, 1976* (Springfield, Va.: CIA, 1976), p. 72; Directorate of Intelligence, *Handbook of Economic Statistics, 1978* (Springfield, Va.: CIA, 1978), p. 76; and, for 1970–1973 figures, Wolfgang Bartke, *China's Economic Aid* (London: Hurst, 1975), p. 21.

to receive economic aid from China during this period. The offer was made as early as three weeks after diplomatic relations had been established. This showed China's satisfaction at having at last found an opportunity in Latin America to practice economic aid on exceptionally good terms. By offering Peru a loan of $42 million, China immediately surpassed the Soviet Union, which had granted a mere $28 million.[36] In 1972, China extended a substantial amount of aid ($65 million) to Allende, an action that was considered partly a response to Soviet ties with that country. However, because of political change in Chile, the aid program remained dormant through the 1980s.[37]

When Beijing offered Guyana an economic aid loan ($52 million) in 1972, China was the first Communist country to undertake such activity in Guyana. On April 9, China and Guyana signed an agreement of technical cooperation, under which Guyana would receive an interest-free loan of $26 million over the five-year period beginning in July 1972. The loan would be repaid over twenty years with a ten-year moratorium.[38] This agreement included the establishment of one or more textile mills, a leather factory, a pig iron plan, and an oil-extraction plant using soybean. These two countries established formal diplomatic relations on June 27. This was the first Chinese diplomatic mission in the Caribbean since initial ties with Cuba were established in 1960.

In addition to financial aid and technical advice, China's contributions to disaster relief in the 1970s were impressive: approximately $1 million to Peru, over $2.5 million to Chile, and over $88,000 to Bolivia, a country that had not even recognized the PRC by then.[39]

In common with the aid of the other major powers, Chinese aid has been an important foreign policy instrument.[40] China's attitude to aid is that it is an "international duty," and "proletarian internationalism" is the guiding principle of its foreign aid.[41] Aid to Latin American countries was a tool China used in its political competition with the two superpowers. Like the superpowers, China is politically motivated; but unlike them, China lacks the ability to support its political objectives.

In some countries, economic aid has become an arena for intense rivalry and struggle for influence not only between China and the West but also between China and the Soviet Union. In this competition, the Chinese have tried to convert quantitative weakness into qualitative strength. Although their aid has been less than that by the Soviets, it has been based on much more generous terms. The most important characteristic of Chinese aid is what is widely acknowledged to be the almost unsurpassed generosity of its terms. In his study *China's Economic Aid*, Wolfgang Bartke indicates:

The most favorable terms China ever granted on repayable loans were offered to Chile (repayment after 50 years!). China's intentions were clear: she wanted to gain a foothold on the Latin American continent which had been closed to her until 1970, having until then been a sphere of influence to the Soviet Union and its satellites. China therefore thought it worth her while to make a generous gesture which would compare favorably with the Soviet Union's very sober terms.[42]

In spite of Beijing's ambition, China lacked the necessary funding for carrying out similar aid programs. Its isolation from the area and lack of knowledge and expertise placed it in a disadvantageous position relative to the U.S. and Soviet diplomacy of aid.

SUMMARY

Growth of Sino–Latin American relations during this period was a general phenomenon related to shifts in international power alignments. Sharpening of conflicts between China and the Soviet Union was an important factor. The United States adopted a policy of rapprochement with China after Nixon's visit to Beijing. A conjunction of forces both inside and outside Latin America and the PRC facilitated a closer relationship. The most important motivation behind the increase in economic relations between China and Latin America was political. The principal objective of China's policy toward Latin America was to gain diplomatic recognition from Latin America and Beijing partly achieved its goal. In the 1970s, Chinese circles of contacts with Latin American states widened. Between 1970 and 1977, Latin American nations formally recognizing Taiwan dropped form twenty to twelve, whereas the number recognizing the PRC went from one to twelve. In addition, although Sino–Latin American trade relations in the 1960s were dominated by Beijing-Havana links, the 1970s witnessed increasing geographical diversification.

On the whole, changes in political setting had a profound bearing on the development of trade relations between the two regions. However, as subsequent chapters reveal trade relations were based not on political factors alone but also on the complementary features of both economies. In brief, in many ways this period was a transitional phase in which Latin American–Chinese relations moved from a rather low to a more significant level. The nature and extent of increased economic relations in the two regions after 1978 is the subject of the next chapter.

NOTES

1. The ultimate meaning of the Sino-Soviet rift became clear after 1968, when Chinese foreign policy seemed to be guided primarily by opposition to the Soviet Union. The Chinese invariably supported Third World movements and governments that opposed the Soviet Union, even if they were repressive dictatorships.

For instance, the Chinese maintained good relations with the Pinochet government of Chile after the coup in 1973.

2. For a detailed study on this topic see John Franklin Copper, *China's Foreign Aid: An Instrument of Peking's Foreign Policy* (Lexington, Mass.: Lexington Books, 1976).

3. For a fuller text of the speech, see *Peking Review*, 15, no. 16 (April 21, 1972), pp.11–14.

4. *Peking Review*, 16, no. 35–36 (September 7, 1973), p. 22.

5. Ibid., p. 22.

6. Roger W. Fontaine and James D. Theberge, eds. *Latin America's New Internationalism: The End of Hemispheric Isolation* (New York: Praeger, 1976), pp. 160–61.

7. Robert L. Worden, "China and Latin America: A 'Last Frontier,'" in *China's Foreign Relations: New Perspective*, ed. Chün-tu Hsüeh (New York: Praeger, 1982), p. 139.

8. *Almanac of China's Foreign Economic Relations and Trade, 1984* (Hong Kong: China Resources Trade Consultancy Co., 1984), pp. 890–902.

9. International Monetary Fund, *Direction of Trade Annual, 1970–1976* (Washington, D.C.: IMF, 1976), p. 95; and IMF, *Direction of Trade Annual 1971–1977* (Washington, D.C.: IMF, 1977), p. 98.

10. Mr. Zhang, a senior Chinese diplomat, has served as the chairman of Chinese Association of Latin American Studies since 1985.

11. Cited in Sha Ding et al., *Zhongguo he ladinmeizhou quanxi jianshi* (Brief History of Sino–Latin American Relations) (Zhenzhou, China: Henan People's Publishing House, 1986), p. 305.

12. Michael H. Erisman, "Cuba's Long March: The Struggle for Third World Leadership," *SECOLAS Annuals*, no. 11 (1980) p. 46.

13. Suk Chin Ha, "The PRC's Influence in Latin America (1949–1973): A Reassessment," *Political Studies Review: The Journal of the Association of Korean Political Scientists in North America*, no. 1 (1985), pp. 118–19.

14. Convenio comercial entre el gobierno de la República de Chile y el gobierno de la República Popular China.

15. *Prensa Latina*, April 25, 1971, quoted in *USSR and Third World*, 1, no. 5 (April 26–June 1, 1971) p. 278.

16. *Almanac of China's Foreign Economic Relations and Trade, 1984*, p. 892.

17. William A. Joseph, "China's Relations with Chile under Allende: A Case Study of Chinese Foreign Policy in Transition," *Studies in Comparative Communism*, 18, nos. 2 and 3 (Summer-Autumn, 1985.), p. 140.

18. Romania was the only other socialist state to maintain relatively normal relations with Chile in the wake of the coup.

19. William A. Joseph, "China's Relations with Chile under Allende," pp. 123–50.

20. Ibid., pp. 145–49.

21. Organization of American States (OAS). Special Consultative Committee on Security, *Against the Subversive Action of International Communism: Analysis of the Second Congress of the Young Communist League (UJC) in Cuba. The Policy of Communist China in Latin America* (Washington, D.C.: OAS, 1972), p. 40.

22. Luo Liecheng, "Development of Economic and Trade Relations between China and Latin American Countries," *Latin American Review* (China), no. 3 (1985), p. 49.

23. *Almanac of China's Foreign Economic Relations and Trade, 1984*, p. 899.

24. Peter Cheng, *Chronology of the People's Republic of China, 1970–1979* (Metuchen, N.J.: Scarecrow Press, 1986), p. 178.

25. The staunchly anti-Communist government of General Jorge Videla was under fire from human rights organizations for its repressive policies and because more than 10,000 people—known as the *desparecidos*—were allegedly killed.

26. Organization of American States (OAS). Special Consultative Committee on Security, *Against the Subversive Action of International Communism: Analysis of the Second Congress of the Young Communist League (UJC) in Cuba. The Policy of Communist China in Latin America* (Washington D.C.: OAS 1972), p. 42.

27. Miguel Alvarez Uriarte and Antonio N. Rubio Sánchez, "Intercambio comercial México–República Popular China," *Comercio Exterior*, 29, no. 4 (April 1979), pp. 494–95.

28. Luo, "Development of Economic and Trade Relations between China and Latin American Countries," p. 49.

29. *Almanac of China's Foreign Economic Relations and Trade, 1984*, p. 897.

30. Cecil Johnson, "China and Latin America: New Ties and Tactics," *Problems of Communism* 21, no. 4 (July-August 1972), p. 64.

31. Alexandre de Souza Costa Barros, "Política exterior Brasilena y el mito de Barón," *Foro Internacional*, 24, no. 1 (July-September, 1983), p. 11.

32. Ibid., p. 11.

33. Michael A. Weininger, "People's Republic of China Latin American Trade Composition and Direction of Trade, 1965–1977," in *Change and Perspective in Latin America: Proceedings of the 1982 Meeting of the Rocky Mountain Council in Latin American Studies*, ed. Richard Bath (El Paso: University of Texas at El Paso, Center for Inter-American and Border Studies, 1982), p. 56.

34. This point is well illustrated in the case of Brazil. Vice-Minister of Foreign Trade Chen Jie was sent to Brasília in August 1974 ostensibly to sign a major import-export agreement. He stayed on after the signing ceremony to make final arrangements for diplomatic recognition several days later. Eight of the first ten Latin American nations to recognize the PRC followed this pattern, though other countries' recognition did not follow so closely on the heels of commercial negotiation. See Robert L. Worden, "China's Foreign Relations with Latin America," in *Dimensions of China's Foreign Relations*, ed. Chün-tu Hsüeh (New York: Praeger, 1977), p. 211.

35. Luo, "Development of Economic and Trade Relations between China and Latin American Countries," p. 49.

36. Wolfgang Bartke, *China's Economic Aid* (London: Hurst, 1975), p. 158.

37. Carol H. Fogarty, "China's Economic Relations with the Third World," in U.S. Congress Joint Economic Committee, *China: A Reassessment of the Economy*, 1975, p. 733.

38. *USSR and Third World*, 2, no. 4 (March 13–April 17, 1972), p. 243.

39. William Ratliff, "Communist China and Latin America, 1949–1972," *Asian Survey*, 12, no. 10 (October 1972), p. 859.

40. For details, see John Franklin Copper, *China's Foreign Aid*.
41. *Peking Review*, 17, no. 43 (October 25, 1974), pp. 16–18.
42. Wolfgang Bartke, *China's Economic Aid*, p. 105.

5

China's Open-Door Policy and Trade with Latin America: 1978–1990

The Chinese economy has undergone a thorough reorganization since the death of Mao Zedong in 1976 and the rise of Deng Xiaoping in subsequent years. China has identified economic modernization as its highest priority. For the first time since 1949, Beijing has accepted the legitimacy of the international order and is seeking normal and stable relations with both superpowers. China has embarked on a sweeping set of policy reforms that have both dramatically accelerated the pace of China's domestic economic development and fundamentally transformed China's economic relations with the outside world. The autarkic policies of the Maoist era have been abandoned, and China has begun a vital transformation toward a pattern of economic growth and development that has led to increasing integration with the world economy. Meanwhile, Beijing is hoping to diversify and expand its exports from raw materials and processed goods to include exports of more refined and technology-intensive products. Here, developing countries are seen as having the best potential. With the advent of China's open-door policy, the 1980s witnessed the beginning of more extensive economic ties between Latin America and China. The new economic relations are characterized by technology transfer, direct investment, extension of credit, and increased trade in commodities. However, so far trade is the most important aspect of economic ties between China and Latin America. The background and implementation of new policy as well as trade relations since 1978 are the subject of this chapter. The opening to the outside world initiated in 1978 has greatly increased the significance of foreign trade within China's economy. In 1988, foreign trade accounted for 28 percent of GDP, whereas the figure was only 10 percent in 1978.[1] China signed several multilateral accords, including the Multi-Fiber Arrangement (MFA), joined major international financial institutions (World Bank and IMF), and applied for membership in the General Agreement on Tariffs and Trade (GATT).

The ending of the Cultural Revolution in 1976 permitted Chinese leadership once more to give serious thought to foreign relations. In the 1980s, Beijing's perception of the global balance of power and China's international environment underwent important changes. From the end of the 1970s to the early 1980s, China was "leaning to the U.S. side." However, since the Twelfth Party Congress in 1982, China declared a return to the policies of Bandung that emphasize the need for peaceful coexistence and independent foreign policy. Only by expanding and diversifying its trade links, regardless of politics, will China be able to pursue a truly independent policy, aligning with neither socialist nor capitalist countries. Thus, ironically, economic interdependence has become a precursor of political interdependence.

During the period under study, Chinese diplomacy increasingly focused on economic issues; even the Chinese themselves called it "economic diplomacy."[2] This method places emphasis on China's international economic, trade contacts rather than on the traditional diplomacy of political, or official, interactions. Chinese decisionmakers believe that a growing economic relationship with Latin America will make ties with that region more stable and durable. After 1978, the Chinese government developed a more active interest in Latin America. The business circles also became increasingly interested in trade and investment opportunities in this area of the world. Trade with Latin America increased continuously since the late 1970s, enabling Beijing to derive economic and political advantages from its contacts with countries in the region.

This chapter is organized in three sections. The first section looks briefly at the significant reorientation in China's policy: the open-door policy since 1978 and independent foreign policy of China in recent years. The second one discusses trends and problems of Latin American economies in the 1980s and their impacts on China's economic ties with the region. The third section presents an overall picture of Sino–Latin American trade. Analysis is also made of the structure and pattern of trade. The chapter concludes with the salient features of China's trade with Latin America. The direct investment and aid program and technology transfer are dealt with in Chapter 6 and Chapter 7.

OPEN-DOOR POLICY SINCE 1978

Because it is well documented, only a brief discussion of China's open-door policy is dealt with here.[3] Chinese planners had previously pursued an import-substitution industrialization policy; foreign trade has historically been small relative to China's total economic activity. The historical turning point for the open-door policy came in December 1978 at the Third Preliminary Session of the Eleventh Central Committee of the Chinese Communist Party (CCP). The communiqué of the Third Plenum announced that China would be "actively expanding economic cooperation on terms of equality and mutual benefit with other countries" and would "strive to adopt the world advanced technologies and equipment." The new outward-looking policy stresses comparative advantage.

Beginning in 1978, the pursuit of economic advantage became an important part of Chinese economic relations with Latin America. Chinese economists no longer argued that the socialist partner should realize a smaller profit than a capitalist investor, in order to make the concept of economic exchange consistent with socialist values and morality. Profit now represented a legitimate part of any economic transaction. For some Chinese policymakers, international trade no longer symbolized exploitation; instead, it became a monetary expression of value, a universal norm of accounting that ensures efficient operations.

Independent Foreign Policy

Since the beginning of the 1980s, China has put great stress on an independent policy and on its ties with the Third World. The Chinese have emphasized their wish for state-to-state relations that increase economic exchanges. Meanwhile, Beijing's Third World policy has undergone a shift from a negative vision of common struggle of global underdogs to a positive and functional notion of North-South and South-South cooperation. In the UN General Assembly, Security Council, and other important UN organizations, Beijing frequently takes the side of Latin America and other Third World nations. According to a study by the Mexican Foreign Affairs Secretariat, China voted with Mexico on 90 percent of twenty resolutions of high priority to Mexican foreign policy concerns during the Forty-Third Session of the UN General Assembly (1988).[4] In its campaign to elect Peruvian diplomat Javier Pérez de Cuéllar as UN secretary-general on December 15, 1981, Beijing scored a major diplomatic victory.[5] The goal of the Chinese policy was to promote friendly relations with all Third World countries, and this necessarily involved supporting the local bourgeoisie—who generally formed government. Relations with radical groups such as Sendero Luminoso (Shining Path) in Peru and the Farabundo Martí Movement for National Liberation (FMLN) in El Salvador are ignored.

Meanwhile, China has abandoned its practice of drawing policy lines based solely on a country's connection with the Soviet Union. In Latin America, China wants better relations with all governments, even if they are pro-Soviet as in the case of Nicaragua under the Sandinistas or Cuba. In the past, China had been afraid of "two, three Cubas" in the Caribbean, and it accused the Soviet Union of using Cuba as an "unsinkable" aircraft carrier in the region. In recent years, trade relations with Cuba have improved steadily. At present, China's primary interest in its relations with Latin America lies in maintaining good relations with all the Latin American countries, regardless of the ideological coloration of the government in power.

NEW TRENDS IN LATIN AMERICA

Apart from economic reforms in China and change in its foreign policy orientation, economic factors in Latin America also affected relations between the two regions. In addition, the Latin American countries changed their perceptions toward China, and this heralded a new era of bilateral economic relations.

After two decades of sustained economic growth averaging approximately 6 percent per annum, the Latin American economies entered a period of recession in the 1980s, in some countries reminiscent of the Great Depression. From 1981 to 1989, per capita product in Venezuela fell 26.6 percent, in Argentina 23.5 percent, and in Mexico 9.2 percent. The only Latin American countries whose per capita GDP did not fall during this period are Colombia and Paraguay.[6] In brief, the 1980s was a "lost decade" for Latin American economic development. This has led their policymakers to review the problem of overdependence on trade with and investment from a few developed market economies as the engine of growth. Slow growth in the major OECD countries contributed to the prolonged recession in international commodity markets and the rise of protectionism in the major OECD markets. Protectionism in particular adversely affected the exports of Latin American primary commodities and manufactures. Latin American countries are making serious efforts to diversify their economic relations so that export growth can be sustained. One notable trend in Latin America since the 1970s has been a shift away from economic nationalism and antidependency directions toward greater economic integration with the world economy. Foreign trade has played an important part in these efforts. By seeking new markets and pushing new products, governments throughout the hemisphere have made a determined effort to increase their export earnings in order to meet their heavy debt-service burdens.

In recent years, Latin American countries such as Brazil, Argentina, and Mexico have turned to new markets among the Third World countries. With industrialization, these countries have developed the concomitant industrial know-how and technology. Exports of industrial services primary to Third World have also grown considerably.[7] Under such circumstances, economic interactions between Latin America and the PRC have expanded markedly.

THE OVERALL PICTURE OF TRADE

Given China's technological and economical underdevelopment, trade with other countries plays an important role in China's own economic development. Trade is of crucial importance in relations between China and Latin America, since their economic interactions in areas such as financial and technical cooperation have not developed significantly. The principal goal of China's new trade strategy is to facilitate and accelerate industrialization by increasing imports of required equipment and raw materials not available at home, and by earning hard currency through the export of fuels and manufactured goods. Trade with Latin American countries is important to this new policy orientation for two reasons. First, Latin America is a newly industrializing region endowed with wide agricultural land and abundant natural resources. It possesses vast potential for development. Second, the region has already grown into an major market for many products China is interested in exporting, such as fuel and manufactured items. In other words, China looks to Latin America as a rich export market through which valuable foreign exchange could be earned.

To make possible the continuous development of their mutual economic relations, China and Latin America have taken several measures conducive to the establishment of diversified cooperation,[8] the main elements of which are a wide range of trade and economic cooperation agreements concluded for various periods of time. These agreements have been of the following types:

- intergovernmental agreements and protocols on trade and payments[9]
- intergovernmental agreements on economic, scientific, and technical cooperation;
- intergovernmental maritime agreements
- specific agreements and arrangements at an enterprise level on inter- or intrabranch cooperation (see Appendix B for details).

By the end of 1990, China had signed long-term trade agreements with thirteen Latin American countries and economic and technical cooperation agreements with ten Latin American countries. In addition, Beijing also signed maritime transportation agreements with five countries in the region, namely, Brazil, Argentina, Chile, Mexico, and Cuba.[10] In 1984, China established a trade center, the China United Trading Corporation, Ltd., Panama, the biggest Chinese export and import company in Latin America. To foster further growth of Sino–Latin American trade, a special comprehensive organization, the China National Latin American Trading Corporation (CNLATC) was set up in 1985 with a branch in Brazil. Other

Chinese import and export corporations have also set up branch offices in Latin America.[11]

Growth of Trade

During much of this period both China's exports to and especially imports from Latin America developed faster than its overall trade.[12] The share of Latin America in its overall trade increased in terms of export from 0.4 percent in 1970 to 1.6 percent in 1989. On the import side, the result was much more impressive. The share of Latin America increased from 0.2 percent in 1970 to 4 percent in 1989.

Sino–Latin American trade, though still insignificant relative to those with other regions, has been marked by remarkable expansion over the last few years. In 1978, the PRC's two-way trade with Latin America broke the $1 billion mark, and by 1990 it soared to $3 billion. However, trade with the region suffered a serious setback between 1986 and 1987. Two factors explain this setback: First, crude oil became the most common Chinese export to Brazil, and the dramatic fall of the price of oil since 1986 resulted in a fall in the value of bilateral trade. In 1987, crude oil represented about 90 percent of China's exports to Brazil. The 1986 total bilateral trade of $1.2 billion was halved to $620 million in 1987. Second, the last decade witnessed the worst and most prolonged recession in many Latin American countries since the 1930s. The recession forced these countries to greatly reduce their imports and to improve their current account balances.

China's Imports from Latin America

The commodity structure of China's imports from individual Latin American countries differs from one to another. Sugar occupies a dominant place in China's imports from Cuba; steel products are imported in relatively big quantities from Brazil, Argentina, and Mexico; aluminum is imported from Venezuela. An important import from Peru and Chile is copper. Latin American agricultural goods have been significant items in trade with China. In the early 1990s China is Uruguay's primary buyer of wool, followed by the Soviet Union, which previously was the biggest wool importer, at 10,000 tons annually.[13] In 1988, China bought half the fish meal that Peru sold on the world market. Each of these commodities uniquely characterizes the local economic foundations of the countries involved. True, China hopes to promote its friendship with Latin America through trade. But Chinese purchases of Chilean and Peruvian copper, for example, are also an economic necessity. As of 1988, there were eight major copper-producing countries in the world: the United States, Chile, the Soviet Union, Canada, Zambia, Zaire, Peru, and Poland. None of these eight countries is Asian, and therefore China must buy copper from other continents.

Imports from Latin America were for a long time dominated by a few items, mostly in the categories of agricultural and mineral commodities. With the new economic policy in China, since 1978 rapid development of industrialization has demanded more raw materials as well as manufactured goods from abroad. Brazil has become a leading Latin American supplier of manufactures to China. In 1988, 36 percent of Brazil's exports to China were manufactured goods.[14] The figure in 1980, in contrast, was only 3 percent. Over the past decade, imports have become more and more diversified. Among the Chinese imports from the region are copper, rough molybdenum, iron ore, zinc, wool, wheat, and cane sugar, with chemical products, light industry products, chemical fibre, and steel products gradually adding to the list in recent years.[15]

Chinese imports have emphasized semifinished goods and industrial materials, especially steel, as well as nonferrous metals. In the late 1980s China overtook the U.S. as Brazil's major market for steel products. The Chinese bought 622,160 metric tons of steel in the first five months of 1985. This represented more than 26 percent of Brazil's steel exports.[16]

In 1984, Chinese imports from Latin America consisted of agricultural products (SITC 1-2), 21 percent; food items (SITC 0), 20 percent; steel and iron, 29 percent (SITC 67); chemical products (SITC 5), 10 percent; and machinery and transport (SITC 7), 11 percent.[17] Yet for some Latin American countries, exports to China remained little diversified; as already noted, they consisted mainly of unprocessed or semiprocessed goods. For example, five items accounted for the bulk of Chile's export to the PRC (92 percent in 1987), as follows: fish meal, 7.1 percent; saltpeter, 2.6 percent; wood, 7 percent; cellulose, 42.7 percent; and copper, 33 percent.[18]

China's Exports to Latin America

China's exports to Latin America were concentrated on just a few products. Since 1980, attempts have been made to diversify the trade structure. In 1989, exports included rice, cotton cloth, petroleum, chemical materials, mineral products, and animal byproducts. China's exports of manufactured goods have increased somewhat extending to textiles and light industry products including a wide range of consumer goods, notably watches, radios, and television sets, as well as arts and crafts. Its exports in the 1980s and early 1990s included machinery and electronics.

No discussion of Sino–Latin American trade would be complete without singling out petroleum and coal products for special discussion. Both are strategic commodities that have played key roles in PRC–Latin American ties. To improve its trade balance, China took vigorous steps to increase its oil production and exports (see Table 5.1). Chinese exports of crude oil began in 1974. By 1980, the export value had reached $286 million. China's share of total export value increased from 10 percent in 1975 to 15 percent in 1980 and 21 percent in 1985. In 1987 the volume reached $300 million.[19] China has discovered more than 160 oil fields and 30 gas fields since 1979. Output in the past decade has been 2.6 times more than the total for the previous thirty years, with China now ranking fifth in world oil production in the 1980s, behind the Soviet Union, Saudi Arabia, the United States, and Kuwait. Brazil bought oil from China on a trial basis in 1978 and then began importing great quantities during subsequent years. In spite of the fact that since 1986 the total volume of China's crude oil export has been cut because of increasing domestic consumption and the Chinese effort to support the mid-1986 agreement by OPEC to curtail production to increase world price, Chinese oil export to Brazil has been increasing steadily. Although this is a modest amount by international standards, it is one of the most important export items China could offer in trade for the goods that it needs from the region. It is thus likely that China's export of oil will be maintained at least at the current level in the years to come.

China has the third largest reserves of coal in the world.[20] The PRC has almost tripled its exports of coal since 1980, with coal its major export to Latin America. Argentina and Chile are the main recipients of Chinese coal. In addition, in 1988 China exported 66,000 tons of metallurgical coke to Peru that replaced Japanese export of that commodity to this market. Latin American countries lack coal, especially good coking coal, and China has a rich resources of coal.[21] It is conceivable that coal from China might find a growing market in Latin America if shipping facilities are improved.

Table 5.1
PRC Crude Oil Production and Oil Exports, 1978–1989 (thousand barrels daily)

Year	1978	1979	1980	1985	1986	1987	1989
Production	2,082	2,123	2,113	2,496	2,613	2,682	2,765
Exports	226	267	265	600	570	545	490
Brazil	1	16	24	47	55	59	47
Chile				1.5	2.4	5.2	

Source: Central Intelligence Agency (CIA), *International Energy Statistical Review*, November 25, 1990, p. 19. The figures for Chile and Brazil for 1986 are from *Almanac of China's Foreign Economic Relations and Trade, 1986, 1988,* and *1990* (Hong Kong: China Resources Trade and Consultance Co., 1986, 1988, and 1990); and from General Administration of Customs of the PRC, *China's Customs Statistics, 1989,* no. 1, and *China's Customs Statistics, 1990,* no. 1 (Hong Kong: Economic Information Agency, 1989 and 1990).

Manufactured goods are China's foremost nonfuel export commodity to Latin America. China exports lathes, tractors, and electric power generating sets for hydroelectric power stations to this region. Over the past few years, China has become the world's fifth largest exporter of ships and is increasing its efforts to open its market in Latin America. In 1988, for the first time a Chinese shipyard won a contract to build two 62,000 metric ton oil tankers for Chile, the first of their kind to be built in China for a Latin American nation. One tanker was delivered in April, 1989, and the other was delivered in 1990.[22] Argentina also plans to import a 65,000 ton oil tanker from China. In Peru, China is expected to sell 500 coupling buses, at a price of US \$47 million.[23]

The armaments industry is one of China's most successful exports. China is known as the fifth largest exporter of arms in the world, after the United States, the Soviet Union, France, and the United Kingdom.[24] These exports generate much-needed hard currency and help to reduce Beijing's trade deficit. Such sales also help to underwrite the government's ambitious Four Modernizations program—the policy to modernize agriculture, industry, science and technology, and national defense. After considering the size of China's trade deficits with Latin America, it should come as no surprise that China has entered into negotiations to sell a variety of arms and arms-related technology to Latin America.[25]

In May 1987, Beijing declared that it was expected to sell its F-7m supersonic fighters (the Chinese version of the Soviet MIG-21) to Brazil.[26] In fact, the transaction was never made. Others said that Brazil was using the Chinese option as a hedge in case other sources did not offer Brazil the terms it sought. Brazil and China are swapping military equipments for electronic components, guided missiles systems, and liquid fuel rockets with China.[27] In 1988, China delivered sixty Hong Jian-73 antitank missiles to Chile.[28] However, it is China's arms technology deal with Argentina that attracted the most international attention.[29] According to British diplomatic sources in Beijing, China successfully negotiated "a secret deal with Argentina to supply technology for the production of antiship and medium-range missiles capable of hitting the Falkland Islands."[30] However, Chinese arms sale patterns and directions follow the logic for market demand factors, not necessarily the logic of foreign policy priorities. On this matter, Dengist unprincipled pragmatism is rampant.[31]

Balance of Trade

Table 5.2 details the export, import, and balance-of-trade of PRC–Latin American trade. Although these figures are in current price, they clearly show that trade has grown dramatically. It may be noted that the PRC has been persistently facing an adverse balance of trade with Latin

Table 5.2
PRC–Latin American Export and Import Values and Balance of Trade (in millions of U.S. dollars)

Year	1950	1960	1970	1980	1986	1989
Total	1.96	31.3	145.8	1,331	1,605	2,968
PRC's Export	0.05	10.3	75.2	488	395	551
PRC's Import	1.91	21.0	70.6	843	1,210	2,741
PRC's Balance	-1.86	-10.7	4.6	-355	-815	-1,866

Source: *Almanac of China's Foreign Economic Relations and Trade, 1984, 1985,* and *1986* (Hong Kong: China Resources Trade and Consultancy Co., 1984, 1985, 1986); and General Administration of Customs of the PPC, *China's Customs Statistics,* 1990, no. 1 (Hong Kong: Economic Information Agency, 1990).

America, which is the only developing region of the world that has had a trade surplus with the PRC. Africa, the Middle East, and Asia all have had trade deficits with China.

The primary reason for China's huge deficit is a similarity in production patterns, in spite of potential for trade expansion. For instance, coffee and coal are the major sources of foreign exchange for Colombia; however, China is exporting oil and coffee, which have little domestic demand in China.[32] Second, some Latin American purchases from China are composed of nonessential consumer goods that in many countries in the region are subject to import permits and quotas. This acts as a disincentive to the sellers of these products and thus depresses the level of Chinese exports. Third, in spite of the fact that China does not need certain agricultural goods from Latin America, it continues to purchase these products in order to implement Chinese foreign policy goals.[33] These imports may entail significant opportunity costs. Nonetheless, in recent years, this has become less common in bilateral trade.

The trade deficit is also caused by the fact that Latin America produces some raw materials the Chinese badly need. China, for its part, manufactures few industrial goods that the Latin Americans must purchase from external sources. From the Chinese perspective, Latin America is more developed than most Asian and African countries and thus better able to absorb Chinese manufactured products. In spite of current setbacks in trade and a trade balance unfavorable to the PRC, the Chinese side is very optimistic about the future of Sino–Latin American trade. Beijing is expecting to double the present volume of two-way trade in the 1990s.[34] Partly for these reasons, Chinese officials have been willing to incur large trade deficits in order to establish themselves in a potentially good market.

Principal Trading Partners

Chinese trade relations with Latin America have not been evenly distributed with all the countries in the region. Analyzed by country, the most important trade partner is Brazil, with 35 percent of two-way trade. Argentina and Cuba constituted the second and third, with 19.4 percent and 14.9 percent respectively. They are followed by Peru, Mexico, and Chile.[35] The volume of trade with these six countries usually makes up 85 percent, in some years even more than 90 percent, of the total trade volume between China and Latin America. The other trading partners in the region include Uruguay, Venezuela, Trinidad and Tobago, and the Bahamas. The total trade volume between China and these four countries is less than $100 million, making up only 5.75 percent of the total volume of Sino–Latin American trade. The trade volume between the remaining three-quarters of the Latin American countries and China is even smaller, consisting of just about 1 percent of the total trade volume between China and the region as a whole.

Of all Latin American countries, Brazil had the highest increase in the relative share of China's trade with Latin America: from 11 percent in 1978 to 35 percent in 1989. Mexico's percentage decreased significantly, from 16 percent to 6.5 percent during the same period.

Brazil

In the past few years, Chinese-Brazilian relations have undergone fundamental changes as bilateral ties have increased and deepened. Chinese trade with Brazil has accounted for 35 percent of Chinese exports to Latin America and about 50 percent of Chinese imports from the area. As mentioned earlier, China exports crude oil and imports mineral products for its modernization efforts. Brazil offers the best hope of accomplishing both objectives because of its immense size and untapped resources.

By 1981, the Brazilian economy, as measured by GNP, had grown to be the tenth largest in the world. The largest country in Latin America, with a population of 140 million, an abundance of natural resources, and an enormous market, Brazil has always had an important position in China's policy toward Latin America. Since the early 1980s, Beijing's trade with Brazil has had an accelerated growth. In 1987, Brazil was China's sixteenth largest trading partner and was the most important trading partner for China in Latin America. As Brazil developed, so did its exports structure. In 1988, manufactured goods accounted for 38 percent of Brazilian export to China; the figure in 1980 was only 3 percent. Moveover, Brazil has the potential to supply China with significant quantities of important raw materials, notably iron ore and timber. Meanwhile, China is keen to diversify its exports from petroleum to rice, corn, cotton, and silk in addition to coal, chemicals, and pharmaceutical products.

The sharp growth of Sino-Brazilian trade since 1978 is partly explained by Brazil's increase in oil imports from China. Brazil imported 24,000 barrels of crude oil daily in 1980, the figure of 1987 reached 59,000 barrels daily. Today, Brazil has become the third largest importer of Chinese crude oil, after Japan and the United States, and China ranks sixth as supplier of oil to Brazil. China could thus be a valuable and reliable substitute when production from the main source tumbles.

In 1988, Brazilian president José Sarney visited Beijing. The two governments signed a protocol on the approval of launching and producing satellites and seven other documents. The seven documents included agreements and protocol on cooperation in the fields of transportation, medicine for preventing and treating epidemic disease, traditional medicine, industrial technology, and power industry, as well as letters of exchange about consular affairs and simplification of visa application procedures.[36] It may be reiterated that Brazil will continue to be the mainstay of China's overall economic relations with Latin America, with the bulk of China's trade with the region centered on this country. In short, the relations between Brazil and China have been based on a remarkable complementarity of their productive sectors and their respective import and export needs. This is reflected in the fact that Brazil is by far China's largest trading partner in Latin America.

Cuba

Since the early 1980s, Havana and Beijing subsequently sought to repair the strains in their relations. China's trade and technological relations with Cuba have improved steadily. The distinguished role of Cuba's leadership in the creation and development of the major organizations of the Third World is well known. Therefore, friendly relations with Havana are very important, especially if China were to gain further support from the Nonaligned Movement and the rest of the Third World and benefit more fully in the areas of economic collaboration. With the improvement of Sino-Soviet relations, Beijing's policy toward Havana has gradually changed. Beijing no longer worries that Havana might fall into the Soviet orbit.

Castro is seen as a "comrade," a word suggesting that there are no serious ideological difficulties between Beijing and Havana. In return, Castro no longer accuses Beijing of "betrayal of internationalism and alliance with imperialism." With the recent changes in Eastern Europe and the Soviet Union, Moscow might redefine its relations with Havana. From Cuban eyes, when the dust of reform settles, the Chinese economic and political order will remain socialist in character; Cubans are confident that Beijing will therefore find more common with Havana than with Moscow and West. In view of this, Havana sincerely hopes that Beijing will become a major economic partner and political supporter, especially since there are fewer socialist-oriented regimes in the world. In the light of the above consideration, Cuban leaders believe that Havana has nothing to lose and everything to gain from expanding relations with Beijing. In brief, both Cuba and China need each other in order to improve their international position. In many areas, China and Cuba have followed parallel policies: a common commitment to socialism, criticism of the U.S. involvement in Central America, support of Sandinistas in Nicaragua, opposition to the U.S. invasion of Panama, and so forth.

Against this background, the 1980s and the early 1990s have seen a growing trade link between China and Cuba. In October 1983, the Cuban minister of external trade, Ricardo Cabrisas, visited Beijing. Cabrisas was the first high-ranking Cuban official to pay a visit to China since the worsening of relations between the two in the mid-1960s. In the same year, the total volume of trade between the two countries more than doubled from 1978. During much of the 1980s, Cuba remained China's second or third largest trading partner in Latin America. In 1989, the two-way trade reached $440 million, about 15 percent of PRC total trade with Latin America.

Accepting an invitation from China's Ministry of Communication to negotiate a maritime transport agreement, the Cuban vice-minister of transport and his delegation arrived in Beijing on February 21, 1984. Agreement on the provisions for the accord was soon reached, and on March 3, 1984, an accord was signed in that city. Following up on their maritime transport agreement, the China State Shipbuilding Corporation sought to obtain an order to build ships for the Cuban government. A barter arrangement was negotiated, swapping ships for sugar. In April 1986, a Chinese shipyard for the first time received a Cuban order for merchant ships. Officials of a Cuban state-owned fishing organization and officials of the Shanghai Shipyard signed a contract in Beijing on April 4, 1986. They agreed to build three 12,600 deadweight ton, technologically efficient, multipurpose ships capable of both 724 TEU (twenty-foot equivalent unit) and 319 FEU (forty-foot equivalent unit) containers. When the container supports are removed, the ships are capable of carrying general or bulk cargos. Credit terms amounting to $30 million were arranged with the China National Machinery Import and Export Corporation and were to be paid for by Cuban sugar shipments over a period of eight years.[37]

Cuban exports to the PRC amounted to $230 million in 1989, compared with only $70 million in 1970. Cuban imports from the PRC increased from $71 million to $212 million during the same period. An economic cooperation agreement and a trade protocol worth $500 million was signed in December 1989, following the second meeting of the Cuba-China Joint Economic Cooperation Commission. This represents an increase of 11 percent over the 1989 figure. The sugar price formula was also signed, but not made public. China pays a preferential price, but one much closer to world prices than is paid by the Soviet Union.[38]

In terms of commodities structure, trade flows remain very traditional. Sugar constitutes an overwhelming share in Cuba's exports to China, which exports mainly manufactured goods and food to Cuba. In 1989, the products making up Chinese exports to Cuba were manufactured products (50 percent), food (34 percent), and chemical products (10 percent). Yet for Cubans, exports to China are still characterized by a low level of diversification that, as already noted, consists mainly of agricultural goods. For many years, Cuba's primary export to China was sugar. The underdeveloped state of the Cuban consumer industry provides China with a sizable market for its light industrial products. Nowadays Chinese consumer goods are popular in Cuba; even Fidel Castro has said openly, "in Cuba no one has never used Chinese-made thermometers, no baby has never used Chinese-made milk bottles, no one has never worn Chinese textiles, and no one has never used Chinese cooling ointment (essential balm)".[39] In the years ahead, Cuba will become more important for Chinese export. This is because of three reasons. First, the Chinese are making a serious bid to diversify their export markets. Second, they regard Cuba as a potentially extensive market for their growing exports of manufactured goods. Third, unlike their trade with other Latin American countries that encountered huge deficits on the Chinese side, their trade with Cuba has been fairly balanced, since the bulk of the bilateral trade has been on a barter base.

Parallel to trade, other areas of economic relations have been enlarged and strengthened. In November 1989, for example, Beijing and Havana signed their second scientific and technological agreement. After a gap of more than two decades, both sides decided to further cooperation in the fields of public health and agriculture, and in the fishery and sugar industries. The document will be in effect for five years.[40]

In addition, industrial cooperation has also become a critical dimension of China's relations with Cuba. In October 1990, China and Cuba signed an economic protocol. Under this agreement, Cuba will use Chinese credit to build factories producing bicycles and electric fans. The factories will use Chinese equipment and will have the capacity to produce 150,000 bicycles and 100,000 electric fans annually.[41] In the same month, the Chinese minister of light industry visited Havana, where the two sides signed an agreement on cooperation of sugar production.[42] The Chinese are also interested in setting up plants producing color television in that country. Although economic aid will remain an important feature of Chinese policy in the Third World, a large-scale commitment to Cuba is highly unlikely.

The recent years have witnessed frequent exchange between two government officials. In June 1989, the PRC foreign minister, Qian Qichen, visited Cuba. This was the first time a Chinese foreign minister made such a trip. On behalf of the Chinese president Yang Shankun, the Chinese foreign minister invited Castro to visit China. The Cuban leader accepted the invitation "with pleasure."[43]

However, because of China's own financial difficulties, China is unlikely to offer significant commitment to Cuba. In addition, since Beijing has other attractive trading partners in the region, such as Brazil and Argentina, Cuba's relative importance in China's Latin American trade has unquestionably diminished. Although Cuba remains one of China's biggest trading partners in the Latin American region, its share in China's overall trade with the region dropped significantly, from 77 percent in the 1960s to 23.4 percent in 1970–1977 and 15 percent in 1989.[44] To sum up, Sino-Cuban relations are expected to be strengthened, but dramatic changes in relations are unlikely to take place quickly.

Argentina

During the military dictatorship (1976–1983), Argentina's trade deficit with the United States increased at a rate more than $2 billion per year, an increase not compensated for by its exchange with the European Community, which was importing less and less from Argentina. This unfavorable international scenario forced the country to trade with the socialist countries. In June 1980, General Jorge R. Videla (1976–1980) became the first South American president to visit China. The atmosphere at talks with Chairman Hua Guofeng and Deng Xiaoping was described by the Chinese side as "sincere, friendly and cordial."[45] During Videla's three-day visit, the two sides signed agreements for economic, scientific, and technical cooperation and cultural exchanges. They also agreed to strengthen cooperation in various fields, including agriculture, raw materials, petroleum, shipping, trade and commerce, fishery, and railway transportation.[46] Politically, the PRC firmly supports Argentina in its sovereign rights to the Malvinas/Falkland Islands on the basis that its claim is just and must be respected by the international community.

Argentina and China have become major trading partners over the last few years. China's need for a reliable supplier of grains and Argentina's need for stable markets for its agricultural exports laid the groundwork for their expanding relations. China has been trying to diversfy its grain suppliers. For instance, despite the Sino-U.S. grain agreement requiring China to purchase a stipulated quantity of grain annually, China turned to Argentina and Canada as alternative sources for grain when she objected to the U.S. textile import policy.[47]

Argentina is the second largest and second most populous country in Latin America, next to Brazil. Having traditionally developed its agriculture, this country became a pioneer in the industrialization of Latin America. Argentina now occupies a leading position in economic and industrial development among the developing countries. It has a diversified industrial structure and can offer not only for domestic consumption but also for export a broad variety of manufactured goods. They range from traditional articles (e.g., leather and agricultural products) to sophisticated technology, including complete industrial plants and equipment.

Argentina also offers the possibility of absorbing China's exports of textiles, ships, and machine tools. Initially, foodstuffs dominated Argentina's exports to China, but manufactured items such as iron and steel products became increasingly important in the commodity structure of trade, especially during the late 1980s. Of Argentina's total imports from China, the percentage of metallurgical products rose from 4.3 in 1978–1979 to 45.7 in 1985–1986. The share of textiles increased from 1.4 percent to 20 percent. Argentina agreed to import 300,000 tons of coal from China between 1989 and 1991 at an estimated cost of $10 million a year.[48]

Despite the rise in two-way trade, China has had a sizable trade deficit with its Latin American trading partners, with Argentina the largest deficit. In 1988 Argentina accounted for 19 percent of China's imports from Latin America, but only 2 percent of China's exports to Latin America. The deficit reached US$400 million; the figure was higher than the total value of Chinese exports to the Latin American region in the same year.[49] In 1989, the trade deficit topped $567 million.[50] With such imbalanced trade, it will be very difficult to reverse the trend.

President Raúl Alfonsín's four-day visit to China in May 1988 offered the Chinese the chance to rectify the bilateral trade balance running strongly in Argentina's favor. The two parties discussed a series of bilateral schemes. These included the following:

- Argentina's renewal of a $300 million credit line to finance imports from China.
- An agreement under which China would supply annually 210,000 tons of coal for the steel industry and 100,000 for thermoelectric power plants. In return, Argentina's Siderca would supply $340 million worth of steel tubes to the Chinese oil industry.
- A scientific and technical cooperation agreement under which Argentina would transfer $50 million worth of equipment for the food-processing, chemical, and agroindustrial sectors.
- An Argentine investment program in livestock breeding, with the investors supplying the cattle, introducing pasture improvement techniques, and managing production.
- The opportunity for fifty-five Argentine firms to test the market for industrial projects valued at $50 million.
- The possibility of setting up joint enterprises for fishing.
- The possible purchase by Argentina of heavy water for its nuclear reactors.[51]

In May 1990, Chinese president Yang Shangkun visited Buenos Aires. In November of the same year, Argentine president Carlos Menem paid a return visit to Beijing. Two sides signed several important agreements. China agreed to participate in an irrigation project in Argentina, to increase the amount of wheat it buys, and to award export credit worth $20 million while Buenos Aires pledged $300 million in export credits to China.

Chile

The last few years witnessed closer trade ties between Beijing and Santiago. From 1984 to 1988, Chile's imports from China increased four times from $12.4 million in 1984 to $55 million in 1988.[52] There have been increasing signs that the trade figures will continue to rise. Chile has been the PRC's main source of copper. In 1983 and 1984, Beijing bought record amounts of Chilean copper as part of a huge increase in total copper imports encouraged by China's booming modernization drive and open-door policy for foreign trade. The other items imported by China from Chile included fish meal, saltpeter, and cellulose.

Chile is important to the Chinese not only because it is the world's largest copper producer and exporter but also because it is a meaningful market for Chinese manufactured products, some of which face increased barriers in Western markets. The Chilean market has also been a highly significant outlet for goods such as crude oil and coal. In 1985, China exported 73,000 metric tons of crude oil to Chile. The figure reached 23,000 metric tons in 1988.

Apart from fuels, Chinese exports to Chile encompass a wide range of manufactured products such as textiles, electric appliances, bicycles, porcelain, gauze for medical use, tools, and machinery. These are mainly consumer-oriented light manufactured goods, but they can provide competition in the Chilean market for similar goods from South Korea and Taiwan. So far such competition has had beneficial effects on Chile. However, as the Chilean economy becomes industrialized and its own manufactured goods become available, such aggressive sale of Chinese goods may create trade frictions. The export of Chinese goods to Chile was successful partly because Chilean governments adopted a coordinated economic policy advocating free trade. Import-export controls were further relaxed and import tariffs lowered from year to year.

The change of government in Chile in late 1989 did not in any way affect Sino-Chilean economic relations. Two-way trade topped $247 million in 1989, making Chile the fourth largest trading partner for China in Latin America. At the conclusion of President Yang Shangkun's visit to Chile in May 1990, the two sides signed a memorandum of cooperation in plant quarantine. During his visit, both Yang and his counterpart Patricio Aylwin expressed satisfaction over their countries' relations. They hoped that such fruitful cooperation would expand to more fields. Yang returned to his country via Easter Island, a route to Latin America the Chinese intend to start using.

Mexico

Beijing has long used Mexico City as a base for expanding its diplomatic, cultural, and political activities in the Caribbean and South America. Relations between China and Mexico improved during the López Portillo and Miguel de la Madrid administrations (1976–1988). Although the share of Mexican trade with China remains small, it moved up gradually, from twenty-third position in 1983 to fifteenth in 1987 in terms of Mexican total exports, and from twenty-sixth to fifteenth in terms of Mexican exports during the same period.[53]

President Portillo visited China in October 1978. During his visit an agreement was signed on tourism cooperation. On October 1981, Premier Zhao Ziyang paid a visit to Mexico; this was the first time that a Chinese premier visited a Latin American country. Chinese sources considered it "a new stage in the development of friendly relations between China and Mexico."[54] In 1984, the two countries signed a maritime cooperation agreement. The under-secretary for economic affairs of the Mexican Foreign Affairs Secretariat, Jorge Eduardo Navarrete, indicated that this agreement would facilitate maritime transportation of passengers and the shipping of goods.[55]

From 1983 to 1987, Sino-Mexican trade was favorable to the Mexican side. The balance of trade in 1983 was $43 million; the figure for 1987 reached $85 million. Mexican exports to China rose from $54 million in 1983 to $130 million in 1987, an increase of about 140 percent. Not only did two-way trade grow in quantity, but the variety of commodities sold increased. The major exports included manufactured goods and metal and mineral products. The major export items in 1987 were iron and steel ingots, copper, and chemical products. Manufactured goods and agricultural products are Mexico's major imports from China. In 1987, imports included computer components, maize, and motorcycle and bicycle parts. Beginning in 1989 with the Carlos Salinas administration, trade relations between Mexico and the PRC have continued to grow consistently. Two-way trade reached the highest level of the past two decades. The overall trade amounted to $190 million, fifteenfold the volume between the two countries when diplomatic ties were established in 1972.

Mexico and Brazil are Latin America's most populous, most highly industrialized countries. Mexico's GNP per capita of $1,760 was only $400 less than that of Brazil in 1988.[56] However, despite the size of its economy, Mexico's importance to China has steadily waned. Mexico's share in Sino–Latin American trade fell from 16 percent in 1978 to 7 percent in 1988 and 6.5 percent in 1989. The reasons are fourfold: First, with the economic reforms in recent years, China's production of cotton has increased rapidly; cotton is therefore no longer on the list of major Chinese imports from Mexico. Indeed, it is even being exported in small but increasing quantities. Second, the economic crisis in the 1980s had a negative impact on Mexico's imports. Third, Chinese exports to Mexico, apart from rice, were made up of a wide range of textiles, household items, and other consumer goods commonly considered "nonessentials" with low-income elasticities of demand. Finally, since crude oil is the major export for both sides, both sides have difficulty increasing trade in this area. Obviously, the Chinese economy is less complementary to the oil-producing states than to other Latin American countries.

Peru

With the launching of China's modernization program and the implementation of its open-door policy, the expansion of trade and economic ties with Latin America was seen as mutually beneficial. Since Peru is richly endowed with natural resources, primary goods such as copper, fish meal, lead, and zinc constitute an important portion of China's imports from that country. Recently, China has become the chief importer of Peruvian fish meal. The Chinese export mainly manufactured goods to Peru. Peruvian prime minister Manuel Ulloa Elías paid an official visit to China in October 1982. One result of his visit was that the two parties signed a $40 million trade contract.[57]

China attaches great importance to its relations with the *Alianza Popular Revolucionario Americana* (APRA). Since Alan García Pérez[58] became president in 1985, relations between the two countries continued to grow. At the same time, Beijing found itself under fire from such groups as the "Maoist" *Sendero Luminoso* guerrillas of Peru, who were blamed for a bomb attack on the Chinese embassy in Lima in 1983 on the anniversary of the birth of Mao Zedong.

On June 15, 1986, Chinese premier Zhao Ziyang and Peruvian prime minister Luis Alva Castro signed a document on the extension of using China's loan for Peru in Beijing. The two leaders also attended a ceremony for an approval instrument concerning an intergovernmental trade agreement and its supplementary protocol between the two countries.[59] Although Peru has been weathering its worst economic crisis of the century, the Chinese have adopted a cautious but active attitude toward business opportunities in this market. Notwithstanding the difficulties, the Chinese steadily expand their trade with Peru, which has become a leading customer of Chinese manufactures and major source of fish meal and copper.

Uruguay

The last few years have also seen a rapid development of Sino-Uruguayan relations in both political and economic spheres. The Sanguinetti government took office in March 1985, ending nearly twelve years of military rule. The civilian government saw the PRC as a potential market of more than 1 billion inhabitants for Uruguayan agricultural and livestock products. Yet the government also understood that any long-term commercial agreement would have to be preceded by diplomatic recognition.[60] In 1988 Beijing established diplomatic relations with Montevideo, which had just severed its relations with Taiwan. After establishing diplomatic ties, two countries signed important economic agreements in which Beijing promised to import up to $150 million per year during the next five years.[61] Wool was the predominant export item; it continues to be so today, though in considerably less relative terms. Uruguay's export to China jumped from $36 million in 1980 to $202 million in 1987. Therefore, the trade with China has provided additional market for traditional Uruguayan exports. Uruguay has imported only a small quantity of machinery and light industry products from China, creating a huge deficit on the Chinese side. In 1989, China imported $110 million worth of goods from Uruguay but exported less than $3 million to this market.

In Uruguay's international economic relations, the PRC occupies an important position. A small country of 3 million people, Uruguay is now China's seventh largest trading partner in Latin America, while China is the third largest customer of Uruguayan products, after Brazil and the United States. However, Isidoro Hodara, director of Uruguay's Foreign Trade Department, said that trading with China could not yet make up for losses of trade opportunities with Taiwan. Commenting on this, a Chinese official said this would be resolved in the course of growing bilateral trade.[62] Expansion of economic relations in this period was accompanied by an active phase of diplomatic relations. Exchange of official visits by the top Chinese and Uruguayan leaders followed. In 1988, Uruguayan president Julio María Sanguinetti paid a visit to Beijing. This was followed by numerous exchanges on government and nongovernment levels between the two countries. In May 1990, Chinese president Yang Shangkun visited Montevideo, where the two sides signed an agreement on animal quarantine and sanitation, a memorandum on cooperation in plant quarantine, and an agreement on cooperation in sports.

SUMMARY

This chapter has discussed Sino–Latin American trade, the most visible part of Beijing–Latin American relations. As observed, the PRC has made great improvements in its relations with Latin American countries. In the 1980s, Sino–Latin American ties were stronger than ever before. The trends and dynamics of trade between China and Latin America in both absolute terms and percentages have been promising because both sides have made efforts to diversify their trade relations.

The chapter has identified six salient features of the PRC's trade with Latin America. First, there is a heavy concentration of primary products in China's trade with Latin America. The most important items on the Chinese export list during this period included crude oil and coal. These became the primary hard currency earners for China, and they will remain so in the years ahead. Excluding energy, the PRC's exports to the region were in commodities where the PRC has a strong advantage, mainly in labor-intensive manufactured goods. Manufactured goods are likely to show a significant rise among Chinese exports to the region by the end of this century if China's economic reforms are successful.

Second, two-way trade is not of crucial importance to either side. Latin American sales to the PRC are helpful to the region's major exporters but not critical for their continued economic growth. Trade with Latin America has never exceeded 7 percent of total PRC trade. However, these long-term relations at the economic level provide a stable market for Latin American exports. Under the policy of modernization, imports such as copper, lumber, lead, and zinc are of course of prime importance. Latin American agricultural exports of wheat, fish meal, and maize have been long-term staples for the PRC's consumption.

Third, Cuba used to be the only country with which China had significant economic relations; now Brazil, Argentina, Chile, Peru, and Mexico, among others, have important trade ties with the PRC. Fourth, the rapid trade growth in recent years has been characterized by a large trade deficit on China's side; thus the trade balance between China and Latin American countries has been markedly in favor of Latin American countries. The imbalance has mounted to roughly 20–30 percent of the total volume of bilateral trade and sometimes even exceeded the volume of total Chinese exports to Latin America. Fifth, the most significant change in the composition of China's international trade has been the relative decrease in agricultural products as a component of imports, and their growth as a component of its exports. For instance, cotton used to be one of the principal raw materials imported by China. From the early 1980s onward, China's importation of cotton from Latin America declined. China is currently exporting both cotton and other agricultural goods to the region.

Finally, China's interest in Latin America clearly has a political dimension. However, in recent years, China's interest has been more economic in its orientation. Current Chinese policy has been based on needs, not grandiose ideology. Latin America could eventually become an immensely important trading partner; consequently, in practical terms, it is the economic aspects of the Sino–Latin American connection that dominate relations between the two regions. In short, economic relations have expanded and broadened since the late 1970s. Not only has the bilateral trade grown in quantities, but the variety of commodities sold has increased. Moreover, several new dimensions have been added in these relations, such as joint ventures and technology transfer. We will examine these areas of economic ties in the chapters that follow.

NOTES

1. World Bank, *World Development Report, 1980* and *1990* (New York: Oxford University Press, 1980 and 1990).

2. Since the 1980s, China has aimed at improving relations with Latin America by establishing a closer economic link.

3. For details, see Sam P. S. Ho, *China's Open Door Policy: The Quest for Foreign Technology and Capital: A Study of China's Special Trade* (Vancouver: University of British Columbia Press, 1984), and Teng Weizao and N. T. Wang, *Transnational Corporations and China's Open Door Policy* (Lexington, Mass.: Lexington Books, 1988).

4. Cited in a mimeograph document of *Consejo Empresarios Mexicanos para Asuntos Internacionales* (CEMAI).

5. In closed session for the election of a new UN secretary-general, China cast sixteen votes to block reelection of Kurt Waldheim. In the end, a compromise Third World candidate, Javier Pérez de Cuéllar from Peru, was chosen.

6. Cited in the *New York Times*, February 11, 1990, E. 4.

7. See "Technology Exports From Latin America," in *Economic and Social Progress in Latin America, 1982 Report* (Washington, D.C.: Inter-American Development Bank, 1982).

8. However, a trade agreement was not essential to trade relations. For example, Guatemala and Panama, while having no trade agreements with Beijing play more important roles in PRC–Latin American trade than do Bolivia and Colombia, both of which do in fact have trade agreements with Beijing.

9. Trade agreements do not imply absolute and rigid commitments in respect to every commodity specified. Commodities traded and their volume/value are not always according to agreed plans. Generally, however, the countries are eager to fulfill their trade plans, and the implementation of these agreements is flexible. This means the agreements are guiding indicators, reflecting the intentions and desires of the trading partners.

10. For details, see Irwin Millard Heine, *China's Rise to Commercial Maritime Power* (New York: Greenwood Press, 1989).

11. Unlike other Chinese national foreign trade corporations which are responsible for certain export goods, for instance, the China Textiles Import and Export Corporation trades only goods related to textiles; CNLATC, in contrast, is authorized to trade all kinds of goods with Latin America. Moreover, CNLATC is capitalized at 10 million yuan. It concentrates on energy, livestock, timber, and iron and steel. It also serves as an agent for producers importing and exporting through barter and for other forms of countertrade as well as for promoting direct trade between regions and China. It planned to open branches in Argentina and Central America during 1988 and in Hong Kong to act as a reexport base for trade with Latin America. However, CNLATC was incorporated into the China National Overseas Trading Corporation in early 1990 as a result of "economic rectification and consolidation."

12. I must emphasize that these rates are derived from data in current prices, since the PRC does not publish data in constant prices for its foreign trade.

13. *Beijing Review* (known as the *Peking Review* before December 1978), 33, no. 23 (June 4–10, 1990), p. 9.

14. General Administration of Customs of the PRC, *China's Customs Statistics* (1989, no. 1, Hong Kong: Economic Information Agency, 1989), p. 64.

15. Guo Chongdao and Li Zhixiang, "Sino–Latin American Economic and Trade Relations in Retrospect and Prospect," *Journal of Chinese People's Institute of Foreign Affairs* (China), no. 8 (June 1988), p. 102.

16. *Asian Business*, 21, no. 11 (November 1985), p. 31.

17. United Nations, *Commodity Trade Statistics*, Series D. 34, no. 17 (New York: United Nations, 1986), pp. 1–8.

18. Rafael Aldunate "Relaciones económicas de Chile con la República Popular China," in *Chile en la Cuenca del Pacífico: experiencias y perspectivas comerciales en Asia y Oceania* (Santiago, Chile: Editorial Andrés Bello 1989), pp. 139–149.

19. Directorate of Intelligence, *China: International Trade Annual Statistical Supplement, 1989* (Springfield, Va.: CIA, February 1989), pp. 1–6.

20. W. C. J. van Rensburg, ed., *Strategic Minerals*, Vol. 1, *Major Mineral-Exporting Regions of the World: Issues and Strategies* (Englewood Cliffs, N.J.: Prentice-Hall, 1986), p. 473.

21. China has 1.5 trillion tons of total resources of coal. China therefore has the world's third largest reserves of coal and is the largest producer of coal.

22. *Renmin Ribao* (overseas edition), June 21, 1990, p. 4.

23. Lima Television Peruana in Foreign Broadcast Information Service, *Daily Report: Latin America* (hereafter cited as FBIS–Latin America), October 10, 1989, p. 75.

24. Stockholm International Peace Research Institute (SIPRI), *SIPRI Yearbook 1988, World Armaments and Disarmament* (New York: Oxford University Press, 1988), Table 7.1.

25. Denis Van Vranken Hickey, "Peking's Growing Political, Economic, and Military Ties with Latin America," *Issues and Studies* (June 1989), p. 126.

26. *Renmin Riblao* (overseas edition), May 9, 1987.

27. *South*, 98 (December 1988), p. 48.

28. *SIPRI Yearbook 1990, World Armaments and Disarmament*, p. 247.

29. Denis Van Vranken Hickey, "Peking's Growing Political, Economic, and Military Ties with Latin America," p. 128.

30. Louise Branson, "Secret Argentine Missile Deal," *London Sunday Times*, May 22, 1988, p. 19.

31. Samuel S. Kim, *The Third World in Chinese World Policy, World Order Studies Program Occasional Paper*, No. 19 (Princeton, N.J.: Center for International Studies, Princeton University, 1989), p. 31.

32. For the Chinese population, coffee still remains an expensive and exotic beverage.

33. This observation is based on my conversations in various research institutes in Beijing in early 1989.

34. Interview with a scholar at the Institute of International Trade of the Ministry of Foreign Economic Relations and Trade (MOFERT) in Beijing in January 1989.

35. General Administration of Customs of the PRC, *China's Customs Statistics,* 1990, no. 1 part 1 (Hong Kong: Economic Information Agency, 1990), pp. 10–11.

36. *Renmin Ribao* (overseas edition), July 7, 1988.

37. *Maritime China* (Summer 1986), p. 101, quoted in Irwin Millard Heine, *China's Rise to Commercial Maritime Power* (New York: Greenwood Press, 1989), p. 78.

38. The Economist Intelligence Unit, *Country Report: Cuba, Dominican Republic, Haiti and Puerto Rico* (London) 1990, no. 1, p. 21.

39. Quoted in *Renmin Ribao* (overseas edition), March 10, 1990.

40. Havana Radio Rebelde Network, November 18, 1989, in Foreign Broadcasting Information Service (FBIS)–Latin America, November 20, 1989, p. 6.

41. *Renmin Ribao* (overseas edition), October 13, 1990.

42. *Renmin Ribao* (overseas edition), October 30, 1990.

43. Xinhua, June 9, 1989, in FBIS–Latin America, June 12, 1989, p. 3.

44. *China's Customs Statistics, 1990,* part 1; and *Almanac of China's Foreign Economic Relations and Trade, 1985* and *1986* (Hong Kong: China Resources Trade Consultancy Co., 1985 and 1986).

45. Richard Breeze, "Peking's Sombrero Diplomacy," *Far Eastern Economic Review,* 109, no. 36 (August 29, 1980), p. 28.

46. *Le Monde,* June 10, 1980.

47. Irwin Millard Heine, *China's Rise to Commercial Maritime Power,* p. 70.

48. Wolfgang Deckers, "Latin America: How the Chinese See the Region," *The Pacific Review,* 2, no. 3 (1989), p. 248.

49. *China's Customs Statistics,* 1989, no. 1.

50. *Beijing Review,* 33, no. 22 (May 28–June 3, 1990), p. 34.

51. *Latin American Regional Reports: Southern Cone* (London: Latin American Newsletter), June 30, 1988.

52. Dirección General de Relaciones Económicas Internacionales, Chile.

53. For detailed discussion on China-Mexico trade, see Segundo Seminario de Comercio entre México y China, *Ponencias del segundo seminario de comercio entre México y China* (Proceedings of the second seminar on Trade between Mexico and China), October 1988, Mexico City.

54. *Beijing Review,* 24, no. 45 (November 9, 1981), pp. 8–9.

55. *Notimex,* July 19, 1984, in FBIS–Latin America, July 23, 1984, M3.

56. World Bank, *World Development Report 1990,* p. 179.

57. *Comercio* (Peru), November 5, 1982, in FBIS–Latin America, November 19, 1982, J1–2.

58. Alan García is the president of the APRA.

59. Xinhua, June 14, 1986, in FBIS-China, June 18, 1986, J5.

60. FBIS-Latin America, December 16, 1985, K1.

61. *Madrid EFE,* August 9, 1988, in FBIS–Latin America, August 10, 1988, p. 27.

62. FBIS-China, November 8, 1988, p. 20.

6

Direct Investment and Aid Program

We examined in Chapter 5 the trade relations between China and Latin America from the beginning of the open-door policy in 1978 to 1990. Parallel to expansion and diversification in trade, other areas of economic relations were also enlarged and strengthened during this period. In recent years, China and the Latin American countries have recognized the importance of mutual direct investment that might come to play in the economic relations between them. With the declaration of the open-door policy, Beijing began in 1978 to invite foreign investors to take part and assist in its modernization programs and from the beginning of the 1980s, to invest abroad. Meanwhile, Latin American countries also began their efforts to set up joint ventures in China.

The economic reforms initiated by the Chinese government and the financial resources needed for the country's own development have led to a thorough revision of China's foreign aid program. While remaining committed to cooperation with the developing countries, Beijing has announced on several occasions that the scale of individual projects will be reduced and that financial assistance will be limited to those countries most in need. Moreover, new forms of mutually advantageous cooperation will be promoted, such as joint ventures and production sharing.[1] During the period under study, the Chinese aid program concentrates on agriculture and light industry projects, which are rather small in scale and limited in funds. In sum, the days when China was willing to throw a substantial amount of money into a handful of countries to fulfill its moral and political commitment to the Third World are gone.

The purpose of this chapter is to show how joint venture has become a critical dimension of China's relations with Latin America, and to ascertain the Beijing–Latin American financial cooperation in the 1980s. After discussion of investment follows an analysis of Beijing's aid program to Latin America and a prediction of the future course of China's economic aid diplomacy in the region.

THE INVESTMENT DIMENSION

We will first discuss Chinese investment in Latin America. Then we will turn to Latin American investment activities in China.

Chinese Investment Activities

Foreign investment has come to play an increasingly important role in the overall Chinese economic strategy, though the amount of total investment is rather moderate.[2] This change in emphasis was influenced by domestic and international economic development. Domestically, in spite of China's vast territorial expanse, with the increasing speed of industrialization, per capita distribution of various kinds of natural resources is far from ample. The demand for most industrial and agricultural products has for a long time outstripped the supply. China is basically deficient in the "ten core commodities" for which UNCTAD has called for special trading arrangements under the proposed Integrated Program for Commodities (IPC).[3] In terms of mineral resources per capita, the world's average level has 10 times the oil, 3.5 times the iron, 8 times the copper, and 4.4 times the gold resources that China has.[4] China also lacks other geographic-specific commodities and forest products. Thus, Beijing is trying to promote joint ventures in natural resources to secure stable supplies.

Internationally, as Chinese manufacturing industries perused an aggressive strategy of expansion in export markets, they began to face problems of import restrictions. Some Chinese exports such as textiles have met with protectionism in the United States.[5] In order to circumvent tariffs and quotas imposed by the United States, several Chinese companies have established their joint ventures in Latin America. In addition, many Latin American countries are already self-sufficient in light industries and have imposed regulations on these imports. Latin American countries are now undertaking economic development projects to achieve higher stages of industrialization. Their major import requirements, therefore, are mainly capital goods. To cope with this situation, some Chinese producers are establishing joint ventures within those countries so that the market may be maintained. The priorities in China's investment in Latin America in the past few years are explained in the following sections.

Joint Development in Natural Resources

Development of Forests. China is seeking to cooperate with Latin American countries endowed with forest resources. For instance, in 1984 a modest $2 million was spent on buying two lumber mills in Brazil. The purchaser (International Forest Import and Export Corporation) intends to export the entire production to China, which has no tropical hardwood reserves.[6] It is the first PRC company to establish roots in Latin America.

Cooperative Fishing. In 1984 China and Guyana set up a joint venture in fishery, fishery product processing, and marketing. Gary Clarke, executive director of Guyana Fisheries Limited (GFL) said, "The venture is a big leap by the Guyana fishing industry and of course will be export-oriented. . . . China will provide eight modern trawlers, as well as processing facilities."[7] Beijing Aquatic Products Corporation and Argentina Fisheries Company; China Tianjing Economic Development Corporation and Ecuador Camilia Company also set up similar joint ventures.[8] On November 27, 1989, the China Agricultural Trust and Investment Corporation signed an agreement in Santiago, Chile, for the purchase of shares worth $18.6 million from the Chile San Johe de Corporation. China's shares make up 25.6 percent of the San Johe de Corporation total. It is China's largest investment project in all Latin American countries.[9] The PRC is also negotiating with Peru and Argentina on establishment of joint ventures in the fishing sector.

Joint Mining. The PRC has been cooperating with a number of countries in iron and gold mining. In Surinam, Beijing is negotiating on the joint venture project of gold mining. In Brazil, the China National Metals and Minerals Import & Export Corporation has established a trading company in Rio de Janeiro dealing mainly in rolled steel, pig iron, and iron ore.[10] In Minas Geras, Brazil, China National Metals and Minerals Import and Export Corporation and Brazilian ITA-MIN Siderúrgica are producing iron jointly. According to *South* magazine, the Chinese recently conducted feasibility studies for two joint ventures in Peru. China will become one of Peru's main trading partners if a proposed three-year mineral contract worth $600 million is signed.[11]

Joint Construction Companies for International Projects

After 1979, the open-door policy led to the formation of Chinese companies providing design, engineering, construction, and labor for projects abroad. The Chinese are attempting to enter the construction business in Latin America (see Table 6.1). One example cited by Mexican officials is a joint operation formed in 1986 between Pemex, the Mexican state oil giant, and the Shanghai Dredging Company to dredge Mexican harbors for 100,000 metric ton vessels, which they say is working very successfully. Sinomex has been expanding operations to Colombia, with prospects for

Table 6.1
PRC Export of Construction and Labor Projects in Latin America, 1976–1988 (in
millions of U.S. dollars)

South America	
Bolivia	5.29
Colombia	33.50
Ecuador	1.86
Guyana	0.69
Peru	5.75
Mexico and Central America	
Mexico	65.51
Honduras	0.01
Nicaragua	1.86
Panama	0.21
Caribbean	
Antigua & Barbuda	2.21
Barbados	4.02
Belize	0.44
Jamaica	1.64
Grenada	0.05
St. Lucia	0.17

Source: Almanac of China's Foreign Economic Relations and Trade, 1989 (Hong Kong: China
Resources Trade and Consultancy Co., 1989).

further business in Argentina, Ecuador, and Venezuela.[12] Elsewhere in
the region, China is involved in the construction of a 500 kilometer railway
in Venezuela. In 1981, the China Civil Engineering Corporation and a
Brazilian construction company, Junior Mendes S.A., signed an agreement to build highways and railroads in the third country jointly.[13] They
built a railroad in Iraq.

Such activities are expected to increase gradually. One article in *China
Reconstruct* observed, "China's resources in manpower and technical
know-how are great and, with more funding, better management, higher
economic results, and the continued strong emphasis on friendship, this
will grow."[14] Although it is widely assumed that overpopulation is
China's greatest problem, the size of the Chinese labor force is also an
asset. In keeping with the widespread commodification of labor, China
has joined the race to outbid Third World countries in exporting cheap
labor. Nevertheless, labor export is unlikely to play a key role in economic
cooperation with Latin American countries, since this area of the globe

also encounters a serious problem of surplus labor. On the other hand, China may not compete for an infrastructure project of the Inter-American Development Bank (IDB) that requires bidders to be members of this institution.

Join Industrial Production

In recent years, the emphasis of Chinese investment abroad has gradually moved to the manufacturing industry. In 1989, the Shanghai Garment Import & Export Company established a joint venture in Mexico. The Beijing Chemicals Import & Export Company is also trying to set up a joint venture to produce candles in Mexico. Some products will be sold locally, but most products are expected to be exported to the U.S. market and to other countries in the region. It is reasonable to expect that such joint ventures will continue to grow.

Though most Sino–Latin American joint ventures are usually a low-technology affair, there are some firms involved in high tech. The China Great Wall Industrial Corporation's (CGWIC) joint venture with Brazil is indicative of both sides' shift toward high technology. Avibrás (Brazilian Air Space Industry) and the CGWIC formed the International Satellite Communication (INSCOM). This firm will sell satellites, launch vehicles, earth stations, and antennas, as well as to market three versions of the Chinese Long March booster and the Brazilian satellite-launching vehicle. In addition, INSCOM will market launch facilities and services in both countries. The joint venture between Brazil and the PRC takes advantages of the complementary nature of their respective space programs. Avibrás is noted for its earth station construction, while the CGWIC offers a proven launch capability. During Chinese president Yang's visit to Brazil, the Brazilian president, Fernando Collor, pointed out that he hoped the cooperation would extend into precision chemicals, new materials, and other fields of advanced technology.[15]

Joint Operation of Restaurants

Generally, the Chinese side is responsible for the supply of cooking utensils, traditional Chinese tableware, furnishings and other decorations, and special condiments and flavorings not available in the local markets. It is also responsible for technical service by providing chefs. Chefs from Sichuan and Liaoning provinces have gone to Mexico, Peru, and Barbados to share their world-famous cuisine.[16] Although the Chinese possess some comparative advantage in running the restaurants, the potential for this business is very limited.

Characteristics of Joint Ventures

What, then, are the characteristics of Chinese foreign investment in Latin America? To begin with, Chinese direct investment is small-scale.

According to incomplete statistics, China typically invests $3 million to $5 million in each enterprise. In most cases, the Chinese share 49 percent of the equity, but sometimes this reaches 90 percent to 100 percent. In the second place, Chinese manufacturing overseas is usually a low-technology affair, serving a market ignored by the multinationals from the developed world. Since a small-scale operation requires little capital or technical input, such operations are designed primarily to handle downstream production. In the third place, Chinese investment can be grouped into two broad categories on the basis of the combination of trade direction. The first category, consisting of trading, manufacturing, and construction, can be considered primarily export related and labor intensive. The other category, consisting of mining, timbering, and fishery, is mainly import oriented and natural resource related. Although there has been increased investment in manufacturing, the bulk of Chinese investment is in resource development and trade-generating activities.

Latin American Investments in China

Since the mid-1980s, Latin American countries have also started to establish joint ventures in China. These investment projects range from copper tubing and coffee processing to oil exploration. The first Latin American direct investment in China was from Chile. In 1988, the Madeco (Copper Manufactures, Inc.) and Codelco (Copper Corporation) and Beijing Nonferrous Metallurgical Company founded the Beijing-Santiago Copper Tubing Company in Beijing, exporting part of its products and selling the rest domestically. The total investment came to $9.93 million, with the two parties providing 40 percent each. The remaining 20 percent is shared by the Bank of China, the Industrial and Commercial Bank of China, and the Midland Bank of Britain. The British loan takes the form of machine tools.[17]

Multinationals from the developed countries have played an important role in Latin American investments in China. Costa Rican tycoon Mauricio Ungar is setting up a joint venture with Swiss and Chinese partners to manufacture light multipurpose aircraft in China.[18] Brazil's Petrobrás is now drilling for oil in the South China Sea with the British BP Petroleum Development.[19] The involvement of multinationals owes much to their knowledge and experience acquired from decades of doing business in China, their better marketing network, and their access to capital as well as to advanced technology.

It is interesting to note that Latin America also views China as a potential base for expanding exports in the region. Mexico, which is looking to wean itself from trade dependence on the United States, is particularly keen. A Mexican company is considering a joint venture in China to make tequila for Southeast Asia. Beijing-Santiago Copper Tubing Company is also looking principally to sell in Southeast Asia, where there is a strong demand for copper pipes for refrigerators and heating and water equipment. A Brazilian instant coffee company (Cacique Enterprise) and the China International Trust and Investment Corporation (CITIC) have jointly invested in an instant coffee processing factory. The Colombian coffee industry has announced that it will invest in a factory for the eventual export of coffee from China.

Although Latin American countries have just begun their investment in China, they are quite successful in this new continent. For instance, the Brazilian contractors who built Itaipu, the world's largest hydroelectric plant on the Paraná River, have won a bid for constructing big Chinese power facilities and are hoping to win more.[20]

Prospects for Joint Ventures

With regard to total Chinese investment abroad, by July 1987 there were about 300 wholly Chinese owned enterprises or joint ventures worldwide with a total investment of about $500 million. China's stake was about half this. Hong Kong and Macao accounted for about one-quarter of the investments, with most of the rest split between the United States, Japan, West Germany, Thailand, and Canada. Latin America, however, accounted for just fifteen joint ventures, with a total investment of $30 million, of which China's stake was $15.3 million.[21]

It is expected that Latin America will figure more prominently in China's calculations. Beijing is aiming to increase overseas investment by concentrating on timber processing, fishing, and iron mining—important sectors in many Latin American countries. Up to 1990, more than twenty joint ventures have been set up by China and the Latin American countries (see Appendix B). Besides, contracts have been signed and negotiated for more than forty other projects.[22]

In short, though mutual investments started only recently, both sides have realized the benefits of joint venture and made every effort to broaden its operation. Chinese investment will continue in the future because some of the same conditions that encouraged it in the past are likely to persist. Nevertheless, unlike the Japanese economy, the Chinese economy is not heavily industrialized. So far no large sums of Chinese money are available for overseas investment. Meanwhile, Latin American countries still belong to capital-deficient countries. Therefore, neither Latin America nor China will be able to undertake major capital investment abroad until each realizes its own industrialization.

CHINA'S AID PROGRAM

The PRC is a small but significant source of air to developing countries. However, within Beijing's foreign aid priorities, Latin America has the lowest position in the Third World, trailing behind the nations of Africa and South Asia. To tighten its link with Latin America, Beijing continues to employ an active economic assistance program as part of its economic diplomacy. Aid to Latin American countries, which had become negligible after 1972, escalated again in 1985, when Primier Zhao Ziyang of China visited four Latin American countries. Visits by other high-ranking Chinese officials followed. In the same year, China provided $2 million to Antigua and Barbados and extended relief assistance to Mexico to help the earthquake victims. During the first half of 1986, four other Latin American and Caribbean countries received new Chinese development loans or grants (i.e., Bolivia, Grenada, Peru, and Surinam), mainly for agricultural projects.[23]

Since the mid-1980s, Beijing's aid program has shifted its attention toward Central America and the Caribbean. In September 1986, China agreed to give Nicaragua $20 million credit (with no interest). According to the then Nicaraguan president Daniel Ortega, the agreement meant Nicaragua "will have immediately disposable resources that will help to alleviate the situation that has been made so grave by the aggression of the United States."[24] Similarly, in 1985 Antigua's deputy prime minister, Lester Bird, reached agreement with China on an aid package in which China would provide a $2 million grant for the development of agriculture, food processing, and fisheries. In addition, Beijing would provide raw materials for light industries and launch several joint manufacturing ventures. Bird praised China for its "willingness to deal with us on a basis of equality and mutual respect." The Antigua official added, "We were also struck by the readiness to accommodate our free enterprise system. . . . No attempt was made by the government to dictate terms."[25]

China's economic and technical assistance program has continued into the early 1990s but is limited to fewer countries, all of which are less developed than the Latin American NICs and have diplomatic relations with Beijing. Except for Peru, which exports copper and fish meal to China, they have no significant two-way trade ties with China, despite the latter's efforts to expand trade. Although economic aid continues to be provided, with few exceptions, on a grant base, Chinese aid for economic development has increasingly taken the form of joint venture and production sharing. According to the Chinese official report, by the end of 1987 China had signed forty-nine agreements of cooperative projects under China's economic aid. Among them, seventeen projects had been completed, ten were under construction, and twenty-two are going to be implemented. The areas of cooperation cover light industry, textiles, agriculture, energy, medicine and health care, construction, animal husbandry, and handicrafts. Most of the cooperative projects have achieved fairly good results and won praise from the recipient governments and people.[26] It should be noted that economic assistance does not cause a drain on hard currency earnings. Two reasons could account for this development. First, the amount of economic assistance to Latin America is small. Second, assistance is mainly granted in forms of goods and technical advisors, not hard currency disbursements.

An examination of the record of Chinese aid bears many of the professed principles. Nevertheless, in the choice of recipients China has been indisputably influenced by political considerations. The Chinese hope that such economic interactions could perhaps promote a more solid political relationship. In the past few years, Beijing, Washington, and Moscow have been in little direct contention in their aid efforts in Latin America. To win diplomatic recognition, Taiwan has intensified its economic aid program in the Latin American region to a degree China cannot parallel.[27] That policy looked quite successful in Central America and the Caribbean region. Over the past two years, four countries in this area, namely, Belize, Barbados, Grenada, and Nicaragua, extended diplomatic recognition to Taiwan in the hope of obtaining aid for development. Under such circumstances, Beijing is certain to increase its aid to this area in competition with Taiwan in the 1990s.

The secondary objective is economic investment in order to open up Latin American markets for mutual commercial interest in the very long run. From the Chinese perspective, an economically stable Latin America could provide China with a valuable market. On the other hand, as John Franklin Copper has noted, China's aid projects have been unselfish in the sense that China has built factories that produce goods that compete with its own exports and frequently tend to reduce the level of trade between China and the recipient country. This has been particularly true of China's aid for the construction of textile mills.[28] For instance, on September 22, 1978, a contract for the supply of equipment and material for the Jamaican Cotton Polyester Textile Company to be built with Chinese aid, was signed in Beijing. Obviously, Chinese aid programs did contribute to the import-substitution projects in Latin America.

With regard to geographic distribution, the bulk of Chinese aid is concentrated in a small number of countries—primarily Chile under Allende, Guyana, Sandinista's Nicaragua, and Peru—that accounted for about 57 percent of total disbursements (see Table 6.2). The geographic distribution of this in the long run reflects to a large extent the desire to strengthen relations with (1) sympathetic governments (Peru, Guyana, and Jamaica under Michael Manley) and (2) politically and strategically important countries (Cuba, Chile under Allende, and Sandinista's Nicaragua).

As Table 6.2 shows, from 1954 to 1989 China granted $314 million in aid to Latin America. That allocation was only 3.2 percent of total PRC aid to Third World countries over the period.[29] The reasons for this low level of aid to Latin America are not difficult to find. First of all, the nations of Latin America are economically more developed than most other

Table 6.2
Chinese Economic Aid Extended to Latin America (in millions of U.S. dollars)

	1954–89	1984	1985	1986	1987	1988	1989
Latin America	314	20	52	10	17	10	0
Chile	65	—	—	—	—	—	0
Guyana	42	—	—	—	6	—	0
Nicaragua	22	—	20	3	—	—	0
Peru	42	—	—	—	—	—	0
Other	143	20	32	7	11	10	0

Source: Directorate of Intelligence, *Handbook of Economic Statistics, 1986* (Springfield, Va.:
     CIA, 1986), p. 114; *Handbook of Economic Statistics, 1987*, p. 115; *Handbook of Economic
     Statistics, 1988*, p. 180; *Handbook of Economic Statistics, 1989*, p. 177; and *Handbook
     of Economic Statistics, 1990*, p. 183.
— denotes data not available.

developing countries. Second, for strategic reasons Latin America is not
a primary concern; other geographic areas closer to China take priority.
Given these considerations, it should not be surprising that Latin America
ranks so low in Chinese aid priorities.

FINANCIAL COOPERATION

With the growth of trade relations, other forms of financial cooperation between China and Latin America have also begun. In 1981, the Bank
of Brazil became the first Latin American bank to set up a representative
office in China. In December 1987, the Bank of China set up a representative office in Panama, the first of its kind in Latin America. The Industrial
Bank of China International Trust & Investment Corporation (CITIC) and
some other Chinese banks are also considering representative offices in
Latin America.

During his visit to China in 1986 Mexican president Miguel de la Madrid
signed an agreement on a reciprocal credit line between the Bank of China
and Mexico's National Bank of Foreign Trade (*Banco Nacional de Comercio
Exterior*) and an agreement for cooperation between the Mexican bank
and the China Council for the Promotion of International Trade (CCPIT).
In 1985, China granted a $20 million credit line to Argentina for the financ-
ing of Chinese exports. Conversely, in May 1988, Argentina renewed a
$300 million credit line to finance imports from China.[30] In addition,
China recognized the important role the IDB plays in the economic and
social development of the Latin American region and is willing to
strengthen its connection with it. It is expected that China will join the
IDB as a nonregional member in the years to come.

At present, Latin American banks have virtually no branch in China, and Chinese banks have hardly any in Latin American countries. Despite agreements on a reciprocal credit line between the Bank of China and its counterparts in Latin America, credit is seldom used because of high fees and little understanding in the business circles of both sides.[31] Generally speaking, so far financial cooperation between China and Latin America is limited by the low level of international trade between Beijing and Latin America and the financial difficulties they are facing. This in turn deters further development of bilateral trade.

In brief, joint venture and foreign aid are used to foster Beijing–Latin American ties. These policy tools are successful. Seventeen out of thirty-two Latin American countries shifted their China policies, leaving by the end of 1990 fifteen mostly small and uninfluential countries still officially recognizing Taipei. In spite of positive impacts, Chinese aid did not have a very widespread effect on the structure of the Latin American economy. The limited amount of resources available is the most important constraint. Of course, it could equally be argued that it was because of the modesty of its foreign aid and direct investment that Beijing has held certain advantages; at least Beijing did not frighten Latin Americans or arouse suspicion or anxiety.

NOTES

1. Organisation for Economic Co-operation and Development (OECD), *The Aid Programme of China* (Paris: Organisation for Economic Co-operation and Development, 1987), p. 10.

2. Interviews with government officials in Mexico, Peru, Chile, and China in 1989.

3. UNCTAD ten core commodities include sugar, cotton, coffee, copper, rubber, tin, cocoa, tea, jute, and sisal. For details, see UNCTAD, *Commodity Yearbook, 1989* (New York: United Nations, 1989).

4. *Beijing Review*, 33, no. 44, (October 29–November 4, 1990), p. 39.

5. Surging Chinese textile exports in the early 1980s made textiles China's number one commodity on the U.S. market and alarmed established textile exporters like Taiwan and South Korea. Against a background of Chinese accusations that the United States was unfairly seeking to obstruct China's natural path, protracted Sino-American textile negotiations yielded a new agreement in December 1987 to limit the rate of increase in Chinese textile exports to the United States to 3 percent annually over a four-year term.

6. *Asian Business*, 21, no. 11 (November 1985), p. 32.

7. The Caribbean News Agency (CANA), August 19, 1984, in *Daily Report: Latin America* (hereafter cited as FBIS–Latin America), August 21, 1984, T1.

8. *South*, 88 (February 1988), p. 21.

9. *Beijing Review*, 32, no. 51 (December 18–24, 1989), p. 37.

10. Wei Yuming, "Boosting Sino–Latin American Trade Relations," *Beijing Review*, 28, no. 43 (October 28, 1985), p. 16.

11. *South*, 88 (February 1988), p. 47.

12. *South*, 88 (February 1988), pp. 21–22.

13. Luo Liecheng, "Development of Economic and Trade Relations between China and Latin American Countries," *Latin American Review* (China), no. 3, 1985, p. 50.

14. *China Reconstructs*, 36, no. 4 (April 1987), p. 31.

15. *Beijing Review*, 33, no. 22, (May 22–June 3, 1990), p. 9.

16. Wei Yuming, "Boosting Sino–American Trade Relations," p. 16.

17. For details, see Carlos Vicuña and Luis Soto, "Negociación y establecimiento de una joint venture en la República Popular China: La experiencia de Madeco y Codelco," in *Chile en la Cuenca del Pacífico: Experiencias y perspectivas comerciales en Asia y Oceania*, ed. Sergio Valdivieso Eguiguren and Eduardo Galvez Carvallo (Santiago, Chile: Editorial Andrés Bello, 1989), pp. 222–231.

18. *Latin American Markets*, June 3, 1988, p. 11.

19. Wei Yuming, "Boosting Sino–Latin American Trade Relations," p. 16.

20. Luo Liecheng, "Development of Economic and Trade Relations," p. 18.

21. *South*, 88 (February 1988), pp. 20–21.

22. Guo Chongdao and Li Zhixiang, "Sino–Latin American Economic Trade Relations in Retrospect and Prospect," *Journal of Chinese People's Institute of Foreign Affairs* (China), no. 8 (June 1988), p. 103.

23. OECD, *The Aid Programme of China*, p. 17.

24. Associated Press cited in *Daily Texan*, September 15, 1986.

25. CANA, July 5, 1985, in FBIS–Latin America, July 8, 1985, pp. S10–11.

26. *Almanac of China's Foreign Economic Relations and Trade*, 1988 (Hong Kong: China Resources Trade Consultancy Co., 1988), p. 435.

27. Taiwan established a $1 billion fund for helping friendly developing countries.

28. John Franklin Copper, *China's Foreign Aid: An Instrument of Peking's Foreign Policy* (Lexington, Mass.: Lexington Books, 1976), p. 142.

29. *Diretorate of Intelligence, Handbook of Economic Statistics, 1990* (Springfield, Va.: CIA, 1990), p. 183.

30. *Latin American Regional Reports: Southern Cone* (London: Latin American Newsletter), June 30, 1988, p. 3.

31. Interviews with the commercial section of the Chinese embassy in Mexico City and the Banco Nacional de Comercio Exterior as well as an official of the Bank of China (BOC) in Beijing.

7

Technology Transfer

Over the last few years, along with increasing trade relations, technological cooperation has become an integral part of China's interaction with Latin America. It has also become a way for China to increase its political and technological leverage in its foreign relations with this region.

Since the late 1970s, Beijing has adopted a vigorous technology transfer policy emphasizing the introduction of advanced technology diversification of sources, and more pragmatic practice of self-reliance. Under such policy, the PRC has been importing technology from the West. On the other hand, in certain types of technology, notably satellite-launching and space technology, China has a comparative advantage. Beijing can also offer some appropriate technology to its counterparts in Latin America. For instance, China is widely recognized as a world leader in small hydropower stations and possesses substantial light industrial technology. In recent years, China has become not only an exporter of raw material such as petroleum but also a potential exporter of advanced technology products. China's technology exports have made huge strides since 1986, when the technology export value totaled only $20 million. In 1989, China's technological exports totaled $895 million, tripling the figure of 1988.[1] Considering the difficulties of breaking into the more desirable markets of the industrialized countries, the Chinese have steadily focused their technology exports on the Third World. Up to 1990, Beijing had scientific and technological agreements with twelve Latin American countries, namely, Brazil, Mexico, Argentina, Venezuela, Chile, Colombia, Ecuador, Nicaragua, Peru, Guyana, Cuba and Trinidad and Tobago and nuclear agreements with Argentina, Brazil, and Chile.

One driving force for China's increasing activities in Latin America is competition with Taiwan. Since 1963, Taiwan has sent numerous technical missions to Latin America in the fields of agriculture, fisheries, mining, and industry. At present, there are fourteen agricultural technical mission, five fishery technical missions, and one handicraft and bamboo mission in the region. There is also a Taipower technical mission (in Honduras) and a mineral technical mission (in Guatemala). The members of these missions total more than 170 people. Sinotech Engineering Consultants, Inc., has also sent hydroelectric experts to work in the Dominican Republic.[2]

Since the early 1980s, China has attempted to diversify the type of technology it is introducing, so that China can maintain its economic independence from foreign sources. Beijing believes the West is unwilling to transfer advanced technology to China. The newly industrializing countries (NICs) have, on the contrary, shown greater flexibility, in order to become more competitive in the world market. Therefore the Chinese believe technology transfer with the NICs is important. Meanwhile, the Chinese also believe that Latin American NICs, particularly Argentina, Brazil, and Mexico, could use their close connections with Western countries and transnational corporations to make key technologies and equipment available to China. Given these considerations, Beijing has been trying to tighten its technical ties with this region in recent years.

In order to realize the above goals, China has participated in Technological Cooperation among Developing Countries (TCDC), a program which was developed by the United Nations Development Program (UNDP). Recent TCDC projects include building centers for biogas development and setting up facilities for small hydropower generation, sericulture, and integrated fish farming.[3] Playing an active role in the TCDC not only raises China's stature in the Third World but also helps the Chinese export more technology there.

The Latin Americans, on their part, also want to absorb the technology from the socialist countries in order to break the de facto high-technology blockage imposed by the West. In view of this, they have strengthened their technical ties with China. In fact, some Latin American countries have also exported technology for many years.[4] Brazil, Mexico, and Argentina's present level of industrial development and external economic relations open up new "nontraditional" possibilities for economic cooperation with the socialist countries. These countries have shown they can produce locally a wide range of manufactured goods, including machinery and equipment, and promote exports of these goods, as well as of turnkey plants to other markets.[5] Chinese authorities recognize that their sales of technological exports are probably smaller than Brazil's current level, hovering around the Brazilian level of in the early 1980s. In addition, Latin America possesses a relatively larger pool of skilled technological manpower. In certain fields, Latin American countries have achieved great success. For instance, several Argentine scientists have earned Nobel prizes in medicine and chemistry. Clearly, in the emerging Sino–Latin American technological cooperation, each side has its own technological advantages.

TECHNICAL COOPERATION WITH BRAZIL

Among Latin American countries, Brazil and China's scientific cooperative ties have progressed the furthest. Since the PRC and Brazil established diplomatic relations in 1974, contacts between the two countries' scientific and technological circles have increased steadily. After 1980, when China and Brazil exchanged seven study groups, the pace of development of Sino-Brazilian links quickened markedly. By 1982, the two nations had signed cooperative agreements and have since that time exchanged groups concerned with such fields as computer technology, rubber production, and patent laws.[6]

Brazil has an export capacity in nuclear power plant components, fuel rods, and uranium mining technology that interests China. In 1984, China and Brazil signed a nuclear cooperative agreement aimed at sharing technology that had been developed in both countries for peaceful uses of atomic energy. On January 14, 1988, they signed a second nuclear accord for industrial cooperation in developing reactors and other nuclear projects under International Atomic Energy Agency (IAEA) supervision.[7] China has sold its oil-drilling exploration technology to Brazil. Petrobrás, the Brazilian state oil company, is offering China its experience in offshore drilling in exchange. Brazil wants to tap China's extensive experience in biogas, while China is studying the effectiveness of Brazil's production and use of gasohol.

During the visit of Brazilian president José Sarney to Beijing in July 1988, the two countries signed an aerospace cooperative agreement that involves the joint production of satellites. Funds totaling $150 million have been allocated for the project, of which $45 million will be provided by Brazil. The first satellite, called the China-Brazil Earth Resources Satellite (CBERS), is scheduled to be launched from Shanghai in 1992. A second satellite, to be launched from the Alcantara base in Brazil in 1994, is still in the preliminary planning stages. Both satellites will be built by the Space Research Institute (INPE) of Brazil with Chinese assistance. A Brazilian spokesperson stated that the agreement would be an important step in breaking the de facto high-technology blockage imposed by the superpowers.[8] Another advantage for Brazil is the cheap price. According to the Brazilian project manager, if Brazil were to take part in a similar project with a Western nation, it would be twice as expensive.[9] Before departing for China, Brazilian science and technology minister Luiz Henrique da Silvera said the CBERS "will supply images of every point in Brazil" aiding environmental, meteorological, and agricultural research. Undoubtedly, the launching of Brazilian satellites will provide China with hard currency and experience.

In August 1990, two Chinese firms won a bid to provide aerial photogrammetric services for a World Bank–financed project in Brazil. This is the first time China's remote-sensing aerial photogrammetric technology will enter the world market. The operation, at a cost of some $7 million, will turn out 2,218 orthophoto maps. According to Xinhau News Agency, the Oriental Scientific Instruments Import and Export Corporation under the Chinese Academy of Science and the China Coal Aerial Photogrammetry and Remote Sensing Corporation would soon send personnel and equipment to carry out the project covering an area of 67,000 square kilometers.[10]

TECHNICAL COOPERATION WITH MEXICO

Soon after establishing diplomatic relations with China in 1972, Mexico became the first Latin American country to cooperate with China in the fields of science and technology. In September 1975, China and Mexico signed a scientific and technological cooperative agreement and have since held seven related meetings and taken part in 120 exchange programs.[11] Through technological exchange, the Chinese have benefited from Mexican instruction on coal-mining and orange-growing techniques. In return, Mexico has profited from the exchanges by learning about China's traditional medicine, its freshwater fishery and silkworm-breeding methods, its production and utilization of marsh gas, and its irrigation and ceramics processes.[12] In May 1990, Chinese president Yang Shangkun visited Mexico. During his visit, China and Mexico held their seventh governmental economic and trade meeting, discussing the possibilities of cooperation in the petrochemical industry, deepwater fishing, manufacturing, and the launching of communications satellites. In November 1990, both sides signed dozens of contracts under which China could export to Mexico technology in the field of electronics, chemistry, medicine, fishing, agriculture, construction materials and textiles.[13]

TECHNICAL COOPERATION WITH ARGENTINA

China's cooperation with Argentina, which began in 1974, has been equally as successful as its efforts in Mexico and Brazil. After signing a scientific and technological cooperation agreement in 1980 in Beijing, China and Argentina held a scientific and technological meeting in 1983 in Buenos Aires, during which delegates agreed to a cooperative plan for fiscal year 1984.

Of all the Latin American nations, Argentina has the most advanced nuclear technology for both experimental and electricity-generating purposes. The first Latin American nuclear power station, "Atucha-1" with a 320-MW capacity, has been in service in Argentina since 1974. A second nuclear plant with a capacity of 600-MW at Embalse on the Río Tercero (Córdoba) started up in 1983. Whereas China has long since surpassed Britain and France as the world's third nuclear power, the PRC is a latecomer in the field of peaceful use of nuclear technology, Argentina possesses the expertise and technology to help China. In view of this, China signed a nuclear cooperation agreement with Argentina in 1984. According to Argentine foreign minister Dante Caputo, this agreement referred to nuclear energy plants, the fuel cycles, low-power reactor, training, and transfer of technology. Under this agreement, Argentina could grant technical aid to the PRC.[14] In return, China sold heavy water to Argentina.[15]

Argentina has traditionally exported meat, packaged cereals, milk products, and vegetable oil to industrialized countries. In China, food consumption has increased and tourism is on the rise, creating a demand for Western food. To meet this demand requires new food-processing equipment or improvements in existing equipment. In view of this, Argentina offered to help China improve existing meat-slaughtering plants to meet international standards and to provide technical assistance to China for processing edible oil. Argentina is hoping to import Chinese porcelain containers for its local wines and is interested in buying traditional Chinese medical herbs. Joint fishery projects on the Argentine coast are planned. Chinese technicians will be trained in Argentina. In June 1988, a new scientific and technical cooperation agreement was signed between Beijing and Buenos Aires. Under this agreement, Argentina would transfer $50 million worth of equipment for the food-processing, chemical, and agroindustrial sectors.[16]

In the rest of Latin America, Beijing is now supplying fish-breeding technology to Guyana and Ecuador, mining technology to Bolivia, and biogas technology to Chile; Beijing also cooperates with Chile in Antarctic exploration. In November 1989, Beijing and Havana signed the second scientific and technological agreement, after a gap of more than two decades, deciding to further cooperation in the fields of public health and agriculture, fishery, and the sugar industry. The document will be in effect for five years.[17] In May 1990, China and Uruguay signed a cooperation agreement on animal quarantine and hygiene and a cooperation memorandum on plant quarantine; later that month, Chinese officials signed a similar memorandum with Chile.[18]

CHARACTERISTICS OF TECHNOLOGY TRANSFER

Compared with technology from the industrialized countries, Chinese technologies have the advantage of being labor intensive and relatively cheap, making them a more attractive buy for many Third World countries. Although technologies from Latin America are not equivalent to those of the North, the Chinese found the former readier to transfer them.[19] Generally speaking, technology transfer between China and Latin America includes

- technologies competitive with those of developed countries (such as space technology of China).
- technologies competitive with those provided by industrialized countries but adapted to local needs (such a nuclear technology in Brazil and Argentina and the coal-mining technology of China).
- technologies not overlapping those from industrialized countries; these are in areas of technological activity specific to particular developing countries either because of the characteristics of their recent industrialization (such as a small hydropower station in China) or because of the natural resource endowments (such as gasohol in Brazil or food processing technology in Argentina).

So far, the major partners of technological cooperation are NICs in Latin America. These NICs have acquired considerable Western technologies and have the ability to duplicate transferred technologies. However, there is little contact between China and the rest of Latin America, which has a much lower capacity to absorb technology. Even for the NICs, current technical cooperation is of marginal significance in their total technology acquisition. Several factors may explain this. First, the bulk of technical cooperation is sponsored by the Chinese government and by its counterparts in Latin America. Recent economic difficulties have negative effects on the further development. For example, the launching of the first Sino-Brazilian satellite was postponed fifteen months because Brazil delayed in making its contribution of $6 million due in 1989.[20] Second, for a long time, major sources of technology for both sides were those of developed countries. As a result, Chinese scientists and their counterparts know little about each other. Third, Technological Cooperation among Developing Countries (TCDC) is directly affected by the technological advancement of the nations concerned. However, it is still the West that produces the most advanced technology, which developing countries need to develop their national economy.

As mentioned earlier, further growth of cooperation is expected in the energy sector, where Mexico has already proved to be a suitable partner for China. The development of cooperation in the peaceful use of nuclear energy could also become an important issue in mutual relations. Opportunities also exist in some other fields, such as iron and steel production, fisheries, and the food industry. Undoubtedly, China and the Latin American countries are seeking the know-how they need to break the high-technology monopoly of the rich countries. In addition, certain Chinese labor-intensive technologies may prove more adaptable to Latin American conditions than the technology of the West. In sum, mutually beneficial economic ties have served as the engine pulling Sino–Latin American technological cooperation forward. Yet the prospects for greater economic interactions will largely depend on how China's economic reforms and open-door policy continue to unfold and how Latin America copes with its current recession.

NOTES

1. *China Daily*, March 12, 1990.

2. *Republic of China Yearbook*, 1990–91 (Taipei: Kwang Hwa Publishing Co., 1990), p. 237.

3. For detailed information, see United Nations Development Program (UNDP), *Cooperation South* (formerly by *TCDC News*), 1988–1990.

4. See "Technology Exports from Latin America," *Economic and Social Progress in Latin America, 1982 Report* (Washington, D.C.: IDB, 1982), and Sanjaya Lall, ed., "Exports of Technology by Newly-Industrializing Countries," special issue of *World Development*, 12, no. 5–6 (May–June 1984), pp. 471–660.

5. See "Science and Technology in Latin America" and "Comparative Indicators of the Results of Scientific and Technological Research in Latin America," in *Economic and Social Progress in Latin America, 1988 Report* (Washington, D.C.: IDB, 1988).

6. Huang Ying, "China, Latin America Expand Technical Links," *Beijing Review*, 28, no. 43 (October 28, 1985), p. 18.

7. Madrid EFF, January 16, 1988, in FBIS–Latin America, January 20, 1988, p. 35.

8. *Times of the Americas* (August 24, 1988), p. 6.

9. *Development Forum*, 18, no. 2 (March–April 1990), p. 5.

10. Xinhua, August 26, 1990, in Foreign Broadcasting Information Service (FBIS)–China, August 27, 1990, p. 25.

11. Interview with an official of the Chinese embassy in Mexico City in July 1989.

12. Huang Ying, "China, Latin America Expand Technical Links," p. 18.

13. *Renmin Ribao* (overseas edition), November 17, 1990.

14. María Soledad Gómez, "Relaciones de China con América Latina y el Caribe durante 1985," *Documento de Trabajo*, no. 312, Programa FLACSO–Santiago de Chile, p. 25; FBIS–Latin America, April 18, 1985, B5.

15. *Noticias Argentinas*, November 7, 1985, in FBIS–Latin America, November 8, 1985, B1.

16. *Latin American Regional Reports: Southern Cone*, June 30, 1988.

17. Havana Radio Rebelde Network, November 18, 1989, in FBIS–Latin America, November 20, 1989, p. 6.

18. *China Daily*, July 23, 1990.

19. Interview with an official of the China State Science and Technology Commission in Beijing in January 1989.

20. *O Globo de Río de Janeiro*, December 21, 1989, p. 30, in FBIS–Latin America, December 27, 1989, p. 43.

8

Problems and Issues in
Current Economic Relations

From the materials covered in previous chapters one can see that economic relations between China and Latin America have advanced fairly smoothly in the past twenty years. In order to determine how realistic prospects are for deepening Sino–Latin American economic ties, it is important to identify and weigh obstacles that constrain the establishment of such ties. This chapter is divided into three parts. The first analyzes mutual problems the two regions face in developing their economic ties. The second outlines the problems China is encountering. The third part deals with the difficulties Latin America confronts. The chapter closes with some conclusions.

PROBLEMS COMMON TO CHINA AND LATIN AMERICA

Transportation

First of all, China and Latin America are physically far removed from one another. For China, Latin America is the most remote area of the world. For a timber mill joint venture between Brazil and China in the Amazon, transportation costs to the Chinese are bound to be formidable. The lumber will have to be shipped 1,000 miles downriver, loaded onto seagoing vessels, and taken halfway around the globe. Some bilateral agreements on navigation do exist,[1] but the irregularity of some lines that service the majority of Latin American countries create problems in the dates of receiving as well as the delivery of the merchandise. This raises the cost of storage and produces delays in the payments of the merchandise against the presentation of shipment documents. During the early

1960s, China's merchants had fewer than thirty ships. Over the past two decades, maritime shipping capacities greatly increased. In 1987, China ranked ninth in tonnage of oceangoing merchant ships and fourth in commercial shipbuilding among the world's maritime nations.[2] However, only in 1989 was one regular commercial steamliner established by the Chinese to facilitate transportation between China and Latin America.[3] There is no regular flight between the two regions. Many goods have to be shipped through Hong Kong or other ports before arriving in Latin America. It is quite common to take six months, and even a year, to transport goods from China to other parts of the Pacific Ocean.

Transportation problems are more serious for the Latin American countries that do not have their own maritime fleet.[4] This maritime transportation irregularity in trade with China is greater in the case of Central American countries.

Foreign Exchange Bottleneck

One key factor for the low volume of trade between China and Latin America is the persistent hard currency shortage. The last decade in Latin America has been dominated by the debt crisis that erupted in 1982. Many countries have drastically cut their imports, especially of consumer goods. In the 1990s, external debt may well continue to cast a long shadow over the future growth and relative importance of Latin America as an export market. The same is also true for China. Yet because of its status as a net exporter of nonrenewable resources and its cautious approach to borrowing in international financial markets, the PRC is not confronted with the balance-of-payment adjustment problems faced by Latin American countries. Nevertheless, China does not have enough foreign exchange to meet all the pressing needs of its economy.

Lack of hard currency and indebtedness to the developed market economy counties have compelled both China and Latin America to adopt countertrading policies in their bilateral trade.[5] In addition, presently Latin American financial institutions have virtually no branches in China, and Chinese banks have hardly any branches in Latin American countries. This situation, which results from the low level of international trade between the two regions, deters the further development of bilateral trade.

Lack of Mutual Understanding and Awareness

Latin American countries are trying to shift their focus of trade to the Pacific Basin. Even so, moving from centuries-old ties to the United States and Europe is difficult. For instance, the lack of knowledge of existing trade opportunities and market requirements are still a constraint for the development of mutual trade. Very few Latin American businesspeople speak Chinese, which is essential for doing business with China. Even fewer are fully aware of the current situation and conditions in China. Information about Chinese goods is often poor, and buyers must attend the Canton Fair or product-specific minifairs. This can be expensive (especially for Latin American small traders) and time consuming for busy executives. An article in the *Beijing Review* observes, "There are still people who are not well-informed about China, some of whom even have misgivings. This is only natural, given distance and insufficient contact between China and Latin America. Of course, China does not know very much about Latin America, either."[6] In many cases, goods sent to Latin America did not correspond to specifications. This is because the PRC suppliers do not sufficiently understand Latin American market requirements.

Chinese research on Latin America is very limited. During the first decade of the PRC, only the Guatemalan Revolution (1954) gained passing attention. The Institute of Latin American Studies under the Chinese Academy of Social Sciences (CASS) was not established until 1961 and was closed for about ten years during the Cultural Revolution. It was not until 1979 that China began to publish studies on Latin America through the journal *Latin meizhou yanju* (Latin American Studies). Only in 1986 did the Ministry of Foreign Economic Relations and Trade (MOFERT) set up a special section under its International Trade Research Institute to look into the emerging Latin American market. As far as Latin America is concerned, there are even fewer scholars specializing in Chinese affairs.[7] That there is an almost total lack of knowledge in Latin America about economic resources and technological development taking place in China not only represents a major obstacle to the expansion of Latin America's present tenuous economic, financial, and technological relations with China but also makes any preliminary diagnosis of prospects for such a rapprochement very difficult.

Advertising of Chinese commodities in Latin America is mostly conducted by sale agents, for Chinese foreign trade firms hardly advertise. Advertisement of Latin American products in China is even rarer. In many instances, Latin Americans simply do not know what is available. Equally significant is the cultural gulf dividing the Chinese and the Latins. The Oriental culture of the Chinese has little in common with that of Latin America, which is derived partly from European culture.

Differences in Trade Practices and Economic Systems

For a long time, the PRC sought to adopt an economic system patterned along Soviet lines and embodying both Marxist principles of ownership and control of resources and Stalinist strategy of rapid industrialization managed by a highly centralized, command economy. As it has evolved, however, the Chinese economy today is much less of a command economy than is the Soviet economy, with greater use of market incentives and decentralized decision making. It is, of course, still a highly planned socialist economy very different from the market economy of Latin American countries. The foreign trade of China is regulated by economic plans that decide the export volume and value. The socialist trade organizations make their purchases by complying with the central government's plan. The recent restructuring of China's economies and trade systems has also added to the complexity. Among Latin American businesspeople, D/A (documents against acceptance) and D/P (documents against payment) are very common, whereas Chinese merchants are accustomed to accept a letter of credit (L/C) for a business transaction. In addition, Chinese businesspeople still find it difficult and inconvenient to obtain visas and set up representative offices in Latin American countries. Indeed, trade cannot be promoted effectively unless freedom of travel exists.

Competitive Aspects of Economic Relations

China is emerging as a new force on the regional and world economic stage. During 1978–1989, China's real GNP and per capita GNP grew considerably faster than the global and developing-country average growth rates. A rapidly growing Chinese economy may threaten the shares of the world's trade and capital other developing countries can obtain. China's economic growth has been associated with, and facilitated by, outward-looking trade and industrial development policies. China's entry into the world market may have considerable effects detrimental to Latin America. Competition is keen in attracting foreign investments and aid, earning foreign exchange, obtaining a greater share in world trade, and exporting labor.

Aid

Coincidentally, China cut its new aid commitments to the developing countries at the same time it began to compete with other developing countries for aid from the international market. China's loan quotas, even for soft loans from the World Bank and the United Nations agencies, are necessarily large because of its level of development and size of population. China's entry into the loan market has led to a redivision of the available resources, leaving less for other developing states. The problem is more severe today as the international economy is contracting and the developed counties are reducing their contributions to international aid organizations.

Foreign Direct Investment (FDI)

Despite considerable progress, the PRC remains in the process of industrialization and desires foreign capital for its development. International investment provides needed economic input, technical skill, and marketing networks. In recent years, China has been the largest recipient of direct foreign investment among all developing countries.[8] From 1979 to 1987 China attracted more than $7 billion of direct foreign investment for over 8,000 enterprises and projects at a time when the flow of private foreign capital had virtually dried up. Not surprisingly, many Latin American governments are growing concerned over the long-term consequences of the massive diversion of Western resources to development in China at the expense of other needy developing countries. According to one UN report:

If one were to make any generalizations about the flows of FDI in the world economy during the 1980s, three overall trends can be seen to be emerging: (1) a marked shift of flows away from developing countries and toward the industrialized countries; (2) the eclipse of Latin America as the major host region in the developing world; (3) the emergence of China as a major host country.[9]

Just as important is Chinese competition for scarce international capital. A major Chinese attraction to the foreign investor, including Latin America, is China's plentiful and inexpensive labor force. In recent years, nearly 45 percent of Chinese exports were labor-intensive products. An important Chinese objective in establishing special economic zones is to woo foreign capital and technology by making available inexpensive labor in a hospitable environment. After revamping its laws on foreign financing and ownership and entering free-trade talks with the United States, Mexico is pitting itself against southern China for foreign investment dollars. Thus, China and Latin America are competing to attract foreign investors from Japan, the United States, and Western Europe to engage in manufacturing for domestic and export markets.

Export of Labor

Although overpopulation is China's major problem, the size of the Chinese labor force is also an asset. In keeping with the widespread commodification of labor, China has joined the race to outbid Third World countries in exporting cheap labor. At present, China actively promotes the business of "international labor cooperation" to capitalize on its human resources. Obviously, China's new aggressive approach to explore cheap labor puts it in direct competition with the Third World.

Xue Muqiao, a leading Chinese economist, noted that China's comparative advantage is its large supply of labor, low wages, and natural resources. Therefore, he concluded that "for sometime to come, we must make use of our rich natural resources, as well as develop more labor-intensive industries and less capital and technology-intensive ones."[10] Developing countries can be defined as being scarce in both physical and human capital and abundant in unskilled labor. Clearly, China and Latin America share the similar comparative advantage of abundant labor; and they confront similar problems, that is, a shortage of capital and advanced technology. This constitutes a serious limitation to the trade between the two regions.

Competition in the International Markets

China exports four bulk commodities that have implications for Latin America: oil, coal, tin, and tungsten. To improve its trade balance, China has taken vigorous steps to increase its petroleum production and export. Likewise, China turned out 1.05 billion tons of raw coal in 1989, thus becoming the largest coal producer in the world. In the same year, China exported 15.29 million tons of coal, compared with 3.12 million tons in 1978.[11] Venezuela and Mexico are today among the world's major oil-exporting countries. Colombia has the largest and highest-quality coal reserves in Latin America and is also emerging as a potentially strong player in the world market.[12] So far Chinese crude oil and coal have posed no direct threat to Latin American producers simply because of China's small market share in the region. Indeed, it is probable that competition will increase as Latin American oil and coal development proceed and as China begins to compete even more vigorously in fuels

China's role is even more important with regard to tungsten. The U.S. Bureau of Mines estimates that China has the world's largest tungsten in wolframite and scheelite, its reserves are equivalent to three times those of the rest of the world, and its export of tungsten has accounted for up to 50 percent of tungsten world trade.[13] A very large fraction of tungsten production—in 1987, 53 percent—is of Chinese origin. Latin American major producers—Peru, Guatemala, and Bolivia—represent only about 6 percent of the world tungsten market.[14] Chinese market operations will therefore continue to influence price. China could supply a wide range of manufactured goods and industrial raw materials to Latin America, but it would be difficult for China to buy crude oil, tungsten, and coal from the region in exchange, since China is also an important producer of these products. Obviously, it is difficult for China to enlarge trade with countries that have similar resource endowments.

In spite of China's currently more "aggressive" trade expansion,[15] China is not ready to be a strong competitor in the world market except with respect to a limited number of products such as petroleum products and some light industrial goods. Research conducted by Bruce D. Larkin in 1986 indicates that "China is selling widely and assertively to raise funds for the purchase of high technology from Japan and other industrial states. As a consequence, China is seeking market shares previously won by other Third World states.''[16] But this is not true of Sino–Latin American ties. It is interesting to note that major competitors of the PRC's trade with Latin America are not from the West but from NICs of Asia, notably, South Korea and Taiwan (see Table 8.1). With China's successful industrialization efforts, China's export of textiles, garments, footwear, toys, and household electrical appliances has increased rapidly. Consequently, Chinese goods compete fiercely with similar goods from the Asian NICs. In the years to come, competition will become more severe in the machinery and consumer electronic industries. Chinese goods do not compete with such popular U.S. articles as automobiles, computers, and chemical and pharmaceutical products. Nor does China offer capital goods such as aviation equipment and precision instruments. In almost every other field, Chinese manufactures enjoy notable success in the Latin American markets, for almost all of them are lower in price than U.S. or European goods. Direct competition with either industrialized countries or less-developed countries is less likely because the product mix is different.

Increasing levels of trade and investment between China and Latin America have also been sources of friction. In the present international economic climate, these frictions seem more likely to increase than decline. On the whole, however, China is more of a complementary trading partner than a competitor to Latin America.

Dependence on the West

Latin American countries (except Cuba) are still highly dependent on the developed market economy countries, which until now have accounted for the most important share in both exports and imports of the region. This tie has generated and imposed a tendency to imitate certain

Table 8.1
Trade between Taiwan and Latin America (in millions of U.S. dollars)

	1977	1978	1979	1986	1989
Taiwan's Imports	177	202	228	573	1,580
Taiwan's Exports	303	434	587	928	1,100
Taiwan's Balance	126	232	359	355	-480
Total	477	636	815	1,500	2,680

Source: *China Yearbook 1980*, (Taipei: China Publishing Co., 1980); *Republic of China: A Reference Book* (Taipei: Hilit Publishing Co., 1988); and *Rupublic of China Yearbook 1990–91* (Taipei: Kwang Hwa Publishing Co., 1991).

lifestyles and patterns of consumption from the developed countries, whose effects reach almost all productive apparatus. Latin American and Caribbean countries have discovered that the trade cord that binds them to the huge U.S. market is harder to loosen than they had anticipated. The magnetlike effect of the U.S. market became apparent during the 1980s as country after country struggled to earn the export dollars needed to pay its debts. In 1988, 44 percent of Latin American and Caribbean exports went to the United States, against just 34 percent in 1980. The figure is tantalizingly near the all-time high of 45 percent of thirty years ago.[17] In addition, one of the primary operative consequences of the interactions of the economies of Latin American countries with those of Western industrialized countries has been the adaption of their productive apparatus to imported techniques destined to supply the demand and to satisfy standards of imitative consumption.

Likewise, Beijing perceives the West as the main source of capital, expertise, market, and technology to be used to step up China's modernization drive. Various Chinese leaders have expressed admiration for the advancement of Western technology and press for the transfer of this technology to China in a variety of areas.

Lack of Competitiveness

China has been undertaking economic reform since 1978. Vigorous efforts are being made to adapt its products and services so as to satisfy the specific requirements of the world market more effectively, as well as to develop more dynamic marketing activities. Despite the economic reforms, the program will not transform the Chinese economy overnight from a poor-quality, inefficient producer into a competitive producer of high-quality manufactured goods. The problem of inadequate competitiveness with respect to manufactures still persists. Insufficient supplies of spare parts and after-sale maintenance are among the most evident issues, which in effect increase the import price of the products. For China, manufacturing high-quality products will be essential to compete in Latin American markets, for there will be no shortage of alternative products.

There are similar problems on the Latin American side. With the increasing trade interactions, Latin American countries want to sell their manufactured goods to China, rather than be suppliers of raw materials.[18] The difficulties Latin American manufactures have in entering the Chinese market are due to a number of causes. The low relative competition of various Latin American manufactured products stand out. Low level of quality and delays in the delivery period are causes as well. Naturally, China and Latin America can benefit from increasing participation in the world economy only if they become competitive international trade participants.

Political Uncertainty

Generally speaking, there is a circular relationship between political stability and economic development. Political stability provides a basis for economic growth, which contributes to an improved standard of living, thereby promoting stability. Yet politics in China has traditionally been a negative influence because of ideological movements that disrupt the economy with periodical policy shifts contributing to uncertainty and failures to take advantage of international trade. China is well known for its astonishing experiments. In experimenting with the Great Leap Forward and the Commune System, thousands of people died of hunger; in experimenting with the Cultural Revolution, the entire society was brought to the verge of collapse. The toll in human suffering was heavy, to say nothing of holding the country back in education, science, and technology. Any future turmoil will bring even greater damage to the Chinese economy, for Chinese exports are largely labor-extensive manufactures and therefore quite susceptible to political disruption.

Political factors have had a very important influence on Chinese policy toward Latin America, most often as a constraint, but more recently as a stimulus. Following Mao's death, a more pragmatic leadership emerged, and economic rather than ideologic development became the predominant societal as well as foreign policy goal. Yet it is widely recognized that large political uncertainties cloud China's future.

Latin American political instability and the traditional anti-Communist elites are also factors affecting Beijing's involving in Latin America. Over the past few years, the PRC has moved from ostracism to acceptance in Latin America. It by no means follows that Beijing has significant political and economic influence in the region. On the contrary, by the end of 1990, only seventeen out of thirty-four countries in the region officially recognized China. Even China's relations with its socialist partners, Cuba and Nicaragua, have been erratic in the past decade.

SPECIFIC PROBLEMS OF CHINA

On the Chinese side, there are three factors that influence the extent to which Latin America will be able to serve as a market and a producer for China. They include underdevelopment of the Chinese economy, inadequate energy production, and the possible decrease in imports of agricultural products.

Underdevelopment of Chinese Economy

To provide a context for the following discussion, Table 8.2 presents a few general figures on China's role in the world economy. The numbers

Table 8.2
China in the World Economy, 1988

	World	China	China's Share (%)
Population (million)	5,000	1,088	21.8
Area (million km)	150	9.6	6.4
GDP ($ billion)	17,018	372	2.2
Value added in manufacturing ($ billion)	3,511	92.8	2.8
Exports ($ billion)	2,627	47.5	1.8

Source: World Bank, *World Development Report 1990* (New York: Oxford University Press, 1990).

show that the country's population density is about three times the world average. China's GDP and value added in manufacturing, about 1.8 percent and 2.8 percent of the world total, demonstrate the country's economic underdevelopment. On a per capita basis, Chinese output is only about one-tenth of the world average. Exports correspond to only 11 percent of China's GDP and account for 1.6 percent of global foreign trade.

In light of its vast territorial expanse, manpower, military capability, and ideology, the PRC is an important power in the world today. However, China is still a developing country, whose economic and technological development are at a correspondingly low level. On an absolute level, China is a very poor, backward economy. The great bulk of its enormous population is engaged in agriculture, and the level of productivity in industry is extremely low. In terms of GNP per capita, China is one of the poorest countries in the world. According to 1990 World Bank figures, China's GDP per capita was as low as $330, less than that of Haiti ($380). The Latin American figure of the same year is $1,830, five times that of China's figure.[19] China's trade turnover per capita is $93, certainly well below that of Latin America. Clearly, the underdevelopment of the Chinese economy places China at a severe disadvantage in developing its relations with Latin America.

China's economic readjustment, in effect since 1988, will probably continue to limit overall economic performance until it succeeds in modifying the serious contradictions and bottlenecks that developed in the Chinese economy during the previous twenty years. China's ability to help Latin American countries is, however, limited. Its economic aid to developing nations is small because of China's own underdeveloped economy. China is no match for either Washington or Moscow in providing economic assistance to the Third World countries. Therefore, although there are some favorable reasons for China's role concerning Latin American countries, there are also great limiting factors.

Inadequate Energy Production

One of the most significant trends in China's foreign trade since the 1970s was the increasing share of natural resource exports as a proportion of overall exports.[20] Much of this can be attributed to China's emergence as a petroleum and coal exporter. Chinese policy statements and investment commitments provide indications that the Chinese wish to increase mineral and energy resource exports as a part of an overall policy to increase exports of selected products. Although this could provide additional income and other benefits to the Chinese, there are limitations to this policy.

Lack of an adequate social and physical infrastructure is perhaps the single most significant limitation on China's ability to become a large mineral exporter. Such infrastructure limitations also limit China's attractiveness for would-be outside investors. China has an advantageous reserve position in coal. However, mining as well as infrastructure problems could prevent the Chinese from realizing this potential. In addition, the future of oil exports is uncertain because of slower-than-anticipated offshore development and growing internal demand.

Possible Decreasing Import of Agricultural Products

A final factor on the Chinese side is the fate of the Chinese import of grain and cotton. Agricultural products are "major items" that China imports from Latin America. Wheat has been a significant Chinese import from the region. Before 1983 China was one of the world's largest importers of raw cotton. These imports averaged around 100,000 tons annually but climbed to a peak of nearly 900,000 tons in 1980. A dramatic increase in domestic cotton production filled domestic demand, and exports exceeded imports in 1983. In 1987, China shipped raw cotton to Asian and European markets at the price of $770 million.[21] China recently shifted from importer to exporter of corn and soybeans.

With its modernization effort, China might increase domestic production of grain and reduce grain imports in the long run. Nevertheless, if China cannot realize its modernization goals, it will continue to purchase large quantities of such products from Latin America.

SPECIFIC PROBLEMS OF LATIN AMERICA

It is also true that Latin America is plagued by some problems that discourage the PRC from making further efforts to develop stronger trade, investment, and technological links with it.

Impact of the Current Recession

While total regional production increased from $873 billion in 1980 to $968 billion in 1988, for a gain of 12 percent (compared with an increase of 78 percent between 1970 and 1980), the population of Latin America went up nearly 20 percent during the same period, rrom 347 million in 1980 to over 414 million in 1988. As a result, in eight years per capita GDP in the region fell by 7 percent ($176), after climbing by almost 40 percent between 1970 and 1980 (more than $700).[22]

Because of the critical economic situation many Latin American countries have gone through since the early 1980s, restrictive measures to imports as well as some protectionist measures have been adopted. These measures have been implemented to protect the development of some sectors of national industry in order to face balance-of-payments difficulties. Latin America has chronically faced a balance-of-trade deficit, and this deficit tended to reduce its overall import volume.

Trade Balance

Another factor that holds back the expansion of trade between China and Latin America is the glaring trade deficits in favor of the latter. From 1950 to 1988, China ran up a cumulative trade deficit with Latin America of more than $10 billion.[23] Because Chinese exports to Latin America remain at a low level, this deficit must be covered by surpluses of credit from Western countries plus sales of gold. China's import capacity is largely determined by the actual availability of foreign exchange from export earnings, supplemented by external borrowing. Given this constraint, any measures that reduce the availability of foreign exchange to China have a negative impact on its flows of trade. Various factors specific to Latin American countries, such as price, quality, or delivery period, could also contribute to a halt in the growth of the traded products.

SUMMARY

To sum up, to date Chinese activities in Latin America are still limited; China is still a marginal player in this region. Although economic and political contacts are successfully institutionalized, relations between China and Latin America are not without strains; there are still serious transportation, financial, and marketing constraints to be overcome. These constraints signify that a large-scale expansion of trade between China and Latin America is unlikely in the near future. On the whole, however, China is more of a complementary trading partner than a competitor to Latin America. By a combination of constructive diplomacy, selective aid programs, and increasing trade relations, the PRC has in recent years enhanced its role in Latin American countries. Moreover, there exist immense potential and wide prospects for deeper cooperation, which will be discussed in detail in Chapter 9.

NOTES

1. Up to 1990, China had signed maritime agreements with five Latin American countries, including Mexico (1984), Cuba (1984), Brazil (1980), Chile (1973), and Argentina (1980), but Chile did not ratify the maritime agreement after the downfall of Allende. In 1986, the China National Metals and Minerals Import and Export Corporation and the China Ocean Shipping Company set up the Latin America–Asia Transportation Agency in order to secure maritime transportation between China and Latin America.

2. For details, see Irwin Millard Heine, *China's Rise to Commercial Maritime Power* (New York: Greenwood Press, 1989).

3. Beginning in June 1989, China set up regular commercial steamliners between China and Latin America; a ship leaves Shanghai and Tianjing for South America every month. So far this is the only kind of regular commercial steam service between China and Latin America.

4. On this topic, see UN Economic Commission for Latin America and the Caribbean (ECLAC), *Basic Concepts of Maritime Transportation and Its Present Status in Latin America and the Caribbean* (Santiago, Chile: ECLAC, 1987).

5. For more detailed studies on China's barter trade practice, see Marisela Connelly, "Comercio de trueque y comercio compensatorio China," *Estudios de Asia y Africa*, 24, no. 2 (1989). For a good account of Latin American experiences on countertrade, see the report by Isidoro Hodara, "Compensation Trade, Experience of Some Latin American Countries, "(UNCTAD/ECDC/Misc. 20).

6. *Beijing Review*, 28, no. 43 (October 28, 1985), p. 4.

7. To my knowledge, only the Centro de Estudios de Asia y Africa del Colegio de México, the Instituto de Estudios Internacionales de la Universidad de Chile, and the Universidad de Buenos Aires have conducted any research on China.

8. Nicholas Lardy, *Economic Policy toward China in the Post-Reagan Era* (New York: National Committee on United States–China Relations, 1989), p. 4.

9. UN Center on Transnational Corporations (UNCTC), *Foreign Direct Investment in Latin America: Recent Trends, Prospects and Policy Issues*, 1986, p. 1.

10. "More on Economic Reform" (special interview), *Beijing Review*, 23, no. 36 (September 8, 1980), p. 20.

11. For details, see "China: The World's Largest Coal Producer," *Beijing Review*, 33, no. 20 (May 14–20, 1990), pp. 17–21.

12. In the last decade, Colombian exports of coal rose from $10 million to an estimated $432 million. See *Latin American Special Report*, SR-90-02 (April 1990), p. 11.

13. Chin E., "The Mineral Industry of China," in U.S. Department of the Interior, Bureau of Mines, *Minerals Yearbook, 1987*, Vol. 3 (Washington, D.C.: U.S. GPO 1989), p. 220.

14. UNCTAD, *Commodity Yearbook, 1989* (New York: United Nations, 1989), p. 365.

15. For instance, in 1989 more than 100 Chinese trade delegations and groups visited Mexico. However, very few Latin American businesspeople have ever visited China.

16. Bruce D. Larkin, "Emerging China's Effect on Third World Economic Choice," in *China and the Third World: Champion or Challenger?* eds., Lillian Craig Harris and Robert L. Worden (Dover, Mass: Auburn House, 1986), p. 101.

17. *South*, 109 (November 1989), p. 28.

18. Interviews with officials of the Mexican and Peruvian governments in the summer of 1989.

19. See World Bank, *World Development Report 1990* (New York: Oxford University Press, 1990), pp. 178–79. It is thought that there is an large downward bias in arriving at China's GDP because its socialist economic structure contains many nonmarket economic activities as well as an undervalued service sector.

20. For detailed discussion on China's mineral production and trade, see James P. Dorian and David G. Fridley, *China's Energy and Mineral Industries: Current Perspectives* (Boulder, Colo.: Westview Press, 1988), and "China," *Strategic Minerals*, ed. W. C. J. van Rensburg, Vol. 1: *Major Mineral-Exporting Regions of the World: Issues and Strategies* (Englewood Cliffs, N.J.: Prentice-Hall, 1986).

21. Directorate of Intelligence, *China: International Trade Annual Statistical Supplement, 1989* (Springfield, Va.: CIA, February (1989), p. 5.

22. *Economic and Social Progress in Latin America, 1989 Report*, (Washington, D.C.: Inter-American Development Bank, 1989), p. 1.

23. *Almanac of China's Foreign Economic Relations and Trade, 1984* and *1988* (Hong Kong: China Resources Trade Consultancy Co., 1984 and 1989).

9

Prospects for Future Economic Relations

As can be seen from the preceding chapters, politics has been a powerful agent in the growth and change of Sino–Latin American relations. In the future, however, underlying economic factors will exert greater influence on the Sino–Latin American connection. This has already become a clear trend. China's relations with most countries in the region are already normalized, and its international relations are increasingly conducted pragmatically. The emerging Sino–Latin American economic relationship will therefore depend more on the structural characteristics of the Chinese and Latin American economies. China's position today is favorable as far as Latin America is concerned. Relations created by past and more recent Chinese immigrants as well as by recent economic ties constitute an excellent basis for close cooperation. China has maintained friendly relations with the Latin American countries, and no tense situation is anticipated. In addition, Chinese positions in international politics lead to no conflicts of interests with Latin America. Notwithstanding its increasing level of involvement in Latin America, and its growing importance in the global strategic balance and world economy, China will remain a regional Asian power; its influence in Latin America will be limited over the next few decades. The most likely scenario is that if China persists in its open-door and reform policy and succeeds, it will become an important trading partner for Latin America within the next two or three decades.

In spite of restraints mentioned in Chapter 8, there is apparently great potential for closer economic ties between China and Latin America. The first section of this chapter compares the salient macroeconomic characteristics of China and Latin America. The second one explores the potential of such relations. The third section examines various future scenarios of and trends in Sino–Latin American economic relations in the 1990s and beyond; it also addresses the relationship between these trends, as well as some of the reasons behind them.

COMPARISON OF THE MACROECONOMIC CHARACTERISTICS OF CHINA AND LATIN AMERICA

Comparison of Economic Structure

Table 9.1 compares several major macroeconomic characteristics of China and Latin America. The population of China is about 1.1 billion, which is almost three times that of Latin America, even though the area of China is only one-half that of Latin America. China is one of the most densely populated countries in the world. In terms of natural endowment, China is poor in natural resources except for some minerals such as tungsten and coal. Even the level of agricultural production is not sufficient to support the food needs of the population. Therefore, China's source of economic growth is its human resources, rather than its natural resources. Making a good contrast, Latin American economies are generally known to be resource based, with primary products constituting the mainstay of their exports.

Table 9.1
Salient Macroeconomic Characteristics of China and Latin America

Items	Year	Unit	China	Latin America
Population	1988	million	1,088	413.6
Area		1,000 km	9,561	20,548
Density of population	1986	per km	112	20
GDP per capita	1988	U.S. $	330	1,840
GDP annual growth	80–88	%	10.3	1.5
Trade/GDP	1987	%	28	22

Source: Unesco, *Statistics Yearbook, 1988* (New York: Unesco, 1988); and World Bank, *World Development Report 1990* (New York: Oxford University Press, 1990), Tables 1, 3, 4, and 14.

Even though China is recognized as a country with rapid GNP growth in the past decade, its per capita GDP is $330, well below that of Latin America. It may be stressed that the conventional GNP measures are inherently biased against a socialist economy with a large segment of non-market activities and an undervalued service sector, so that the real material content of the Chinese GNP should be much higher than indicated in Table 9.1.

China and Latin America differ also in industrial structure. In spite of its relatively low per capita income, China has a larger manufacturing sector (34 percent) than Latin America (27 percent).[1] The 1988 shares of agriculture, industry, and service were 32 percent, 46 percent, and 21 percent of GDP respectively. In the case of Latin America, the figures were 10 percent, 39 percent, and 52 percent respectively in the same year.[2] In 1987, according to the *World Development Report 1990*, China's value added in manufacturing came to $92.8 billion, as compared to $79 billion for Brazil, $36 billion for Mexico, and $22 billion for Argentina. Within manufacturing, the value of machinery and transport equipment came to $25 billion for China compared to $21 billion for Brazil, $15 billion for Argentina, and $14 billion for Mexico.[3] Obviously, industry and manufacturing play a more important role in the Chinese economy.

On the other hand, China's service industry is extremely backward, accounting for only 21 percent of GDP. China's commercial, financial, and technological consulting services are all underdeveloped. In contrast, Latin America has a comparatively highly developed service industry that accounts for 51 percent of GDP. Finance, commerce, transport, and tourism have long been the pillars of the region's economic development.

Table 9.2 characterizes the changing structure of production in the two regions. The Chinese manufacturing industries portion of the GDP increased from 31 percent in 1965 to 33 percent in 1988. A big decrease in the share of output occurred in agriculture thanks to the Four-Modernizations program in recent years. Agriculture dropped from 44 percent to 32 percent over the same period. The PRC witnessed phenomenal economic growth in the past decade. Its GDP annual growth was 10.3 percent during 1980–1988, among the highest in the world.[4] This contrasted sharply with the economic recession of Latin America in the 1980s.

With the growth of its economy, China has risen from a backward agricultural state to a fairly advanced industrial-agricultural country. Economic reforms since 1978 have shifted China toward a more market oriented and open economy. A rapidly growing Chinese economy with a greater role in world economy has wide-ranging implications for various countries, including those in Latin America. Meantime, Latin American countries are also rapidly industrializing and promoting the export of manufactures. The Latin American economies are basically open and outward-looking, with foreign trade and foreign investment playing a

Table 9.2
Structure of Production, 1965 and 1988 (percentage of GDP)

Unit	China		Latin America	
	1965	1988	1965	1988
GDP $billion	67.2	372	95.3	808
Agriculture	44	32	16	10
Industry	39	46	33	39
(Manufacturing)	31	33	23	27
Services	17	21	51	52

Source: World Bank, *World Development Report 1990* (New York: Oxford University Press, 1990). Table 3, pp. 182–83.

Table 9.3
Structure of China's Merchandise Exports and Latin America's Imports of Commodities (percentage in total export or import)

	China's Exports	Latin American Imports
Primary commodities	27	27
Machinery & transport equipment	4	35
Other manufactures	69	38
Total	100	100

Source: World Bank, *World Development Report 1990* (New York: Oxford University Press, 1990), pp. 206–7.

crucial role in their economic growth. Exports have been an engine of economic growth in Latin America for a long time. Generally speaking, China and Latin America belong to the Third World but differ in terms of industrial structure and resources, and therefore the two have the potential to be complementary.

Comparison of Foreign Trade Structure

Despite certain similarities in export patterns, as noted in Chapter 8, both sides have many commodities to exchange. In 1988, China's shares of (1) primary commodities, (2) machinery and transport equipment,[5] and (3) other manufactures[6] in total merchandise exports were 27 percent, 4 percent, and 69 percent respectively. The shares of the same products for Latin America in total 1988 imports were 27 percent, 35 percent, and 38 percent respectively (see Table 9.3). Thus, other manufactures weigh heavily for China's exports and Latin America's imports. This suggests, of course, the potential for considerable trade of such commodities, flowing from China to Latin America.

More specifically, Table 9.4 compares China and Argentina, Brazil, Chile, Mexico, and Peru on their major manufactured goods exports by Standard International Trade Classification (SITC).[7] The table indicates that China's exports are relatively concentrated in basic and miscellaneous manufacturing (SITC 6 and 8), whereas those of Argentina, Brazil, Chile, and Mexico are more concentrated in chemical and machinery and transport equipment (SITC 5 and 7). As for the imports, Chinese manufactured imports were dominated by basic manufactures. Miscellaneous manufactures (SITC 8) accounted for only a very minor share; this reflected China's policy of importing mainly producer goods rather than consumer goods. There is a similar situation in the export structure of primary goods. As can be seen from Table 9.5, China's primary goods exports are somewhat concentrated in fuels and agricultural raw material, whereas Brazil, Peru, and Chile are more concentrated in mineral ores and metals.

The increased importance of Chinese exports of petroleum has not adversely affected Latin American petroleum producers. Chinese crude oil has not competed directly with Mexican and Venezuelan petroleum exports to Latin American markets. This is basically because China is a

Table 9.4
Product Distribution of Manufactured Goods Exports of China and Major Latin American Countries, 1984 (in percentage)

SITC	Argentina	Brazil	Chile	Mexico*	Peru	China
Chemical (5)	27.6	19	34.9	11.8	11.3	11
Other manufactured goods (6+8-67-68)	41.7	43.4	41.7	26.2	75.7	76.7
Machinery and equipment (7)	30.8	37.5	23.4	60.4	12.9	12.3
Total manufactured goods export	100	100	100	100	100	100

Source: UNCTAD, *Handbook of International Trade and Development Statistics, 1987 Supplement* (New York: United Nations, 1988).
*Figures are for 1985.

Table 9.5
Product Distribution of Primary Goods Exports of China and Major Latin American Countries, 1984 (by percentage)

SITC	Argentina	Brazil	Chile	Mexico*	Peru	China
All food items 0+1+22+4	86.7	70.7	25.3	10.6	24.7	32.7
Agricultural raw material 2-(22+27+28)	4.3	13.3	10.5	1.11	5.9	12.2
Fuels 3	4.8	.65	1.37	79.7	37.3	49.3
Ores & Metals 27+28+67+68	4.2	15.3	62.8	6.24	56.8	5.28
Total primary goods exports	100	100	100	100	100	100

Source: UNCTAD, *Handbook of International Trade and Development Statistics, 1987 Supplement* (New York: United Nations, 1988).
*Figures are for 1985.

"silent member of OPEC"[8] China and Bolivia are principal producers of tin, antimony, and tungsten. In 1988, China and Bolivia signed an agreement to cooperate in the producer price for antimony concentrate and other minerals.[9] Bolivian mining minister Jaime Villalobos emphasized the importance of this agreement: "I believe that this agreement will benefit the two countries because the market of this important mineral can be defended, if the two countries implement a strict policy in accordance with this contract."[10]

In the third country markets, there has been no major conflict between China and Latin American countries so far. For instance, bilateral trade with the United States is still of considerable importance in the international economic relations of both China and Latin America. And the countries all understand that no NIC could achieve a breakthrough without first capturing its share of the U.S. market. Even so, to date there is no friction between the PRC and Latin America in this market because China and the Latin American countries have in fact their own distinct exports to the U.S. market. For instance, in 1988 the major Chinese export commodities to the United States were clothing (24 percent), toys (20 percent), fabrics (7 percent), telecommunication equipment (6 percent), petroleum (5 percent), household electronic appliances (5 percent), and travel goods and handbags (5 percent).[11] In the same year, the "big items" that Latin American countries exported to the U.S. market were machinery and transport equipment (28 percent), mineral fuels (20.6 percent), and agricultural commodities (15 percent).[12]

Potential threats to PRC manufacturing exports lie in the further industrialization efforts of Latin American NICs such as Brazil and Mexico. Yet areas of mutual benefit are great and will continue to expand. For instance, booming Sino-Brazilian trade is based largely on the exchange of Chinese oil and coal for Brazil's iron ore and manufactured products. It is evident that trade transactions among countries with different resource endowments constitute the dynamic components of Sino-Latin American trade.

In brief, the trade between the two regions coincides with the comparative advantage of each side. Latin America, endowed with plentiful natural resources, could export to China more resource-intensive items such as chemicals and mineral products. The Latin American countries have large exportable surpluses of primary commodities, and they could in many instances increase their production without great difficulties. China, endowed with plentiful human resources, could export to Latin America more skill- and labor-intensive products such as textiles, clothing, and light industrial products. China's exports are expected to rise over the next fifteen years, but the competition with Latin American products will not be great. In general, China's increased role in the international economy should be beneficial to Latin America. The complementarities between China's energy and cheap light industrial goods and Latin American mineral products and food suggest a natural basis for economic exchange.

Capital and Technology Exchange

As discussed in Chapter 7, technology transfer between the two regions is largely untapped and so potential to increase such transfer is enormous. Some Latin American countries, such as Brazil, Argentina, and Mexico, have an industrial base and a degree of technological sophistication that, though not as advanced as that of the United States or Japan, would be suitable and affordable for China. Conventional arms, oil exploration equipment, electronics, and expertise in the construction of hydroelectric power plants are all areas available to the Chinese.

However, China and Latin America have insufficient capital. They have implemented active policies for attracting foreign capital. Although they engage in some mutual investment, Chinese investment in Latin America represents only a tiny percentage of total foreign investment in the region, and vice versa. China and Latin America are unlikely to invest abroad on a large scale until they realize industrialization at home.

POTENTIAL FOR CLOSER ECONOMIC TIES

The people of China and Latin America make up 30 percent of the world's population. Their land mass makes up 20 percent of the world land area. Despite rapid growth in the past decade, Sino–Latin American trade accounts for only a tiny proportion of Chinese and Latin American total external trade. Under normal circumstances, the volume of trade between China and the Latin American nations makes up only 1 percent of the total volume of Latin American foreign trade and 3 percent of China's total. The bulk of Sino–Latin American trade is concentrated in six Latin American countries, namely, Brazil, Argentina, Cuba, Chile, Peru, and Mexico (in decreasing order). Trade with the rest of Latin America is numerically insignificant. The most noticeable factor in Sino–Latin American trade has been the low level of Chinese exports. The small share represents unexploited potential markets, or room for future expansion. Financial and technological cooperation is also very limited. In short, Sino–Latin American relations are still underdeveloped.

Potential of the PRC

The PRC has more than 1.1 billion inhabitants and its GNP is expected to reach $1 trillion by the end of this century. China is now among the world's top twenty trading nations in terms of total value of imports and exports and is the world's ninth largest producer of goods and services. Today China is first in the world in output of grain and meat, for the people's food; of coal and cement, for fuel and construction; of textile fabric, to clothe the people; and of items as bicycles and washing machines to make their lives easier. In some other fields, China is in the world's top five (such as television sets, number two; steel and electric power, number four; crude oil, number five.[13] Moreover, China has applied to become a contracting party to the GATT and has indicated a willingness to abide by GATT rules.[14] As President Yang Shankun made quite clear, China's objective is to become prosperous and powerful—a world power.[15] According to an estimate by the U.S. Commission on Integrated Long-term Strategy in early 1988, China will have the world's second largest GDP by the year 2010.[16] Most analysts agree that China's economy is likely to continue to grow at a relatively high rate but somewhat below the record-setting pace of the last decade. There is no consensus on China's future role in the world economy. It is obvious, however, that Chinese foreign trade will grow along the path of economic reforms, even if slowly. By the year 2000, China expects its total foreign trade to reach the goal of $160 billion, four times the 1981 level. If this objective is achieved, China will rank among the largest foreign trade countries in the world and its presence in the world market will be significant. China's importance as a supplier to Latin American states will increase as it provides more goods that Latin Americans need. In turn, China will create stronger demand for Latin America's products.

Certain features in the system of foreign trade management in China create some difficulties for the development of its trade. Economic reforms now under way are expected to stimulate trade exchange. They are expected to have a positive impact on China's trade and economic relations with the outside world, including Latin America. For example, up to now the Chinese have not established direct contacts with major sellers of some Latin American export commodities (such as fish meal); hence the prevalence of the indirect purchase of such commodities through third parties. Economic reform is likely to reduce, if not eliminate, this problem.

Potential of Latin America

Latin America's GDP per capita of over $1,800 is higher than that of either developing Asia or Africa. The combined Latin American GDP is about $810 billion, almost twice that of the whole African continent. Major Latin American countries have become semi-industrialized states with diverse resources. Their needs are wide and they have a variety of products to offer. Not surprisingly, Latin America constitutes one of the largest import markets in the developing world, with total imports near $85 billion in 1985, or almost one and a half times the level of African imports.[17] By 1980, Brazil was exporting more manufactured goods than any other upper-middle-income country except the "Gang of Four" (the four Asian NICs).[18] Meanwhile, Argentina, Mexico, Colombia, Chile, and Uruguay recorded notable increases since the 1960s. In addition, Latin American countries are richly endowed with natural resources and produce many products for which China has a continuing demand.

The Latin American economies are now passing through the most severe economic disturbances of the past fifty years. It is likely that the 1990s will witness a modest economic growth in the region. On the debt front, though, Latin America is still under a heavy strain of payment imbalance. Total disbursed external debt was estimated at $426 billion in 1988, a significant decrease from the previous year ($441 billion).[19]

Diversifying Strategies of Both Sides

The growth of Sino–Latin American trade is broadly in line with the long-term strategy of market diversification to which the Chinese and Latin American governments have committed themselves. For instance, at present China is trying to import iron ore from both Brazil and Chile. From the Latin American standpoint, the PRC is also one of the potential big new markets among developing regions. As one article of the *Times of the Americas* concludes:

China offers a huge and new market for Latin America's exports, and it is a market that assumes an even greater potential in the face of an expected surge in American protectionist trends in the years ahead. By the end of the century, China may have become Chile's largest purchaser of copper, and the business communities of both countries are aware of the importance of establishing the necessary infrastructure that will permit present commerce to expand.[20]

Impact of Changing Economic and Export Strategies

Since the late 1970s, China has been pursuing a strategy of combining import substitution with an export-oriented economy. In China, four special economic zones (SEZs), and fourteen coastal cities plus Hainan Island, have been opened to foreign capital. They are strategically located to buy raw materials and sell products. It is in manufactured goods, which have risen to account for 73 percent of China's total exports,[21] that future export earnings lie. Given the abundant supply of low-wage labor, China's comparative advantage is in manufactured goods and the Chinese should be able to make advances in exports of light manufactured goods. Export potential also exists in other manufactured goods such as metal products, machinery and transportation equipment, and handicrafts.

At the same time, Latin American countries are turning away from import substitution to export-oriented strategies. Most Latin American countries have adopted an economic policy of growth through trade. Trade as an "engine of growth" is a widely spread and shared concept among these countries. In view of higher protective measures in the OECD countries, further export diversification has been called for, as well as more trade, rather than the pursuit of inward-looking policies. As noted, China and Latin America are facing a serious external debt problem. To overcome it, they have resorted to engaging in more trade, with trade surplus perceived as the solution to the problem. On the other hand, a prominent feature of the latest round of economic policy efforts is the decision to "open up" long-protected national economies to foreign competition. Even more than Chile, Mexico has led the way in this—and in Mexico the result has been an import boom. The new governments in Venezuela, Argentina, Brazil, and Peru have announced their intention to tread the same path. The motive for trade is as strong in Latin America as it is in China. It is logical that under such a strategy both China and Latin American countries will further their contacts with the rest of world.

Increasing Ties among Nations of the Pacific Rim

During the past decade, the world has been on the verge of a Pacific century; interactions among the Pacific Rim nations have increased significantly. A. W. Clausen, the then president of the World Bank, noted,

"In the Pacific Basin, from China to California, there may well be the most dynamic part of the world economy for the rest of the century—a vast and expanding market."[22]

Since the 1960s, Latin America has sought to diversify the markets for its exports and the sources of its imports by reducing excessive reliance on the West. Latin America's preference in this regard is for regional economic integration. But owing to a lack of complementarity, the Latin American states have achieved only limited success in actually integrating their economies, breaking down trade barriers, or promoting economic development.[23] One alternative for Latin America is to turn to the Pacific Basin, including China. Beijing also attaches great importance to its relations with the Pacific Rim, and in 1986 it became a member of the Pacific Economic Co-operation Conference (PECC)—which was established in 1983 and is the most promising forum for Pacific cooperation.[24] According-ing to the opinion of the chairman of the Hong Kong Metropolitan Bank, "In China's view the Pacific Ocean is not an obstacle to trade and cultural exchanges but a cause for mutual cooperation. The Pacific Basin represents a natural trading hinterland for the Chinese economy."[25]

Moreover, modern technology has reduced the importance of temporal and spacial distance and helped Asia and Latin America draw closer to each other. The emergence of the "Pacific era" has accelerated this pro-cess. Communication via commercial and cultural exchanges serves to stimulate and motivate the desire to understand one's trading partners more fully. In spite of mutual efforts, so far Brazil, Argentina, and Cuba, the countries of the Atlantic coast, remain China's three most important trading partners. This situation is unlikely to change in the near future.

In the past few years, the commercial sections of Chinese embassies in Latin American countries have been strengthened considerably.[26] Many Chinese companies now have representatives in major Latin American cities. This factor, together with the frequent exchange of trade and economic delegations as well as the hosting of trade exhibitions, will acquaint China and Latin America with each other's economic develop-ment and the possibilities of fruitful and mutually advantageous economic cooperation.

Role Played by the Overseas Chinese

Chinese emigration is another mechanism that has promoted com-munication with the outside world. As early as 1585 traces of the first Chinese in Mexico can be found.[27] In 1810, the Portuguese contracted with several hundred Chinese workers to plant tea in the capital of Brazil. This is the earliest record of Chinese migration to Brazil. *Cha*, the Por-tuguese word for tea, is a transliteration of the Chinese word for tea. The nineteenth century also saw the rapid influx of a large number of Chinese

immigrant laborers to Peru, Mexico, and the Caribbean. These Chinese
were employed substitutes for the black slaves who were then in short
supply. Toward the end of the nineteenth century about 300,000 Chinese
migrated to Latin America.

Available data show that the Chinese are found in all Latin American
countries. There are at present some 250,000 Chinese settlers and their
descendants in Latin American countries, of which about 100,000 are in
Brazil and Peru (see Table 9.6).[28] Through their skills and efforts, the immigrants established themselves and became a part of middle-class society. In some countries, the immigrants' contribution as pioneer
agriculturalists came to be appreciated. Nowadays the descendants of
earlier Chinese settlers are assimilated into Latin American society and
actively working in each country as useful citizens.[29] Some of them have
occupied central positions in Latin America political life. For instance,
the former president of Guyana, Arthur Chung, is a man of Chinese
descent. In Peru, several Chinese descendants serve as congresspeople.[30]

Broadly speaking, the influence of Chinese immigrants on Sino–Latin
American economic relations has not been very great. This is partly
because the bulk of Chinese settlers have been engaged in restaurants,
hotels, cafes, laundries, and other small businesses, not in foreign trade
or manufacturing industry. The second reason is that the overseas Chinese
seem to have manifested little enthusiasm for identifying with mainland
China in their respective countries.

Although their effects on trade have been negligible, Chinese settlers
have played an important part in Chinese investment in Latin America.
When Chinese firms establish joint ventures, local Chinese settlers or their
descendants often participate in the companies as partners. Some local
Chinese are also employed by such companies to facilitate labor management by helping communicate between local employees and Chinese executives. An Argentine Chinese even donated two pieces of his land to
the general manager of the China Technology Development Corporation
in order to build two special economic zones in Argentina.[31]

Political Relations

It is important to note that both sides have genuine interest in establishing mutually beneficial relations. This interest has been reflected in
the frequent exchange of official delegations, sometimes at the head-of-
state level,[32] and the conclusion of trade, economic, and technical cooperation agreements. China now has diplomatic relations with seventeen
Latin American and Caribbean nations. The rest of them maintain links
with Taiwan but are expected to abandon this policy eventually. Expanded
diplomatic relations will continue to provide a natural avenue for fostering trade.

Table 9.6
Overseas Chinese in Latin America

Country	Number of Overseas Chinese
Mexico	20,000
Central America and the Caribbean	
Cuba	15,000
Honduras	2,500
Costa Rica	4,500
Panama	30,000
Nicaragua	13,500
El Salvador	630
Dominican Republic	5,000
Trinidad and Tobago	5,000
Jamaica	30,000
Barbados	50
Antilles	1,400
Bahamas	200
South America	
Colombia	5,000
Venezuela	12,000
Ecuador	10,400
Peru	30,000
Brazil	45,000
Bolivia	900
Chile	2,000
Paraguay	2,000
Uruguay	200
Guyana	6,000
Surinam	7,000
French Guyana	700
Total	248,980

Source: Committee of Overseas Chinese Economy in Ten Years, *Shi Nian Lai Hua Qiao Jin Ji, 1972–1981* (Oversease Chinese Economy in Ten Years, 1972–1981) (Taipei: Ch'iao wu wei yuan hui ti san ch'u, 1981), pp. 211–35.

China claims that in common with countries in Latin and Central America it has a history of colonialism, and like them it desires a peaceful international environment and demands the right to an independent foreign policy and the freedom from intervention. In the United Nations China has frequently voted with Latin America on issues such as regional disbarment, aid, development, decolonization, and apartheid. China also maintains that it and the Latin American countries are all developing countries. Geographically, the vast Pacific Ocean lies between China and Latin America; therefore, there have been no border disputes between them. In contrast with the complex issues between the United States and Latin America, and China with its Asian neighboring countries, no factor detrimental to the existing cordial relations between China and Latin America appears to exist. In brief, despite differences in political systems, bilateral political relations are generally satisfactory.

Internationally, China not only has become a strategic ally of the United States but also is improving its relations with another superpower. Soviet leader Mikhail Gorbachev's four-day visit to China in May 1989 signaled the end of two decades of Sino–Soviet hostility. The talk between Gorbachev and Deng Xiaoping proclaimed the beginning of "normal" state-to-state relations, while the meeting later the same day between General Secretaries Zhao Ziyang and Gorbachev was hailed as the "natural restoration" of party-to-party relations. Beijing thus no longer needs to worry about assault from the Soviets or the Americans when fostering its relations with the countries in the "backyard" of the United States.

In sum, the future trade and economic relations between the PRC and Latin America seem to be encouraging, implying further increases in economic interdependence. After forty years of cooperation, China and Latin America have become intertwined in many aspects. Their trade and economic cooperation will be further developed and diversified in the coming years. One of the few major problems in China's relations with Latin America in the post-Mao era was the suspending of diplomatic ties with Grenada, Belize, and Nicaragua over their recognition of "two Chinas."

SCENARIOS FOR FUTURE DEVELOPMENT

Given the aforementioned trends in China and Latin America, what kind of scenario can be written for the region? Three scenarios are briefly considered here.

China as a Major Foreign Power in Latin America

Some see China as a NIC that is rapidly upgrading its production technology and aggressively seeking international markets, becoming another, potentially more powerful Japan.[33] The Chinese presence has been growing significantly in Latin America, especially over the past twenty years. But neither its present nor its future possibilities should be exaggerated. Power in the modern world requires a strong economic base, communication, and heavy industry in particular. The PRC is seriously deficient in these respects. Therefore, China will not have the economic depth to become a superpower for several decades.

By the end of the century, China will still belong to the low-income group of countries, even if it succeeds in maintaining its impressive GNP growth attained in the past decade.[34] China is no match for either Washington or Moscow in providing economic assistance to Latin American countries. Beijing has not made available any large amounts of economic aid to Latin America partly because of China's own underdeveloped economy. So, although some political and historical reasons favor China's role concerning Latin American countries, there are also great limiting factors.

China could emerge as a major foreign power in Latin America provided that certain conditions are met. These conditions include political stability, success of economic reform, and adequate power and transportation systems. Additionally, China might increase its role in mineral and manufacture exports primarily by attracting foreign involvement in Chinese projects. China's difficulty in meeting the above conditions is apparent. To make matters worse, insufficient finances, an inadequate educational system, and a shortage of skilled workers are additional problems.

China's approach to the Third World has been determined by broader Chinese foreign policy concerns. China continues to give top priority to security and development concerns, which will force Chinese leaders to focus paramount attention on Chinese relations with the United States, the Soviet Union, and the developed countries.[35] The Third World countries that appear most important to China are those with a direct and important role to play in providing China with an environment in which to develop its economy. The other countries are of secondary importance.[36] Under such circumstances, China's economic ties strongly favor the developed world and its own neighboring Asian countries.

Realistically, that China will become a "second Japan" in Latin America is unlikely in the foreseeable future. Considering that its present available resources remain limited, China will continue to be a regional Asian power instead of a world power. Therefore, its influence over Latin America will remain limited for the next two or three decades. But given China's size and potential resources, the PRC may one day join the major foreign powers in Latin America. Political factors and economic constraints make such an eventuality only a very long-term possibility, however.

China's Decreasing Role in Latin America

The second possible scenario is that a post-Deng leadership may seek to curtail its ties to the outside world and to revert to a more traditional, self-sufficient, Stalinesque centralized economic system. As a consequence, China would return to its pre-1970s relationship with Latin America, becoming less of a market and less of a supplier. But the closed-door policy would not be tolerated long by China's young and talented population. Moreover, in recent years China has gradually become involved in the interdependent world economy. The PRC, which lacks many resources and must rely on the world market for its light industrial products cannot afford to be inward-looking. On the other hand, the reforms have simply gone so far that it may not be possible for hard-liners to reverse them.

Although a slowdown of industrial production is under way, it is unlikely that China will witness a reversal to the self-reliant development of pre-1978. Almost all of China's leaders support economic reform and an open-door policy, though there are major differences of opinions over how fast and how far these reforms should proceed. Therefore, this scenario is also unlikely to take place. But the possibility of a return to Maoist economic policies, involving autarky and a deemphasis on trade with the outside world, cannot be ruled out.

China as an Important Trading Partner

The third, and the most likely, possible trend is the continuation of the ongoing process of increasing ties between China and Latin America. Current leaders are unlikely to lead China back toward the radical Maoist experiments of the past, yet they are more likely to pursue the policies of a centralized open economy rather than a market-oriented open economy. There have been some changes in the post-Tiananmen period. Some important aspects of economic reform have been postponed indefinitely. On the other hand, China's policy in world affairs continues to pursue the same broad objectives that shaped Mao and Deng's foreign policy after the founding of the PRC in 1949. Virtually all of China's leaders have endorsed the strategy of export-oriented development in China's coastal areas. In the light of all these considerations, China will in all probability maintain an open-door policy to the rest of the world. Therefore, it is anticipated that the basis for future trade relations between the PRC and Latin America will continue to be favorable, implying further increases in economic interdependence.

SUMMARY

China and Latin America are both huge continental land areas whose combined foreign trade constitutes more than 10 percent of total world trade. Both areas are rich in manpower, and both are still in the throes of economic development. For the Sino–Latin American relationship to endure, China's political stability is a necessary but insufficient condition. The growing relationship must also be forged on some viable economic foundation such as mutually beneficial trade relations. The complementarities between China's energy and cheap light industrial goods and Latin America's mineral and agricultural products suggest a natural basis for economic exchange. Potential threats to China's type of exports lie in the further industrialization efforts of Brazil, Mexico, Argentina, and Chile. The Chinese may in the future shift into the export of machinery, electronics, and more highly processed manufactured goods. Areas of mutual benefit are great and shall continue to expand into the future.

The present international situation is favorable to the PRC in spite of the recent political turmoil. The complementary character of the relationship between the Chinese and Latin American economies is unquestionable, for China needs to import the raw materials and food Latin America can supply, whereas Latin America needs the cheap light industrial products as well as the fuels the PRC can provide. The exchange of Latin American products such as copper, steel, iron, and agricultural goods for Chinese coal, crude oil, and cheap light manufacturing goods reflects a natural division of labor. Clearly, the economic structures of China and the major Latin American countries are largely complementary and therefore are conducive to trade expansion; but those of China and the fuel-exporting countries, such as Mexico, Venezuela, and Colombia, are to some extent competitive. To sum up, the most likely trend is that if China persists on its open-door and reform policy course and is successful, it will become an important trading partner for Latin America in the next two or three decades.

NOTES

1. Because manufacturing is generally the most dynamic part of the industrial sector, its share of GDP is shown separately.

2. World Bank, *World Development Report 1990* (New York: Oxford University Press, 1990), pp. 182–83.

3. Ibid., pp. 188–89.

4. Ibid., Tables 1 and 3.

5. Machinery and transport equipment are the commodities in SITC section 7.

6. Other manufactures represent SITC sections 5 though 8 less section 7 and divisions 67 and 68.

7. Standard International Trade Classification (SITC) is used here for the formatting of the data. The one-digit code is as follows:

0 Food and live animals chiefly for food

1 Beverage and tobacco

2 Crude materials, inedible, except fuels

3 Mineral fuel, lubricants, and related materials

4 Animal and vegetable oils, fats, and waxes

5 Chemicals and related products

6 Manufactured goods classified by material

7 Machinery and transport equipment

8 Miscellaneous manufactured articles

9 Commodities and transactions not classified elsewhere in SITC

8. Since 1986, the total volume of China's crude oil export has actually been cut in order to support the mid-1986 OPEC agreement to curtail production to increase the world price of oil.

9. *La Paz la Red Panamericana*, January 10, 1989, in *Daily Report: Latin America* (hereafter cited as FBIS–Latin America), January 11, 1989, p. 42.

10. Ibid.

11. U.S. Commerce Department quoted in CIA, *Chinese Economy in 1988 and 1989: Reforms on Hold, Economic Problems Mount*, p. 14.

12. U.S. Department of Commerce, *Highlights of U.S. Exports and Imports Trade* (December 1988) (Washington, D.C.: U.S. Department of Commerce, Bureau of the Census, 1988), B12-B14.

13. Israel Epstein, "The 1990s—Bridge to the Future," *China Today* (formerly *China Reconstructs*), 39, no. 1 (January 1990), p. 13.

14. See Chen Dezhao, "China and the GATT," *Australian Outlook: The Australian Journal of International Affairs*, 43, no. 1 (April 1989), pp. 36–43.

15. Cited in Gerald Segal. "As China Grows Stronger," *International Affairs*, 64, no. 2 (Spring 1988), p. 231.

16. Commission On Integrated Long-Term Strategy, *Discriminate Deterrence* (Washington, D.C.: GPO, 1988), p. 7.

17. UNCTAD, *Handbook of International Trade and Development Statistics 1987 Supplement* (New York: United Nations, 1988), pp. 5–6.

18. The Asian NICs are Hong Kong, Taiwan, South Korea, and Singapore.

19. *Economic and Social Progress in Latin America, 1989 Report*, p. 25.

20. *The Times of the Americas*, July 1, 1987.

21. *World Development Report 1990*, p. 208.

22. Speech given at the Asia Society, June 2, 1982.

23. Jack W. Hopkins, "Latin America in the World," in *Latin America: Perspectives on a Region*, ed. Jack W. Hopkins (New York: Holmes & Meier, 1987), p. 283.

24. For details, see Akira Chiba, "Pacific Co-operation and China," *The Pacific Review*, 2, no. 1 (1989), pp. 44–56.

25. Quoted in Walter Sanchez Gonzalez, *Relations between Latin America and Asia: Interactions and Political Implications* (Santiago, Chile: Instituto de Estudios Internacionales, Universidad de Chile, 1985), p. 29.

26. According to the *China Daily* (May 23, 1990), China has set up economic or commercial offices in seventeen Latin American countries.

27. Sanchez Gonzalez, *Relations between Latin America and Asia*, p. 28.

28. For more information on Chinese immigration in Latin America, see Eugenio Chang Rodriguez, "Chinese Labor Migration to Latin America in the Nineteenth Century," *Revista de Historia de América*, no. 46 (1958), pp. 375–99.

29. For a detailed study on the economic status of the Chinese in Latin American countries, see Committee of Overseas Chinese Economy in Ten Years, *Overseas Chinese Economy in Ten Years, 1972–1981* (Taipei, 1981), and Man-Shik, Min, ''Far Eastern Immigration into Latin America,'' *Korea and World Affairs: A Quarterly Review*, 11, no. 2 (Summer 1987), pp. 331–49.

30. Sha Ding et al., eds., *Zhongguo he ladinmeizhou guanxi Jianshi* (Brief History of Sino–Latin American Relations) (Zhenzhou, China: Henan People's Publishing House, 1987), p. 331.

31. *China Daily*, March 12, 1990.

32. In 1985, Chinese premier Zhao Ziyang visited Latin America. Chinese president Yang Shankun visited Mexico, Brazil, Chile, Argentina, and Uruguay in May 1990. Since 1980 seven presidents and four prime ministers from Latin America have officially visited China. There have also been visits from parliamentary delegations from Bolivia, Peru, Cuba, Colombia, Jamaica, and Trinidad and Tobago.

33. On this topic, see Gerald Segal, ''As China Grows Stronger,'' *International Affairs*, 64, no. 2 (Spring 1988).

34. China has set for itself the goal of increasing its per capita GNP to $800–$1,000 by the end of this century.

35. The Chinese openly acknowledged their part in the greater power triangle (the United States, the Soviet Union, and China).

36. For an assessment of China's relations with the Third World, see Lillian Craig Harris and Robert L. Worden, eds., *China and the Third World: Champion or Challenger?* (Dover, Mass.: Auburn House, 1986).

10

Summary and Conclusions

The preceding chapters examined economic relations between China and Latin America from 1949 through 1989. During this period, China's trade relations with Latin America went through four stages: nongovernmental trade in the 1950s; predominantly Sino-Cuban trade in the 1960s; the expansion of Latin American regional trade relations from 1970 to 1977; rapid trade growth since the initiation of the open-door policy in 1978. China's role in Latin America has grown consistently since the early 1970s. It was noted at the beginning of this study that China is now playing a more active, more effective, and more influential role in the international economic relations of Latin America than at any previous time. Given this groundwork, it is now time to address the questions posed in Chapter 1 in light of the data and analysis presented here.

This study of Sino–Latin American economic relations reveals that their development was affected by ideological motivations, economic interests, and international power politics. Sino–Latin American relations were shaped by profound changes in the internal economies of the countries involved and by changes in the world economic and political environment. For many years, most Latin American countries and China were practically isolated from each other as a result of the cold war climate prevailing in world politics, and the lack of significant economic ties linking the two regions. With the establishment of diplomatic relations between Beijing and many Latin American countries, this situation was reversed. Recent years have witnessed a boom in Sino–Latin American economic relations.

Among the factors that contributed to the development of mutual relations, the dynamic economic growth of China and Latin America is particularly noteworthy. Between 1958 and 1978 Latin America more than quadrupled its GDP, which developed in this period at an average annual growth rate of 5.5 percent, that is faster than the other developing areas (except oil-producing countries) and the developed market economy as a whole. Meanwhile, China has experienced an even more dynamic growth of its economy in the same period. In recent years, China has relied increasingly on external economic factors in its efforts to assure sustained economic growth. Consequently, growth of foreign trade has substantially exceeded that of the national economy, and this trend is expected to persist in the future.

CHINA'S POLICY GOALS IN LATIN AMERICA

Beijing has long-range and short-range goals for its relations with Latin American counties. In the first two decades of the People's Republic, Beijing encouraged developing countries to undermine the territorial, strategic, political, and economic dominance of the West. Trade was often used as a tool for attaining political as well as economic objectives.

During much of the 1960s, the Chinese were convinced that the Cuban Revolution would herald the spread of other revolutions in Latin America and so China consistently made attempts to encourage Latin American Communists and non-Communist leftists to undertake protracted armed struggle to overthrow existing governments. These revolutionary hopes never materialized, however. Armed struggle failed to achieve predicted successes, and Cuba became economically and politically isolated from Latin America. In the 1970s, Beijing sought to use trade and aid to build political support and eventual diplomatic recognition in Latin America. With the winning of diplomatic recognition from most Latin American countries, and the economic reforms since 1978, trade has become less politically motivated.

Since the late 1970s, Chinese policies toward Latin America have become increasingly pragmatic. The PRC's current trade goals include (1) opening new markets for Chinese manufactured goods, (2) diversifying Chinese raw materials suppliers, (3) strengthening its diplomatic ties with Latin America, and (4) promoting the region's economic development. It has become apparent that Beijing's more flexible and economically pragmatic approach to Latin America allowed China to garner major economic benefits, including access to new technology and new markets for Chinese exports.

For a long time, Chinese ideology has stressed the common interests of the PRC and Latin America. The efforts to make common cause with Third World countries against a mutual enemy may be considered a congenial imperative of Chinese policy toward Latin America. Thus, support for and solidarity with the Third World is indeed a basic principle in Chinese foreign policy; such identification will continue undiminished even if China becomes a rich and powerful state.[1] China's long-term goals are to achieve formal diplomatic relations with all Latin American countries and to develop beneficial economic and technical ties with them. Beijing has pursued these long-term aims since the early 1970s and will continue to do so in the 1990s. Overall, these objectives have largely been achieved. Beijing has managed to improve its relations with all the countries in the region, including Cuba. Cooperation now occurs in economic, financial, and technological arenas.

CONSISTENCY AND CHANGE IN CHINA'S LATIN AMERICAN POLICY

As has been observed, the consistency of China's Latin American policy is apparent. However, there have been significant changes over the last four decades.

From "People's War" to Economic Development

In the 1960s, China's advocacy of wars of national liberation in Latin America was the main policy theme. Since 1970, China has deliberately omitted articulating the need for a people's war against governments in the Third World. At the same time, Beijing has encouraged the Latin American regimes to achieve economic development and to seek autonomy from the industrialized nations, and the United States in particular. Since the beginning of the 1970s, China has assured that a prosperous, stable Latin America serves Chinese interests. This policy change coincided with the general easing of tensions between the PRC and the United States. The rationale for the change in Chinese policy involves the following elements:

1. Expecting that Latin American development would bring China long-term economic returns, China endorses regional unity and autonomous economic development. The PRC believes that Latin American economic development will strengthen political stability in the region. Accordingly, the Chinese are ready and willing to cooperate with Latin American countries in their process of economic development.

2. Supporting economic growth in the regions also reflects Beijing's willingness to separate economics from politics. Therefore, Beijing retains strong links with both pro-Soviet Cuba and pro-U.S. regimes in the region.

3. Having their experience with Cuba and radical guerillas in the 1960s, Chinese leaders have been extremely cautious in their response to recent revolutionary governments/movements in Latin America.

4. Contributing to Latin American modernization will also allow China to pursue its foreign policy goals: to resist the superpowers' influence in the area and to tighten China's ties with the region.

The central goal of Chinese policy is to promote friendly relations with the developing countries, and this necessarily involves supporting the local elite who generally form governments. Compared to that of the 1960s, China's Latin American policy since the early 1970s has been much more accommodating to established governments, less concerned with insurrectionary movements, and based on the belief that the Third World was a progressive international force. Simultaneously, the CCP has been trying to establish relations with nationalist parties such as Mexico's Partido Revolucionario Institucional (PRI) and Peru's Alianza Popular Revolucionario Americana (APRA), while cooling relations with more radical parties.[2] The shift first became evident in February 1979 when CCP officials attended the fiftieth anniversary of the PRI, Mexico's ruling party. China now claims to have established relations or contacts with some twenty-six political parties in Latin America.[3]

From Economic Independence to Interdependence

In the past, China maintained a "self-reliance" model for its economic development and supported a policy of "economic independence" for Latin America. Like the *dependistas*, they considered that political and, more importantly, economic dependence on the West remained the main obstacle to genuine development in Latin America. According to the then-prevailing Chinese view, the struggle for political independence by a Third World country would remain incomplete unless it was followed by a nationalized and self-sufficient economy. For that purpose, China firmly supported Latin American economic nationalism, such as nationalization of foreign capital in the early 1970s.

Post-Mao China has shifted from *dependencia* theory to the Western neo-realist liberal theory of global interdependence.[4] "Self-reliance" disappeared from Beijing's pronouncements, open-door policy—"make full use" of foreign trade, technology transfer, and loans and investment—replaced self-imposed isolation. In recent years, the term *interdependence* has gained currency in Chinese official publications, China has been increasingly involved in the changing and interdependent global economy. Professor Huan Xiang, the then director-general of Center for International Studies of the State Council, pointed out, "The closely interdependent world market has taken the place of regional and national self-reliance and closed doors."[5] On several occasions, Chinese scholars criticized the dependency theory.[6] China's view on the nature of the international economy, namely, its globally interdependent character, reflects Beijing's interest in world economic coexistence rather than confrontation. Likewise, today Beijing encourages Latin American countries not only to maintain agreeable relations with the West but even to compete with these countries to attract scarce foreign capital from Japan, the United States, and Western Europe. It appears that in the years ahead, China will continue to serve as a force for stability and prosperity in Latin America.

From Cultural to Economic Diplomacy

The evolution of Chinese policy from its establishment in 1949 to the present has been marked by a fundamental shift from "cultural diplomacy" to "economic diplomacy." Because the Chinese lacked normal diplomatic channels and had very limited economic resources in the early years of the PRC, they relied almost exclusively on their cultural contacts and exchange to build bridges between the newly established People's Republic and Latin America.[7]

Since 1978, Chinese foreign policy priorities have shifted to the economic sphere. The PRC consistently emphasizes economic rather than political relations.[8] Not surprisingly, Chinese interests are now focused on trade and investment, while purely political affairs are regarded relatively unimportant. Over the past few years, most Chinese missions have been business ones. Since the late 1970s, economic relations have become a fundamental element of the new stage of Sino–Latin American relations. During his 1985 visit to Bogota, Colombia, Premier Zhao Ziyang informed a number of Latin American diplomats, "If you have difficulties in establishing diplomatic relations with China, we can start with economic relations and trade.[9] In brief, economic diplomacy has enabled China to maintain friendly relations with politically diverse nations while pursuing its economic objectives.

Generally speaking, since the late 1970s, Beijing's Latin American policy has demonstrated a significant level of flexibility and pragmatism. The PRC is prepared to adopt a flexible response to new development in the region; and in most cases, such reactions are conducted in conformity with China's open-door policy, which links China and its future with the international economy. Although communism remains the PRC's unchangeable ideology, governing domestic policy, it plays a much less influential role in its foreign policy. In addition, there are important continuities with the past. A Third World nation as well as a potential superpower, China continues to pursue two separate ends in its foreign relations: to champion the causes of the Third World against the superpowers while at the same time doing everything possible to enhance its own development and security.

EXTERNAL INFLUENCES ON SINO–LATIN AMERICAN ECONOMIC RELATIONS

In international affairs each state is more or less affected by the behavior and reaction of other states.[10] Relations with other foreign powers have, as noted, played an important role in Sino–Latin American relations since the postwar period. Here we examine three such actors: the United States, the Soviet Union, and Taiwan.

The U.S. Factor

In the earlier years of the PRC, Beijing-Washington relations were an important influence on Sino–Latin American relations. The emergence of Sino–Latin American relations over the last two decades and their continuation today can be seen as a response to the changing international environment, in which the dominant position of the United States is increasingly weakening.

External factors significantly constrained Chinese–Latin American relations in the early stage. Since 1949, the PRC was faced with a hostile policy of "containment" by Washington, which not only forbade U.S. trade with China but also pressured other states not to recognize China, to ban Chinese access to strategic materials, and to hold economic relations with China to a minimum. This policy was effective for many years. For historical and ideological reasons, China was closely associated with the Soviet bloc in its early years. In this initial period, China not only lacked the interest and means to pursue an ambitious Latin American policy but also understood that such a policy would have amounted to a direct challenge to the dominant power's hegemony. In the absence of diplomatic relations and in view of Latin America's alliance with the United States, the Chinese attitude toward Latin America was influenced by the state of Sino–American relations. United States policy toward China changed substantially beginning with the Nixon administration. The Nixon and Carter administrations increasingly sought to control trends in the Third World via the intermediary of détente and triangulations with China and the Soviet Union, as if these two states had the capacity to impose constraints on the dynamics of change in the Third World.[11]

Latin American relations with China were partly shaped by the U.S. position: Once the United States recognized the PRC, the Latin American states followed suit. Prior to Nixon's visit to Beijing, most Latin American countries were hesitant to seek reconciliation with Beijing in part because they feared that failure to support Washington's position might have adverse economic or political repercussions. Nixon's visit automatically removed from Latin American countries the U.S. pressure that prevented them from establishing or improving diplomatic relations with the PRC.

United States–Latin American relations have changed over the past decade. With the erosion of U.S. hegemony over the region, Latin American countries have gained greater autonomy in their foreign affairs. The independent political initiative of the Contadora Group of the mid-1980s is just one example of this trend. (The Contadora Group consists of

Mexico, Panama, Venezuela and Colombia, the four countries that met in January 1983 to initiate a process of international consultation to promote a negotiated peace in Central America.) However, they are still developing countries that depend on trade, credit and technology with the United States. Thus, fluctuations in Washington's China policy will continue to have an impact in Latin American relations with China.[12]

The Soviet Factor

China's overall relations with the developing areas have also been strongly influenced by its political relationship with the Soviet Union. Chinese and Soviet policies toward Latin America were complementary and harmonious until the Sino-Soviet split in the early 1960s. Until then, in fact, the Chinese consistently stressed the Soviets' leadership in promoting the aims of the Communist system in Latin America. Rising Sino-Soviet tensions in the 1960s led to an intense schism between pro-Chinese and pro-Soviet elements in many Latin American Communist parties and the rapid deterioration of Chinese relations with most of their Latin American Communist comrades for two decades.[13] For the same reason, Havana-Beijing relations worsened. They did improve noticeably only after the beginning of normalization between Beijing and Moscow.

Until the beginning of the 1980s, the Soviet Union was a major concern in China's policy toward Latin America. As a result of the Soviet invasion of Czechoslovakia in 1968 and the growing military confrontation along the long frontier between China and the Soviet Union, Beijing began to regard Moscow, rather than Washington, as its principal strategic adversary. Consequently, China's policy toward Latin America came steadily to assume an anti-Soviet rather than an anti-American character. China's strategic concern about being militarily encircled by the Soviets was to some extent reflected in its relations with Latin America. This is particularly true, of course, in the instance of deterioration of Sino-Cuban relations. But this also helps explain in part China's close relations since 1973 with the Chilean military government; Pinochet made anti-Sovietism a centerpiece of his foreign policy.

With the Sino-Soviet rapprochement, Beijing and Moscow have been less critical of each other's policies in the Third World. Beijing took a neutral position toward U.S.-Soviet rivalry in Central America. Competition with the Soviets no longer weighs heavily in China's Latin American policy.[14] In spite of the fact that China and the Soviet Union have normalized their relations in recent years, there can be no return to the kind of Sino-Soviet relations that existed in the 1950s. Since 1989, Chinese and Soviet Latin Americanists have exchanged academic delegations; however, there is no indication that the two major powers are coordinating their policies in Latin America. Meanwhile, the possibility of a renewed Sino-Soviet conflict still exists.

As Sino-Soviet relations began to relax, Sino-Cuban relations also showed signs of improving. However, in view of Cuba's heavy reliance on Moscow, China-Cuba economic relations will continue to be tied closely with Beijing-Moscow bilateral relations. Although economic aid will remain an important feature of Chinese policy in the Third World, a large-scale commitment to Cuba is highly unlikely.

In sum, since the mid-1980s the Soviet impact on Sino–Latin American relations has been somewhat reduced. Compared with U.S. influence on Sino–Latin American relations, the Soviet impact is modest except in the case of Cuba. On the other hand, the Chinese appear to use any opportunity offered to replace outgoing or declining Soviet involvement. Chile was often cited in this respect. For instance, the Chinese not only refused to interrupt diplomatic relations after President Allende's downfall but actively encouraged trade between the two countries.[15] Though Beijing and Moscow have normalized their relations in the past few years, there can be no return to the Sino-Soviet relationship that existed in the 1950s. China is no longer closely aligned with the Soviet Union.

The Taiwan Factor

The Taiwan question is one of the most sensitive issues in China's foreign policy. A strong motivation in Beijing's Latin American policy is Taiwan's influence in the region.[16] Beijing-Taipei diplomatic competition in Latin America since 1949 is an extension of the general political and economic competition between the two governments (see Table 10.1). Latin America has become increasingly important to Taiwan. As of December 1990, Taiwan maintained diplomatic relations with twenty-seven states in the world; fifteen of them are in Latin America.[17] Not surprisingly, Taiwan policymakers aim to reduce Taiwan's reliance on U.S. and Japanese markets and instead to compete with them, becoming a major trading partner with Latin America and Eastern Europe.

Trade also follows and stabilizes the diplomatic flag in Latin America. The past few years have witnessed considerable exchanges of dignitaries between Taiwan and Central American countries, as well as efforts to expand trade with these countries. Taiwan has become a good market for agricultural products and raw materials from Latin America, even for those countries with which it has had no official relations, including Chile, Colombia, Peru, and Venezuela. The two-way trade between Taiwan and the Latin American countries reached more than $2.68 billion in 1989 compared with only $477 million in 1977.[18] Taipei has also set up representative offices in Latin American countries having no diplomatic relations with Taiwan, such as Argentina, Brazil, Chile, Peru, Ecuador, Venezuela, and Colombia.[19]

Table 10.1
Diplomatic Relations with Latin America: PRC versus Taiwan (as of February 1991)

	PRC	Taiwan
South America		
Argentina	2/19/72	
Bolivia	7/9/85	
Brazil	8/15/74	
Chile	12/15/70	
Colombia	2/7/80	
Ecuador	1/2/80	
Guyana	6/27/72	
Paraguay		7/8/57
Peru	11/2/71	
Surinam	5/28/76	
Uruguay	2/3/88	
Venezuela	6/28/74	
Mexico and Central America		
Mexico	2/14/72	
Costa Rica		1941
El Salvador		1941
Guatemala		1935
Honduras		1941
Nicaragua*	12/7/85-11/7/90	11/6/90
Panama		1909
Caribbean		
Antigua & Barbuda	1/1/83	
Bahamas		1/10/89
Barbados	5/30/77	
Belize*	2/6/87—10/23/89	10/13/89
Commonwealth of Dominica		5/10/83
Cuba	9/28/60	
Dominican Rep.		
Grenada*	10/1/85—8/8/89	7/20/89
Haiti		
Jamaica	11/21/72	
St. Kitts-Nevis		10/9/83
St. Lucia		5/7/84
St. Vincent		8/15/81
Trin. & Tobago	6/20/74	

Source: *Shijie zhishi nianjian, 1987* (World Knowledge Yearbook, 1987) (Beijing: Shijie Zhishi Chubanshe, 1987), pp. 710–16, and *Renmin Ribao*, 1987–1990.
*The PRC suspended its diplomatic ties with Grenada, Belize, and Nicaragua in recent years because their governments "resumed" diplomatic relations with Taiwan.

Taiwan has proven to be one of the most important models of how free enterprise unleashes economic growth. Many Third World nations, particularly in Latin America, look to Taiwan as a model for their economic development. Taipei has also enhanced its position in the Caribbean through economic and technological assistance.[20] Beijing, however, has fewer aid arrangements with the countries in this area. Partly due to its close economic relations with Taiwan, Costa Rica has maintained important ties with almost all the socialist countries with the exception of the PRC.[21] Some Caribbean countries, which did not profit handsomely from trade and aid programs from China, recently restored their political and economic ties with Taiwan. For instance, in January 1989, the Bahamas extended diplomatic recognition to Taiwan. Grenada and Belize recognized Taiwan as the government of China in mid-1989, and Nicaragua switched its embassy from Beijing to Taipei in late 1990.

The Sino-Soviet quarrel tended to puzzle Latin American leaders. But to Latin Americans, the Beijing-Taipei competition in the Western Hemisphere was probably more welcome than annoying. Most Latin American countries were fully aware that the more intense the competition between Beijing and Taipei, the better their chances for exploiting and taking advantage of it. Although diplomatic ties were established between the PRC and many Latin American countries, these countries still maintain commercial ties with Taiwan. For certain Central American and Caribbean countries, two-way trade with Taiwan will be larger than that with the PRC in years ahead. Various Taiwanese trade offices are active in South America and Mexico. This state of affairs is unlikely to change in the medium or even long term. As elsewhere, Beijing has ruled out any moves by Latin American governments to establish or maintain diplomatic relations simultaneously with Beijing and Taipei. Undoubtedly, Beijing is likely to increase its trade and aid programs in the years ahead in order to keep Beijing–Latin American relations strong. Over the long run, because of differences in size, population, military strength, natural resources, and diplomatic power between Beijing and Taipei, Taiwan will find it more and more difficult to compete with the PRC in Latin America.

Japan has emerged as a major source of economic influence in Latin America, rivaling the United States and overshadowing Western Europe. Yet so far Japan has very little influence on Chinese relations with Latin America.

In summary, in the past decades China's relations with Latin America actually and largely hinged on its relations with the two superpowers. When its relations with one or two of them changed, its relations with the countries of Latin America changed accordingly. However, with Latin America's and China's effort to diversify their international economic relations, foreign factors will assume a less influential role in the growth of Sino–Latin American relations. In short, China will probably play a more active role in the economic and political affairs of Latin America, but it has its own independent way of pursuing its goals in this part of world.

IMPLICATIONS FOR THE UNITED STATES

In the postwar period, U.S. economic engagement in Latin America was overwhelming; but since the late 1970s, Chinese influence has been rising steadily. Growing ties between China and Latin America have clear implications for the United States. The implications of the "Chinese role in Latin America" are mixed, but the positive implications appear to far outweigh the negative ones.

On the negative side, China's interest in gaining access to Western capital, markets, and technical assistance creates some problems for U.S. policy in the Third World. All three of these commodities are in short supply, and the United States will have to weigh the new requests made by China against the longer-standing demands of other developing countries. Clearly, China may compete with Third World countries for scarce U.S. resources and for entry into an increasingly protectionist U.S. market.[22] Arms transfers from China may become another point of disagreement. Prior to the 1960s, most military hardware for Latin America was supplied by the United States, but this picture has changed entirely during recent decades. Now Western Europe, the Soviet Union, and Israel as well as China provide vast amounts of arms to the region.[23]

On the positive side, U.S. policymakers can claim several gains from China's changing relations with Latin America. A good example is that now Beijing firmly supports regional economic development instead of encouraging armed struggle. Many agree that China is no longer exporting revolution. Harry Harding concluded that China now refrains from actively supporting revolution in developing countries aligned with the United States. On a wide range of specific Third World issues, China has become much more supportive than obstructive of U.S. foreign policy actions and objectives.[24]

All things considered, present PRC involvement in Latin America has been largely compatible with Western interests and is likely to remain so for the immediate future, provided that Beijing continues its current policy direction in support of economic development and regional stability. However, because Beijing's influence in Latin America is limited and its economic resources are in short supply, China's impact on U.S. relations with Latin America should not be overestimated. China's present role in Latin America will continue to grow, but China will not be in a position to challenge the U.S. role in the region very soon.

LATIN AMERICAN MOTIVES AND GOALS

Since the 1970s, the Latin American states have attempted to diversify their international relations, seeking friends and trading partners wherever they might be found. The goal has been to replace dependence on the United States with international interdependence. In return, nonhemispheric actors have become increasingly interested in Latin America for political and economic reasons. Before the 1970s, Latin American policy toward China was based mainly on political considerations, whereas today economic interests are paramount in Latin America's relations with China. For example, Brazil has held a hard line against communism for years but has become China's largest Latin American trading partner. A growing number of countries like Argentina, Chile, Uruguay, and Cuba are finding the PRC a profitable customer. The favorable trade balance on the Latin American side is a dramatic example. However, there are at least four motives common to all countries: (1) to find new customers for exports, (2) to acquire imports from new sources of supply, (3) to conserve foreign exchange through barter trade, and (4) to improve terms of trade, with mutually beneficial exchange and credit on favorable terms. When Montevideo established relations with Beijing in February 1988, Uruguayan foreign minister Enrique Iglesia made it clear that "China is a massive market and has far greater potential for us than Taiwan. Establishing relations with China is a decision based on political realism."[25]

Political objectives in Latin American trade with China are not wholly absent. Many view it primarily as a means of strengthening their negotiating position vis-à-vis the United States and other developed countries.[26] Some Latin American countries clearly like to use their Chinese connections to break, or at least reduce somewhat, their dependence on the United States. Beijing's support for the Latin American position on a variety of North-South and South-South issues has helped to pave the way for improving relations with Latin America. As the then president of Brazil, João Baptista de Oliveira Figueiredo, observed during his 1984 visit to Beijing, "Our common interests will be further expanded as our two countries are sharing more views in international issues."[27] Given this background, since the early 1970s China has increasingly become a source of trade, credits, technical assistance, and political support for Latin American countries.

IMPLICATIONS FOR SOUTH-SOUTH COOPERATION

A salient feature of the Third World political economy during the past two decades has been the establishment of South-South cooperation,[28] also known as economic cooperation among developing countries (ECDC). Since the early 1980s, China has redefined its support of the New

International Economic Order (NIEO) in favor of South-South cooperation (collective self-reliance). South-South cooperation and a North-South
dialogue were said to be two interrelated aspects of the same process of
transforming the old economic order into a new one.[29] When Deng
Xiaoping met with Uruguay's President Julio María Sanguinetti, he said,
''China's policy is to establish and develop relations with Latin American
nations. We will work together with Latin American countries to set an
example of South-South cooperation.''[30] Thus, Deng saw South-South
cooperation as the theoretical basis of China's economic relations with
Latin America. The Chinese predict great potential for South-South
cooperation. They consider that by the end of the century the developing countries will create 27 percent of the world's industrial output and
share 28 percent of the international trade.[31]

Theoretically, South-South cooperation is based on barter, joint ventures, preferential prices, and transfer of technology—all elements that
China claims are visible in its relations with Latin America.[32] In recent
years, both China and Latin American countries have stressed South-
South cooperation as a means of avoiding the obstacles entailed in trading
with the Western nations. In the long term, if China and Latin America
are successful in their modernization and cooperation efforts, likely consequences include the following:

- A sustained growth of economic relations could assist both sides in their development efforts, particularly in strengthening economic structure, diversifying
  markets and sources of supply, and increasing export sales, thus contributing
  to better use of human and natural resources on both sides.

- Direct trade between the two regions avoids the protectionist measures increasingly imposed by the OECD countries and eliminates the intermediary role of
  multinational corporations. Direct trade has also fostered specialization in production without the fear of overdependence on Western economic structure.

- Although Chinese–Latin American trade accounts for a very small percentage
  of China's and Latin America's total trade during the period covered in this
  study, the development of such trade tends to reinforce cooperation among
  developing countries and lessen their heavy dependence on the West.

- Technology transfers between China and Latin America are breaking the traditional monopoly that industrialized countries have held on this commodity,
  spurring increased international competition in this highly controlled market.

- Since exports of capital goods to industrialized countries may not be possible
  at first, the more accessible developing countries' markets can offer opportunities
  to advance up the ladder of technological sophistication.

Nevertheless, some important limitations to South-South trade should
be mentioned. First, like Latin America, China has an expanding market,
and it is short of capital and technology. In contrast, the West has plenty

of capital and technology coupled with insufficient markets. Second, financial and technological factors are important constraints, limiting the size of South-South cooperation. Therefore, in the near future, cooperation among developing countries can only complement their trade with industrialized countries at best. It should be mentioned here that in some sectors, such as coal and crude oil, China and Latin American exporters are competitive.

According to official Chinese sources, South-South cooperation is not an alternative to North-South relations. It is, rather, a more realistic path toward independent national economies, strengthening Third World solidarity, increasing the South's bargaining power, and generating new momentum for stalled global negotiations. The expansion of Beijing–Latin American ties partly results from intergovernmental policies of diversification, but mainly from market forces.[33] Despite the proclamation of "South-South cooperation," China's trade is heavily skewed to the West. As a Chinese economist argued, "Since both sides are developing countries, production levels are not high, and the export commodities structures are in general similar, therefore the relative share of the Third World countries in our total trade volume is not comparable to the industrially developed countries."[34] This represents a justification on the basis of comparative advantage for the somewhat small share of trade with developing countries.

It should be stressed that the growth of Latin American relations with China has not lessened their relations with the West in a significant way, although their relations with the United States in terms of trade did expand during the past decade. Neither have Sino–Latin American ties brought any notable change in internal class forces or the pattern of economic development.

IMPLICATIONS OF EVENTS IN TIANANMEN SQUARE, 1989

The military crackdown on the Chinese students' movement on June 4, 1989, also known as the June 4 Event, has tremendous implications for China's politics and economy. Many substantial foreign policy gains achieved during a decade of reforms have been jeopardized. Notwithstanding its worldwide impacts, The Tiananmen tragedy has had comparatively little impact on Sino–Latin American economic relations. This is partly because trade between China and Latin America accounts for only a small percentage of China's total external trade, and partly because most Latin American countries have been moderate in their responses to the Tiananmen Square incident.[35] The Latin American stand on the Tiananmen incident was greatly appreciated. Just a year after Tiananmen, China's President Yang Shangkun was invited to visit five Latin American countries (Mexico, Uruguay, Brazil, Argentina, and Chile), where he was accorded a warm welcome. His visit brought these countries nearer to each other.

Nevertheless, the June 4 Event has indirectly affected Sino–Latin American relations. On the one hand, tensions in relations with the United States and Western Europe have served to increase China's tendency toward closer ties with Latin America. Chinese embassy officials interviewed believed that although there might be a setback in China's total external trade, China's trade with Latin America will increase as China furthers its trade activities in the Third World, and especially in Latin America.[36]

On the other hand, any slowdown of economic reform within China will hurt China's trade with Latin America in the long run. Since China's long-term comparative advantage lies in manufactured goods, a dynamic export sector depends on significant further reforms of China's still predominantly state-managed industry, which has shown very little sign of substantial improvements in its efficiency since reforms began. More satisfactory export performance will depend also on improvement in the foreign trade system as well as an abandonment of the long-standing Chinese goal of eventual self-sufficiency. In addition, China's current efforts to cut back "unproductive" and unauthorized investment projects as a way of curtailing inflationary measures in the domestic economy may reduce demand for some Latin American exports. Many agree that China would go through a difficult period of transition before it could resume dynamic higher growth.

Further development of the Chinese economy hinges on internal political stability. This depends essentially upon whether the present leadership in Beijing can effect a smooth transition of power once Deng Xiaoping and other aging leaders pass from the scene. A few scenarios could be drawn for the next few years. In the worst, China would be ruled again by Maoist-oriented leaders, thus impairing China's relations with Latin America. More optimistically, a stable China dedicated to orderly economic development would contribute to its own economic growth, and relations with other countries. The present Chinese administration has reaffirmed its current policy of economic reform and the open-door policy, but it remains to be seen whether this policy will be carried over into the post-Deng period.

Taken together, the Tiananmen Square event has had little immediate effect on Sino–Latin American relations. But if China's market-oriented economic reform and its open-door strategy are reversed, such relations will be negatively affected in the long run.

NATURE OF CHINESE–LATIN AMERICAN TRADE RELATIONS

China's economic relations with Latin America—just like those of other major powers—have been as much an extension of foreign as economic policy.[37] Although there is no evidence of neocolonialism in Sino–Latin American relations, some authors allege that China–Third World trade has this feature.[38] Moscow spokespersons used to accuse Beijing of following a self-serving line that sought to exploit the nations of Latin America for its private ends, subordinating their real interests to its own big-power chauvinist aspirations to attain global hegemony.[39] These statements are debatable. First of all, it is true that in the 1960s and 1970s China's imports consisted primarily of natural or processed primary commodities from Latin America, and this region as a whole had few manufactured goods exports to China.[40] However, Latin American exports of manufactured goods have registered rapid growth in recent years. The ratios of manufactures have accounted for 37 percent of total commodity exports in the Brazilian case, 34 percent for Mexico, and 26 percent for Argentina.[41] Yet this ratio varies from case to case. It has been observed empirically that the goods China exports to less-developed countries tend to be more capital intensive than those China exports to more developed one's. For instance, China's exports to Chile and Cuba show a general predominance of manufactured products, and Beijing chiefly imports raw material from these countries in return.

Second, unlike the "dependent" trade relationship between developing countries and the West, the trade relations between Latin America and China are still quite limited. Third, China has constructed aid projects in production lines that have made its own exports redundant (e.g., the construction of a textile mill in Jamaica). Finally, available evidence suggests that Latin America has received fuels, manufactures, and food stuffs from China, all of which has helped the region in its plans for economic development and trade diversification. Chinese aid-cum-trade packages have had a positive effect on growth and development in Latin America.[42] In a nutshell, growth of Sino–Latin American trade over the past several decades has led to greater interdependence among the economies of China and many Latin American countries. This has been beneficial to the countries involved.

However, such interdependence is of limited significance for both sides. Undoubtedly, China is very low on the list of priorities of Latin American foreign policy and vice versa. China's international relations are concentrated on the United States and the Soviet Union. Relations with Japan and Western Europe are on a second level. Next come relations with Asian neighboring countries; on the fourth level are China's relations with Latin America, only slightly above relations with African countries.[43]

FUTURE PROSPECTS FOR CHINESE–LATIN AMERICAN ECONOMIC RELATIONS

Despite the Soviet Union's notable influence in Latin America, and the continuing U.S. view that Latin America remains within its "sphere of influence," it is anticipated that the PRC will become an important trading partner in Latin America in the next twenty or thirty years. Trade relations between Beijing and Latin America improved significantly in the 1980s. As discussed in Chapter 9, the most likely future scenario is that Chinese–Latin American relations continue in a positive direction.

Clearly, for Sino–Latin American relations to endure and prosper, China's political stability is a necessary but insufficient condition. Stronger relations must also be forged on a viable economic foundation such as mutually beneficial trade. There have been some internal changes in the post-Tiananmen period. But externally, China's policy in world affairs continues to pursue the same broad objectives that shaped Deng Xiaoping's foreign policy since 1978.

Future cooperation between China and Latin America will also be influenced by international actors like the United States, the Soviet Union, and Taiwan, with which China has considerably improved relations since the early 1980s. China today is in a favorable situation as far as Latin America is concerned. Ties created by Chinese emigrants, old and new, as well as by recent economic initiatives have produced an excellent basis for continuing cooperation. Friendly relations have been established and maintained with Latin American countries, and no conflicts are anticipated.

To sum up, Sino–Latin American economic ties have become less ideological.[44] In the last decade, China's trade and aid policy, which had been politically motivated, has been geared to the economic needs of both sides. It is the varying degrees of economic complementarities that are the main determinants of the extent of Chinese relations with Latin American countries. Mutually beneficial economic ties have served as the engine pulling Sino–Latin American relations forward. Given the potential of both sides, one might reasonably expect China to become an important trading partner of Latin America in the years to come. Yet the prospects for greater economic interactions will depend largely on how China's economic reforms continue to unfold and how Latin America copes with its economic difficulties and maintains political stability.

NOTES

1. Samuel S. Kim. "The Third World in Chinese World Policy." *World Order Studies Program Occasional Paper*, no. 19, (Princeton, N.J.: Center for International Studies, Princeton University, 1989), p. 1.

2. The CCP's general secretary, Mr. Hu Yaobang, told the Peruvian prime minister, Manuel Ulloa Elías, "We are willing to establish ties with nationalist parties and Communist parties of the Third World countries." For details, see *Beijing Review*, 25, no. 42 (October 18, 1982), p. 6.

3. Lillian Craig Harris, *China's Foreign Policy toward the Third World* (New York: Praeger, 1985), p. 101.

4. Samuel S. Kim, "China and the Third World: In Search of a Peace and Development Line," in *China and the World: New Directions in Chinese Foreign Relations*, 2d ed, ed. Samuel S. Kim, (Boulder, Colo.: Westview Press, 1989), p. 159.

5. Huan Xiang, "International Conflicts and Our Choices," *Beijing Review*, 27, no. 48 (November 26, 1984), p. 16.

6. For details, see Zhang Sengen and Wang Ningkun, "Latin American Studies in the People's Republic of China: Current and Future Prospects," *Latin American Research Review*, 23, no. 1 (1988): 123–32.

7. Further details are given in William Ratliff, "Chinese Communist Cultural Diplomacy toward Latin America, 1949–1960," *Hispanic American Historical Review*, 49, no. 1 (February 1969), pp. 53–79.

8. According to the Chinese official source, this economic diplomacy is characterized by foreign affairs work serving peace, development, and Four Modernizations. Economic cooperation takes precedence over political relations and the former's success will promote the latter. See *Wen Wei Pao* (Hong Kong), December 4, 1985, p. 3.

9. "Zhao in Bogota: Old Friend Comes Home," *Beijing Review* 28, no. 45 (November 11, 1985), p. 6.

10. Lloyd Jensen, *Explaining Foreign Policy* (Englewood Cliffs, N.J.: Prentice-Hall, 1982), p. 242.

11. Gabriel Kolko, *Confronting the Third World: United States Foreign Policy, 1945–1980* (New York: Pantheon Books, 1988), p. 297.

12. Robert L. Worden, "China and Latin America: A 'Last Frontier,'" in *China's Foreign Relations: New Perspectives*, ed., Chün-tu Hsüeh, (New York: Praeger, 1982), p. 136.

13. For more information on the Sino-Soviet split and its impact on Latin America, see H. Michael Erisman, "Conflicto Sino-Cubano: la lucha por influencia en el Tercer Mundo," *Areito*, 5, no. 5 (1979), pp. 12–19, and William R. Ganer, "The Sino-Soviet Ideological Struggle in Latin America," *Journal of Inter-American Studies and World Affairs*, 10, no. 2 (April 1968), pp. 244–55.

14. Gorbachev's Chinese policy involves a fundamental shift from the efforts to isolate, weaken, and encircle China that characterized Moscow's policy from 1960 to 1982.

15. Claudio Veliz, "Latin America's Opening to the Pacific," in *Latin America and World Economy: A Changing International Order*, ed., Joseph Grunwald (Beverly Hills: Sage Publications, 1978), p. 125.

16. Ming Chen-hua, *Penetration of Latin America by the Chinese Communists*, Joint Publications Research Service, Publication no. 3498, (New York: JPRS, 1959).

17. They include the Bahamas, Belize, Costa Rica, Dominica, the Dominican Republic, El Salvador, Grenada, Guatemala, Haiti, Honduras, Panama, Paraguay, Nicaragua, St. Kitts–Nevis, St. Lucia, and St. Vincent.

18. *China Yearbook 1980* (Taipei: China Publishing Co.) and *Republic of China Yearbook, 1990–91* (Taipei: Kwang Hwa Publishing Co. 1991), p. 237.

19. *Republic of China Yearbook, 1989* (Taipei: Kwang Hwa Publishing Co. 1989), p. 241.

20. See Yu San Wang, "The Republic of China's Technical Cooperation Programs with the Third World," in *The China Question: Essays on Current Relations between Mainland China and Taiwan*, ed. Yu San Wang (New York: Praeger, 1985).

21. On this topic, see "Costa Rica and Taiwan Join Hands," *The Times of the Americas*, July 27, 1988, p. 12.

22. Harry Harding, "China and the Third World: From Revolution to Containment," in *The China Factor: Sino-American Relations and the Global Scene*, ed., Richard H. Solomon (Englewood Cliffs, N.J.: Prentice-Hall, 1981), p. 290.

23. On this topic, see Isaac Caro, *América Latina y el Caribe en el mundo militar* (Santiago, Chile: Facultad Latinoamericana de Ciencias Sociales (FLACSO), 1988).

24. Harry Harding, "China and the Third World," p. 292.

25. Quoted in *South*, 98 (December 1988), p. 48.

26. For details, see Latin American Economic System, *Latin American–U.S. Economic Relations, 1982-1983* (Boulder, Colo.: Westview Press, 1984), pp. 88–92.

27. "Fruitful Visit by Brazil's President," *Beijing Review*, 27, no. 24 (June 11, 1984), p. 7.

28. The PRC has long considered itself a socialist country belonging to the South. By its own reckoning, China in 1986 stood eighth in GNP. But its position reduced to one hundred thirtieth when the figure is divided by its population of 1.1. billion. See Xinhua, January 15, 1988, in *FBIS-China*, January 15, 1988, p. 13.

29. Samuel S. Kim, "China and the Third World," p. 160.

30. *Renmin Ribao* (overseas edition), November 8, 1989, p. 1.

31. Huan Xiang, "International Conflicts and Our Choices," *Beijing Review*, 27, no. 48 (November 26, 1984), p. 18.

32. Wolfgang Deckers, "Latin America: How the Chinese See the Region," *The Pacific Review*, 2, no. 3 (1989), p. 249.

33. In order to increase trade with Africa, the Chinese government decided to delay imposing customs duty on items exported to Africa until after they are sold. Meanwhile, African products of similar prices, quality, and patterns to those made in other countries would enjoy priority in entering the Chinese market. However, this is not the case in Sino–Latin American trade. See *China Daily* (April 23, 1990) for details.

34. Gan Lun, "Thirty-five Years of China's Foreign Trade," *Guoji Maoyi Wenti* (Problems of International Trade), no. 4 (1984), p. 6.

35. Mexico was the only exception canceling Chairman Yang Shankun's visit in June 1989. However, it invited Yang to visit Mexico City a year later.

36. Interviews with Chinese embassy officials in Mexico City in July 1989.

37. The leadership of the CCP has consistently argued that a nation's foreign policy is essentially determined by domestic conditions.

38. On this subject, see Suzanne Paine, "China's Economic Relations with Less Developed Countries, 1950–1976," in *Economic Relations between Socialist Countries and the Third World*, ed., Deepak Nayyar (London: Macmillan Press, 1977), pp. 208–61.

39. George Ginsburgs, "The Soviet View of Chinese Influence in Africa and Latin America," in *Soviet and Chinese Influence in the Third World*, ed., Alvin Z. Rubinstein (New York: Praeger, 1975), pp. 197–220.

40. On this subject, see Michael A. Weininger, "People's Republic of China Latin American Trade Composition and Direction of Trade, 1965–1977," in *Proceedings of the 1982 Meeting of the Rocky Mountain Council in Latin American Studies 1982*, ed., Richard Bath (El Paso: University of Texas at El Paso, Center for Inter-American and Border Studies, 1982), pp. 51–59.

41. General Administration of Customs of the PRC, *China's Customs Statistics*, no. 1 (1989), pp. 63–66.

42. For instance, Cuba will use Chinese credit to build factories producing bicycles and electric fans in this country. The factories will use Chinese equipment and will have the capacity to produce 150,000 bicycles and 100,000 electric fans annually.

43. The volume of Sino-African two-way trade was less than $1 billion in 1989, much lower than that of Sino–Latin American trade, which reached $2.5 billion in the same year.

44. Beijing used to subsidize a number of foreign language publications to Latin America. Since the late 1970s, the government cut the financial subsidy to such propaganda; as a result of increased cost of publication and economic difficulties in Latin America, subscription to one of the major Chinese official publications *Beijing Informa* (Spanish language edition of *Beijing Review* fell rapidly from 13,000 in 1976 to only 700 in 1988.

Appendix A: Trade Treaties and Agreements between China and Latin America, 1949–1990

ANTIGUA AND BARBUDA

6/7/84	Agreement: Technical cooperation
8/23/84	Protocol: Technical assistance
6/26/85	Agreement: China provides $5 million aid
5/24/86	Agreement: Development
12/12/88	Agreement: Interest-free loan of $1.35 million, and a grant of $0.5 million

ARGENTINA

2/7/72	Agreement: Trade
2/2/77	Minutes: Trade agreement
5/30/78	Document: Trademark registration
5/30/78	Agreement: Maritime transportation
5/30/78	Exchange of Notes: Tax advantages for maritime transportation
5/30/78	Exchange of Notes: Reciprocal registry of wheat, corn, and cotton
5/30/78	Exchange of Notes: Long-term purchase of cotton

Sources: Douglas M. Johnston and Hungdah Chiu, *Agreements of the People's Republic of China, 1949–1967: A Calendar* (Cambridge, Mass.: Harvard University Press, 1968); Hungdah Chiu, *Agreements of the People's Republic of China: A Calendar of Events, 1966–1980* (New York: Praeger, 1981); Peter P. Cheng, ed., *A Chronology of the People's Republic of China from October 1, 1949* (Totowa, N.J.: Littlefield, Adams, 1972); Peter P. Cheng, ed., *A Chronology of the People's Republic of China, 1970–1979* (Metuchen, N.J.: Scarecrow Press, 1986); FBIS, *Daily Report: People's Republic of China;* and *Daily Report: Latin America*, 1980–1990.

6/6/80   Agreement: Granting of $300 million of financial credit to PRC

6/7/80   Agreement: Economic cooperation

6/7/80   Agreement: Scientific and technical cooperation

8/19/83   Agreement: Cooperation in agriculture

8/23/83   Agreement: Trade

5/84   Agreement: Peaceful utilization of nuclear power

11/8/85   Exchange of Notes: PRC grants Argentina $20 million credit line

11/8/85   Protocol: Economic cooperation

5/88   Agreement: Scientific and technical cooperation

5/88   Contract: Argentina set up a model farm in China

5/88   Pact: Animal quarantine

5/88   Agreement: Argentina sells 150,000 metric tons of sugar a year to China for the next 2 or 3 years

BARBADOS

6/80   Agreement: Economic and technical cooperation

1/31/85   Agreement: Technical assistance

6/6/86   Agreement: Economic and technical cooperation

5/11/90   Agreement: Economic and technical cooperation

BELIZE

4/9/87   Agreement: Economic and technical cooperation

BOLIVIA

5/20/86   Agreement: Technical and economic cooperation

10/88   Agreement: Economic cooperation

1/10/89   Agreement: Cooperation in producer price of antimony and other minerals

7/4/89   Contract: Agricultural loan to Bolivia

BRAZIL

8/21/61   Agreement: Trade and payments

6/23/75   Agreement: Representation of pharmaceuticals

1/7/78   Agreement: Trade

11/9/78   Agreement: Exchange Brazilian iron against Chinese oil

5/30/79   Agreement: Maritime transportation

3/25/82   Agreement: Scientific and technical cooperation

8/2/83   Protocol: Scientific cooperation in agriculture, fishery, animal husbandry

12/2/83	Protocol: Cooperation in energy
5/29/84	Agreement: Scientific and technical cooperation
5/29/84	Supplementary protocol to the agreement of Sino-Brazilian trade
10/11/84	Agreement: Peaceful utilization of nuclear power
10/31/84	Agreement: Chinese exports of crude oil to Brazil
11/1/85	Protocol: Iron and steel
11/1/85	Agreement: Economic and trade
11/1/85	Protocol: Geoscience cooperation
1/14/88	Agreement: Nuclear cooperation
7/6/88	Agreement: Cooperation in industrial technology and power industry
7/6/88	Protocol: Construction and launching of two satellites
7/6/88	Protocol: Cooperation in transportation
7/6/88	Agreement: Cooperation in preventing and treating epidemic disease
7/6/88	Agreement: Cooperation in traditional medicine
7/6/88	Agreement: Cooperation in transportation
5/18/90	Agreement: Economic and technical agreement
5/18/90	Protocol: Trade in iron ore, Brazil sends 2 million tons of iron ore per year to PRC

CHILE

10/23/52	Agreement: Trade
4/20/71	Agreement: Trade
8/19/71	Agreement: Telecommunication
6/8/71	Agreement: Economic and technical cooperation
6/8/72	Agreement: Exchange of commodities
6/8/72	Agreement: Trade and payments
6/8/72	Agreement: Long-term trade
1/26/73	Agreement: Maritime transportation
10/5/78	Accord: Sale of copper to PRC
4/14/79	Agreement (verbal): Cooperation in exploration of subsoil and exploitation of minerals and other resources discovered
5/9/79	Agreement: Scientific and cultural
6/4/85	Agreement: Import 100,000 tons of Chinese crude oil
3/17/89	Agreement: Nuclear cooperation
5/89	Agreement: Cooperation in seismology
5/19/89	Agreement: Chile imports trolley bus from China

6/19/89   Agreement: Joint cooperation
5/31/90   Memorandum: Cooperation in plant quarantine

COLOMBIA

7/17/81   Agreement: Trade
12/23/81   Agreement: Scientific and technical cooperation
10/25/85   Exchange of Notes: $5 million credit line between two countries
10/25/85   Agreement: Economic cooperation
10/88   Agreement: Trade

CUBA

12/31/59   Contract: Sugar
7/23/60   Agreement: Trade and payments
7/23/60   Agreement: Scientific and technical cooperation
11/30/60   Joint Communiqué: Trade talks
11/30/60   Agreement: Economic aid
11/30/60   Protocol: 1960 Trade
1/21/61   Contract: Sugar
1/21/61   Contract: Copper ore
3/8/61   Exchange of Letters: Payments (noncommercial)
10/21/61   Agreement: Telecommunications
10/21/61   Agreement: Postal services
1/27/62   Agreement: Radio and television cooperation
1/27/62   Protocol: Radio and television cooperation
4/24/62   Protocol: 1962 trade
8/23/62   Protocol: Scientific and technical cooperation
2/22/63   Protocol: 1963 trade and payments
2/22/63   Protocol: Delivery of goods
2/22/63   Agreement: Loan
2/26/63   Joint Communiqué: Economic talks
6/25/63   Agreement: Cooperation between Academies of Sciences
6/25/63   Agreement: Plan for cooperation between Academies of Sciences
11/14/63   Memorandum: 1964 trade
11/15/63   Protocol: Scientific and technical cooperation
1/15/64   Protocol: Exchange of goods and payments
8/11/64   Protocol: Economic aid
12/31/64   Agreement: Trade (1965–1970)
12/31/65   Protocol: 1965 Trade

12/31/65   Protocol: Delivery of sugar
12/31/65   Protocol: Delivery of goods
1/4/65   Joint Communiqué: Trade talks
5/21/65   Protocol: Science and technical cooperation
5/26/66   Protocol: 1966 Trade
5/27/66   Plan for cooperation between Academies of Sciences
7/6/66   Agreement: Scientific and technical cooperation
3/21/67   Protocol: 1967 trade
7/19/68   Exchange of Letters: Delivery of goods
2/14/69   Protocol: 1968 trade
6/29/70   Protocol: 1970 trade
5/11/71   Agreement: Trade
5/11/71   Agreement: Payments
5/11/71   Protocol: 1971 trade
3/4/72   Agreement: Loan
3/4/72   Protocol: 1972 trade
3/23/73   Protocol: 1973 trade
7/10/74   Protocol: 1974 trade
5/8/75   Protocol: 1975 trade
6/10/76   Agreement: Payments
6/10/76   Agreement: 1976 trade
4/15/77   Protocol: 1977 trade
3/18/78   Protocol: 1978 trade
1/17/79   Protocol: 1979 trade
3/3/80   Protocol: 1980 trade
12/20/80   Agreement: Trade for 1981–1985
12/20/80   Protocol: 1981 trade
12/20/80   Agreement: Payments
3/19/82   Protocol: 1982 trade
3/28/84   Protocol: 1984 trade
5/3/84   Agreement: Maritime transportation
3/1/86   Protocol: 1986 trade
4/21/89   Agreement: Financial cooperation
11/18/89   Agreement: Scientific and technological cooperation

ECUADOR

7/10/75   Agreement: Trade
7/10/75   Agreement: Establishment of commercial offices

2/22/82   Agreement: Sale of 10,000 tons of bananas to PRC
5/17/84   Agreement: Economic, technical, and scientific cooperation
7/7/87   Agreement: Economic and technical cooperation
6/17/88   Three economic cooperation contracts

GRENADA

7/16/87   Agreement: Economic and technical cooperation

GUYANA

11/14/71 Agreement: Import and export
11/14/71 Agreement: Developing trade, etc.
11/16/71 Press Communiqué: Trade talks
4/9/72   Agreement: Economic and technical cooperation
11/8/72   Protocol: Economic and technical cooperation
11/8/72   Agreement: Import and export
10/25/73 Agreement: Import and export
3/14/75   Agreement: Economic and technical cooperation
10/23/75 Agreement: Import and export
12/16/76 Certificate: Handing over a clay brick factory
1/19/79   Agreement: Interest-free commodity loan by PRC
5/15/86   Agreement: Rescheduling of Guyana's debts to PRC
4/27/87   Agreement: Economic and technical cooperation
7/31/88   Agreement: $5.5 million interest-free loan to Guyana
4/12/90   Agreement: Economic and technical cooperation

JAMAICA

2/12/74   Agreement: Economic and technical cooperation
9/26/76   Agreement: Trade
12/13/78 Agreement: Loan
10/15/86 Agreement: Joint venture on textiles

MEXICO

4/22/72   Exchange of Notes: Cultural, scientific, and technical exchanges
10/27/72 Press Communiqué: Trade talks
4/22/73   Agreement: Trade
9/9/75   Agreement: Scientific and technical cooperation
11/8/75   Protocol: Scientific and technical cooperation
11/25/76 Protocol: Scientific and technical cooperation

12/16/77   Protocol: Scientific and technical cooperation

10/27/78   Agreement: Tourism cooperation

2/27/79   Protocol on the fourth conference of the two nations' scientific and technical cooperation

9/15/83   Agreement: Scientific and technical cooperation

7/18/84   Agreement: Maritime transportation

7/18/84   Agreement: Trade

2/17/85   Agreement: Professionals exchange

10/6/87   Agreement: Bank of China and Mexican National Bank of Foreign Trade (Bancomex)

10/6/87   Agreement: Cooperation between the Mexican National Bank of Foreign Trade (Bancomex) and the China Council for the Promotion of International Trade (CCPIT)

1988   Agreement: Reciprocal credits for bilateral trade

NICARAGUA

8/19/80   Agreement: Sale of cotton to PRC in 1981

9/16/86   Agreement: Scientific and technical cooperation

9/16/86   Protocol: Trade

11/6/88   Protocol: Cooperation

PERU

4/28/71   Talk between PRC vice-minister of Foreign Trade and Peruvian scretary-general of the Foreign Ministry

6/15/71   Minutes: Fishery talks

6/16/71   Minutes: Trade talks

11/28/71   Agreement: Economic and technical cooperation

8/9/72   Agreement: Trade

3/21/81   Protocol: China provides small hydropower stations to Peru

7/11/87   Protocol: Peru sells $600 million minerals to PRC

11/2/88   Agreement: Economic and technical agreement

3/26/89   Agreement: Purchase of 500 China-made buses

9/14/90   Agreement: China provides a loan of $6.3 million, and grant for $0.63 million

SURINAM

5/23/86   Agreement: China provides interest-free loan of 15 million guilders (one U.S. dollar, 2.56 guilders)

TRINIDAD AND TOBAGO

7/26/84   Agreement: Trade

1987   Agreement: Trade, economic, scientific, and technical cooperation

URUGUAY

11/56   Contract: PRC purchase of wool from Uruguay

12/17/85   Joint Statement: Promotion of trade

2/3/88   Agreement: Trade

8/8/88   Agreement: Technology

11/7/88   Agreement: Governmental loan to Uruguay

5/26/90   Agreement: Cooperation on animal quarantine and sanitation

5/26/90   Memo: Plant quarantine

VENEZUELA

11/17/72   Minutes: Foreign trade talks

7/16/73   Agreement: Chinese purchases of Venezuelan chemical fertilizer

11/1/81   Agreement: Scientific and technical cooperation

11/1/85   Agreement: Trade

11/1/85   Protocol: Oil exploitation cooperation

10/1/88   Agreement: Hydrocarbons exploration

11/1/88   Agreement: Trade

Appendix B: Major Sino–Latin American Joint Ventures in Latin America

Argentina: China-Argentina Ocean Fishing and Aquatic Products Processing Co. **Partners:** Beijing Aquatic Products Corporation, Argentina Fisheries Co. Ltd.

Argentina: Codepeca (exploration of fish resources in Argentina). **Partners:** Harengus and China National Fisheries Corporation.

Barbados: Kingsboro International Holding Co. Ltd. (knitwear manufacturing and marketing). **Partners:** Jiangsu Provincial International Economic and Technical Cooperation Corporation, Kingsboro Holding Co.

Bolivia: Jinghua Industrial Development Corporation (mining). **Partners:** Beijing International Trust and Investment Corporation, Bolivian Huahua Co.

Brazil: Huaxi Timber Industrial and Trade Co. Ltd. (timber and plywood for export). **Partners:** China International Cooperation Wood Corp., The East Union of Manuas of Brazil.

Brazil: Siderúrgica ITA-MIN Ltd. (iron). **Partners:** China National Metals and Minerals Import and Export Corp., Brazilian ITA-MIN Siderúrgica Ltd.

Brazil: Latin America–Asia Transportation Agency Co. Ltd.(maritime transport). **Partners:** China National Metals and Minerals Import and Export Corp. and China Ocean Shipping Company (COSCO).

Brazil: CITIC-Brazil Trade Ltd. **Partners:** China International Trust & Investment Corporation (CITIC).

Brazil: International Satellite Corporation (sells space satellites, launch vehicles, earth stations, and antennas). **Partners:** China Great Wall Industrial Corporation and Avibrás.

Sources: South, 88 (February 1988), p. 21, FBIS, *Daily Report: People's Republic of China* and *Daily Report: Latin America*, 1980–1990.

Chile: Maquichina. (sales of Chinese machinery). **Partners:** China National Machinery and Equipment Import and Export Corporation.

Ecuador: China-Ecuador Medicine Production Corporation. **Partners:** Shanxi Provincial Medicine Import and Export Corp. Guayaquil.

Ecuador: Huashen Industry Co. Ltd. (produces candles). **Partners:** Sinochem Development Co. Ltd. **Partners:** Sinochem Development Co. Ltd., Cucana Company of Ecuador.

Ecuador: Camelia Co. Ltd. (prawn breeding and processing of aquatic products). **Partners:** China Tianjin Economic Development Corporation, Ecuador Camelia Co. Ltd.

Guyana: Guyana-China Fisheries Ltd. (ocean fishing and processing and marketing of aquatic products). **Partners:** China Agriculture Company, Guyana Fisheries Ltd. (GFL).

Mexico: Chinese Food Restaurant. **Partners:** China Sichuan Provincial Economic and Technical Cooperation Corporation, Mexican Loredo Group de Hotels.

Nicaragua: SINONICA (sells principally Chinese goods in Nicaragua and other Central American countries). **Partners:** China United Trading Corporation, Nicaraguan Immediate Service Company.

Panama: Engineering and Consulting Co. Ltd. **Partners:** China National Complete Equipment Export Corporation, Hong Kong Melihua Hotel Industry Company Ltd.

Panama: Panama Huaxi Timber Industrial and Trade Co. Ltd. (promotes sale of wood in Panama). **Partners:** China International Cooperation Wood Corporation.

Venezuela: Orinoc Industry Co. Ltd. (enamelware and other light industrial products). **Partners:** China Tianjing Light Industry Products Import and Export Corporation, Venezuelan Orinoc Company Ltd.

Selected Bibliography

Adie, W. A. C. "China, Russia and the Third World," *The China Quarterly*, no. 11 (July-September 1962), pp. 200–213.

Agrawal, Govind et al. *South-South Economic Cooperation: Problems and Prospects*, New Delhi: Radiant Publishers, 1987.

Alba, Victor. "The Chinese in Latin America," *The China Quarterly*, no. 5 (January-March 1961), pp. 53–61.

Alatorre, Sala. "Towards the Pacific," *Voice of Mexico*, no. 10 (June-July-August 1989), pp. 52–59.

Alvarez Uriarte, Miguel and Antonio N. Rubio Sánchez. "Intercambio comercial México-República Popular China," *Comercio Exterior*, 29, no. 4 (April 1979), pp. 487–96.

Atkins, G. Pope. *Latin America in the International Political System*. Boulder, Colo.: Westview, 1989.

Avramovic, Dragoslav, ed. *South-South Financial Cooperation*, London: Frances Pinter, 1983.

Bajitov, Rustem. "Pekín y su política en América Latina," *América Latina* (USSR), no. 4 (1979), pp. 35–51.

Bartke, Wolfgang, *The Economic Aid of the PR China to Developing and Socialist Countries*. 2d ed. London: K. G. Saur, 1989.

Berrios Rubén. *Economic Relations between Nicaragua and the Socialist Countries*. Working Papers, no. 166, Washington, D.C.: The Wilson Center, 1984.

Bizzozero, Lincoln, J.. "Toma de decisiones en politica exterior Uruguaya: El caso de las dos Chinas,"*Cuadernos del CLAEH: Revista Uruguaya de Ciencias Sociales*, 13, no. 4 (1988), pp. 71–82.

Bradley, Anita. *Trans-Pacific Relations of Latin America*. New York: Institute of Pacific Relations, 1942.

Breeze, Richard. "Peking's Sombrero Diplomacy," *Far Eastern Economic Review*, 109, no. 36 (August 29, 1980), pp. 28–29.

161

Bustamante, Romer Cornejo. "El comercio exterior de China con América Latina," *Comercio Exterior*, 35, no. 7 (July 1985), pp. 714–20.

Cai Weiquan. "Reflexiones sobre la cooperación económica y comercio entre China y América Latina hacia el futuro." Master's thesis, Centro de Investigación y Docencia Económicas, México, 1986.

Carl, Beveley May. *Economic Integration among Developing Nations: Law and Policy*. New York: Praeger, 1986.

Carlsson, Jerker, and Timothy M. Shaw, eds. *Newly Industrializing Countries and the Political Economy of South-South Relations*. New York: St. Martin's Press, 1988.

Caro, Isaac. *América Latina y el Caribe en el mundo militar*. Santiago, Chile: Facultad Latinoamericana de Ciencias Sociales (FLACSO), 1988.

Central Intelligence Agency. *China: International Trade Annual Statistical Supplement*. 1989.

Chai, Trong R., "Chinese Policy toward the Third World and the Superpowers in the UN General Assembly 1971–1977: A Voting Analysis," *International Organization*, 33 (Summer 1979), pp. 391–403.

Chang Rodríguez, Eugenio. "Chinese Labor Migration into Latin America in the Nineteenth Century," *Revista de Historia de América*, no. 46 (1958), pp. 375–99.

Chang Ya-chun. "On Current Chinese Communist Relations with the Third World," *Issues and Studies*, 18, no. 12 (November 1982).

Chaturvedi, T. N. *Transfer of Technology to Developing Countries: Need for Strengthening Cooperation*. New Delhi: Gitanjali Publishing House, 1982.

Chen Jie. "Trade between China and Latin American Countries," *China's Foreign Trade* (China), no. 4 (July-August 1980), p. 2.

Cheng Fei. "China's Trade with Latin America," *China's Foreign Trade* (China), no. 1 (January-February 1981), p. 62.

Cheng Zhiyun. "La amistad Chino-Mexicana: historia y realidad," *China Construye* (April 1987), pp. 42–45.

Chidzero, Bernard, and Altaf Gauhar. *Linking the South: The Route to Economic Cooperation*. London: Third World Foundation, 1986.

Cohen, Jerome Alan, ed. *The Dynamics of China's Foreign Relations*. Cambridge, Mass.: Harvard East Asian Research Center Monograph, 1970.

Committee of Overseas Chinese Economy in Ten Years. *Overseas Chinese Economy in Ten Years 1972–1981*, Taipei, 1981.

Copper, John Franklin. *China's Foreign Aid: An Instrument of Peking's Foreign Policy*. Lexington, Mass.: Lexington Books, 1976.

——. "The PRC and the Third World: Rhetoric versus Reality," *Issues and Studies*, 22, no. 3 (March 1986), pp. 107–125.

Cruz, Francisco Santiago. *La nao de China*. Mexico: Editorial Jus, S.A., 1962.

Dai, Shen-yu. "Peking and the Third World," *Current History*, 69, no. 408 (September 1975), pp. 75–79.

Davis, Harold Eugene, and Larman C. Wilson. *Latin American Foreign Policies: An Analysis*. Baltimore: Johns Hopkins University Press, 1975.

Deckers, Wolfgang. "Latin America: How the Chinese See the Region," *The Pacific Review*, 2, no. 3 (1989), pp. 246–51.

D'Ignazio, Frederick, and Daniel Tretiak. "Latin America: How Much Do the Chinese Care?" *Studies in Comparative Communism*, 5, no. 1 (Spring 1972), pp. 36–46.

Domínguez, Jorge I. *To Make a World Safe for Revolution: Cuba's Foreign Policy*. Cambridge, Mass.: Harvard University Press, 1989.

Editorial Board of the Almanac of China's Foreign Economic Relations and Trade. *Almanac of China's Foreign Economic Relations and Trade*. 1984–1988. Hong Kong: China Resources Trade Consultancy Co.

Edwards, Sebastian. "The United States and Foreign Competition in Latin America." In *The United States in the World Economy*, ed. Martin Feldstein, pp. 9–77. Chicago: University of Chicago Press, 1988.

Eguiguren, Sergio Valdivieso, and Eduardo Galvez Carvallo, eds. *Chile en la Cuenca del Pacífico: Experiencias y perspectivas comerciales en Asia y Oceania*. Santiago, Chile: Editorial Andrés Bello, 1989.

Erisman, H. Michael. "Conflicto Sino-Cubano: la lucha por influencia en el Tercer Mundo," *Areito*, 5, no. 19–20 (1979), pp. 12–19.

——. "Cuba's Struggle for Third World Leadership," *Caribbean Review*, 8, no. 3 (1979), pp. 8–12.

——. "Cuba's Long March: The Struggle for Third World Leadership," *SECOLAS Annuals*, no. 11 (1980), pp. 40–62.

Ferris, Elizabeth, ed. *Latin American Foreign Policies: Global and Regional Dimensions*, Boulder, Colo.: Westview Press, 1981.

"Fidel Castro on Trade between Cuba and China," *Prensa Latina*. In *Global Digest*, 3, no. 4 (1966).

First Division of the Third Department for Regional Affairs, Ministry of Foreign Economic Relations and Trade. "The Economic and Trade Relations between China and Latin American Countries." In *Almanac of China's Foreign Economic Relations and Trade*, pp. 434–35. Hong Kong: China Resources Trade Consultancy Co., 1989.

Fogarty, Carol H. "China's Economic Relations with the Third World." In U.S. Congress. Joint Economic Committee. *China: A Reassessment of the Economy*, 1975, pp. 730–37.

Ganer, William R. "The Sino-Soviet Ideological Struggle in Latin America," *Journal of Inter-American Studies and World Affairs*, 10, no. 2 (April 1968), pp. 244–55.

Garza Elizondo, Humberto. *China y el Tercer Mundo: teoría y práctica de la política exterior de Pequín, 1956–1966*. Mexico: El Colegio de México, 1975.

Gauhar, Altaf, ed. *Third World Strategy: Economic and Political Cohesion in the South*. New York: Praeger, 1985.

General Administration of Customs of the PRC. *China's Customs Statistics*, 1988–1989. Hong Kong: Economic Information & Agency.

Gene, Gregory. "Peking's Latin Beat," *Far Eastern Economic Review*, 73, no. 38 (September 18, 1971), pp. 56–58.

Gil Villegas, Francisco. "Opciones de politica exterior: México entre el Pacífico y el Atlántico," *Foro Internacional*, 29, no. 2 (October-December 1988), pp. 263–88.

Ginsburgs, George. "The Soviet View of Chinese Influence in Africa and Latin America." In *Soviet and Chinese Influence in the Third World*, ed. Alvin Z. Rubinstein, pp. 197–220. New York: Praeger, 1975.

Ginsburgs, George, and Arthur Stahnke. "Communist China Trade Relations with Latin America," *Asian Survey*, 10, no. 9 (September 1970), pp. 803–19.

Gitli, Eduardo. "Relaciones económicas comparadas con países socialistas. los casos de Argentina, Brasil e India," *Investigación Económica* 47, no. 179 (January-March 1987), pp. 255-76.

Gladue, E. Ted. *China's Perception of Global Politics*. Washington, D.C.: University Press of America, 1982.

Gómez, María Soledad. "Relaciones de China con América Latina y el Caribe durante 1985," *Documento de Trabajo*, no. 312, Programa FLACSO–Santiago de Chile, 1986.

——. "China: el nuevo socio de América Latina," *Separatas Cono Sur*, 3, no. 3 (July 1986), pp. 5-8.

Grunwald, Joseph, ed. *Latin America and World Economy: A Changing International Order*. Beverly Hills, Calif.: Sage Publications, 1978.

Guo Chongdao. "Relaciones comerciales entre China y América Latina," *China Construye* (November 1988), pp. 59-62.

Guo Chongdao and Li Zhixiang. "Sino-Latin American Economic and Trade Relations in Retrospect and Prospect," *Journal of Chinese People's Institute of Foreign Affairs*, (China), no. 8 (June 1988), pp. 100-109.

——. "China and Latin America to Develop Joint Ventures," *Intertrade*, April 1988, pp. 31-32.

Guo Hongshan. "Cooperación e intercambio entre China y Argentina," *China Construye* (August 1988), p. 19.

Halpern, A. M., ed. *Policies toward China: Views from Six Continents*. New York: McGraw-Hill, 1965.

Harris, Lillian Craig. *China's Foreign Policy toward the Third World*. New York: Praeger, 1985.

Harris, Lillian Craig, and Robert L. Worden, eds. *China and the Third World: Champion or Challenger?* Dover, Mass.: Auburn House, 1986.

Havrylyshyn, Oli. *Exports of Developing Countries: How Direction Affects Performance*. Washington, D.C.: World Bank Publication, 1988.

Heine, Irwin Millard. *China's Rise to Commercial Maritime Power*. New York: Greenwood Press, 1989.

Herrera, Felipe. "Latin America and the Third World." In *Latin America and World Economy: A Changing International Order*, ed. Joseph Grunwald, pp. 223-38. Beverly Hills: Sage Publications, 1978.

Hickey, Dennis Van Vranken. "Peking's Growing Political, Economic, and Military Ties with Latin America," *Issues and Studies*, 25, no. 6 (June 1989), pp. 113-31.

Hirst, Monica and Magdalena Segre. "La política exterior de Brasil en 1988: los avances posibiles." *Estudios Internacionales*, 22, no. 84, (October-December 1988), pp. 463-88.

Horvath, Janos. *Chinese Technology Transfer to the Third World: A Grants Economy Analysis*. New York: Praeger, 1976.

Huang Shikang. "La República Poplar China en la Cuenca del Pacífico." In *Chile en la Cuenca del Pacífico: Experiencias y perspectivas comerciales en Asia y Oceania*, ed. Sergio Valdivieso Eguiguren and Eduardo Galvez Carvallo. Santiago Chile: Editorial Andrés Bello, 1989, pp. 22-25.

Huang Ying. "China, Latin America Expand Technical Links," *Beijing Review*, 28, no. 43 (October 28, 1985), pp. 17-18.

Hsüeh, Chün-tu, ed. *Dimensions of China's Foreign Relations*. New York: Praeger, 1977.

———. "China and Latin America: A 'Last Frontier.'" In *China's Foreign Relations: New Perspectives*, ed. Chün-tu Hsüeh, pp. 130–43, New York: Praeger, 1982.

———. *China's Foreign Relations New Perspectives*. New York: Praeger, 1982.

Inter-American Development Bank (IDB). *Economic and Social Progress in Latin America*, Annual Report 1980–1990. Washington, D.C.: IDB.

International Monetary Fund (IMF). *Direction of Trade Statistics Yearbook*, 1980–1990. Washington, D.C.: IMF.

Johnson, Cecil. *Communist China & Latin America, 1959–1967*. New York: Columbia University Press, 1970.

———. "China and Latin America: New Ties and Tactics," *Problems of Communism*, 21, no. 4 (July-August 1972), pp. 53–66.

Joseph, William A. "China's Relations with Chile under Allende: A Case Study of Chinese Foreign Policy in Transition," *Studies in Comparative Communism*, 18, nos. 2 and 3 (Summer-Autumn 1985), pp. 125–50.

Joyaux, François. "La política China en Latinoamérica," *Mundo Nuevo*, 57–58 (March-April 1971), pp. 24–34.

Joxe, Alain. *El conflicto Chino-Soviético en América Latina*. Montevideo: Editorial Arca, 1974.

Kim, Samuel S. *China and the World: New Directions in Chinese Foreign Relations*, 2d ed. Boulder, Colo.: Westview Press, 1989.

———. "China and the Third World: In Search of a Peace and Development Line." In *China and the World: New Directions in Chinese Foreign Relations*, 2d ed., ed. Samuel S. Kim, pp. 148–80. Boulder, Colo.: Westview Press, 1989.

King, Chen. "Relations with Third World and 'Intermediate Zone' Countries." In *China: A Handbook*, ed. Yuan-li Wu, pp. 367–92. New York: Praeger, 1973.

Landau, George, Julio Feo, and Akio Hosona. "Latin America at a Crossroad: The Challenge to the Trilateral Countries," *The Triangle Papers*, 39 (August 1990).

Lee, Joseph. "Communist China's Latin American Policy," *Asian Survey*, 4, no. 11 (November 1964), pp. 1123–1134.

Lewis, W. Arthur. "The Slowing Down of the Engine of Growth," *American Economic Review*, 70, no. 1 (1980), pp. 555–64.

Li He. "Sino-Latin American Economic Relations: Recent Trends and Future Prospects," *Latin American Occasional Papers Series at the University of Massachusetts*, no. 25. University of Massachusetts at Amherst, 1990.

———. "Chinese Immigrants in Peru," *Ibero Americana Nordic Journal of Latin American Studies* (Stockholm, Sweden), 20, no. 2 (1990), pp. 3–16.

Luo Liecheng. "Development of Economic and Trade Relations between China and Latin American Countries," *Latin meizhou chunkan* (Latin American Review), no. 3 (1985), pp. 47–51.

———. "Improve Friendship and Develop Jointly: Accompany Premier Zhao's Visit to Four Latin American Countries," *China's Foreign Trade* (China), April 1986.

Meng Xianchen. "Entrenadores Chinos en América Latina," *China Construye*, May 1987, pp. 46–48.

Menon, B. P. *Bridges across the South: Technical Cooperation among Developing Countries*. New York: Pergamon Press, 1980.

Ming Chen-hua. *Penetration of Latin America by the Chinese Communists*, Joint Publications Research Service publication no. 3498. New York: JPRS, 1959.

Muñoz, Heraldo, and Joseph S. Tulchin, eds. *Latin American Nations in World Politics: Comparative Perspectives*. Boulder, Colo.: Westview Press, 1984.

Nai Ruenn Chen. *China's Economy and Foreign Trade, 1979–81*. U.S. Department of Commerce, 1982.

——. and Jeffery Lee, *China's Economy and Foreign Trade, 1981–85*. U.S. Department of Commerce, 1986.

Oppenheimer, Andrés. "La ofensiva China," *América Economía*, 1, no. 6 (1987), pp. 26–27.

Organization for Economic Co-operation and Development (OECD). *The Aid Program of China*. Paris: Organization for Economic Co-operation and Development, 1987.

Organization of American States (OAS). Special Consultative Committee on Security. *Against the Subversive Action of International Communism: Analysis of the Second Congress of the Young Communist League (UJC) in Cuba. The Policy of Communist China in Latin America*. Washington, D.C.: OAS, 1972.

Paine, Suzanne. "China's Economic Relations with Less Developed Countries: 1950–1976." In *Economic Relations between Socialist Countries and the Third World*, ed. Deepak Nayyar, pp. 208–61. London: Macmillan Press, 1977.

Passin, Herbert. *China's Cultural Diplomacy*. New York: Frederick A. Praeger, 1963.

Pavlic, Breda, et al. *The Challenges of South-South Cooperation*. Boulder, Colo.: Westview Press, 1983.

PRC State Statistical Bureau. *China's Statistics Yearbook*. 1985–1988.

——. *China Trade and Price Statistics*. 2d ed. Hong Kong: Oxford University Press, 1987.

Ratliff, William. "Chinese Communist Cultural Diplomacy toward Latin America, 1949–1960," *Hispanic American Historical Review*, 49, no. 1 (February 1969), pp. 53–79.

——. "Communist China and Latin America, 1949–1972," *Asian Survey*, 12, no. 10 (October 1972), pp. 846–63.

Rensburg, W. C. J. van, ed. *Strategic Minerals Vol. 1, Major Mineral-Exporting Regions of the World: Issues and Strategies*. Englewood Cliffs, N.J.: Prentice-Hall, 1986.

Riedel, James. "Trade as the Engine of Growth in Developing Countries, Revisited," *The Economic Journal*, 94 (March 1984), pp. 56–73.

Robinson, Thomas W. "Restructuring Chinese Foreign Policy, 1959–76: Three Episodes." In *Why Nations Realign: Foreign Policy Restructuring in the Postwar World*, ed. K. J. Holsti, pp. 134–71. London: George Allen & Unwin, 1982.

Roch, Eugenio Anguiano. "China: la política de cooperación con el Tercer Mundo," *Estudios de Asia y Africa*, 15, no. 3 (1980), pp. 515–71.

Rodríguez, José H. "Brazil and China: The Varying Fortunes of Independent Diplomacy." In *Policies toward China: Views from Six Continents*, ed. A. M. Halpern, pp. 457–76. New York: MacGraw-Hill, 1965.

Rodríguez Sacoto, Manuel. ¿*Relaciones con Pekín*? Quayaquil, Ecuador: Casa de La Cultura Ecuatoriana, Núcleo del Guayas, 1973.

Roldán, Eduardo. "La República Popular China y México," *El Universal*, August 13, 1972.

——. "China y América Latina," *Cuadernos Americanos*, 226, no. 5 (September-October 1979), pp. 7–22.

Ruilova, Leonardo. *China Popular en América Latina*. Quito: Instituto Latinoamericano de Investigaciones Sociales, 1978.

Salinas Chavez, Antonio. "La Cuenca del Pacífico: Retos y posibilidades para la economía," *Comercio Exterior*, 39, no. 1 (January 1989), pp. 11–22.

Segundo Seminario de Comercio entre México y China. *Ponencias del segundo seminario de comercio entre México y China* (October 1988). Ciudad de México.

Sha Ding, et al. *Zhongguo he ladinmeizhou guanxi jianshi* (Brief History of Sino-Latin American Relations). Zhenzhou, China: Henan People's Publishing House, 1987.

——. "Chinos de ultramar en América Latina," *China Construye* (February 1987), pp. 56–59.

Sienianwski, Michael. "South America Giant Seeks Stronger Links with Asia," *Asian Business*, November 1985, pp. 30–32.

Su Yuxiang. "Development of Economic and Trade Cooperation between China and Mexico," *China's Foreign Trade* (China), May 1987.

Suárez, Andrés. "Castro between Moscow and Peking," *Problems of Communism*, 12, no. 5 (September-October 1963), pp. 18–26.

Suk, Chin Ha. *Chinese and Soviet Interest in Chile: 1949–Present: A Comparative Study*. Ph.D. diss., George Washington University, 1973.

——. "The PRC's Influence in Latin America (1949–1973): A Reassessment," *Political Studies Review: The Journal of the Association of Korean Political Scientists in North America*, no. 1 (1985), pp. 107–22.

Theberge, James D. "Soviet, East European, and Chinese Communist Trade and Aid with Latin America: Scope and Trends." In *Latin America's New Internationalism: The End of Hemispheric Isolation*, ed. Roger W. Fontaine and James Theberge, pp. 157–71. New York: Praeger, 1976.

Thomas, Harmon C. *A Study of Trade among Developing Countries, 1950–1980: An Appraisal of the Emerging Pattern*. Amsterdam, New York: North-Holland, 1988.

Tretiak, Daniel. *Perspectives on Cuba's Relations with the Communist System: The Politics of a Communist Independent: 1959–1969*. Ph.D. diss., Stanford University, 1974.

——. "China's Latin American Trade," *Far Eastern Economic Review*, 41, no. 4 (July 25, 1963), pp. 221–24.

——. "Peking and Mexico," *Far Eastern Economic Review*, 43, no. 5 (January 30, 1964), pp. 200–202.

——. "Mexican Traders," *Far Eastern Economic Review*, 44, no. 9 (May 28, 1964), p. 415.

——. "Latin America: The Chinese Drive," *Contemporary Review*, 205, no. 1186 (November 1964), pp. 571–76.

——. "China's Tough Brazil Nut," *Far Eastern Economic Review*, 48, no. 3 (April 15, 1965), pp. 122–29.

——. "China and Latin America: An Ebbing Tide in Trans-Pacific Maoism," *Current Scene*, 4, no. 5 (March 1, 1966) pp. 1–12. Reprinted in *The Foreign Policy of China,*, ed. K. C. Chen. Roseland, N.J.: East-West, 1972.

——— . "Cuba and the Soviet Union: The Growing Accommodation," Rand Memoranda, RM–4935–PR (July 1966).

——— . "China's Relations with Latin America, Revolutionary Theory in a Distant Milieu." In *The Dynamics of China's Foreign Relations*, ed. Cohen Jerome Alen, pp. 88–106. Cambridge, Mass.: Harvard East Asian Research Center, Harvard University, 1970.

Ulloa Elías, Manuel. *La era del Pacífico*. Lima, Peru: Ministero de Economía Finanzas y Comercios, Oficina de Comunicaciones, 1983.

United Nations. *Salient Features of Economic Cooperation among Developing Countries*. 1977.

——— . *Commodity Trade Statistics*, 1985–1989.

United Nations Conferences on Trade and Development (UNCTAD). *Cooperative Exchanges of Skills among Developing Countries*. 1978.

——— . *Commodity Yearbook*. 1985–1989.

United Nations Development Program (UNDP). *Cooperation South*, 1988–1990.

United Nations Economic Commission for Latin America and the Caribbean (ECLAC). *International Economic Relations and Regional Co-operation in Latin America and the Caribbean*, Santiago, Chile, 1987.

United Nations Educational, Scientific and Cultural Organization (UNESCO). *Statistics Yearbook UNESCO*. 1985–1989.

United States Congress. Senate. Committee on the Judiciary. Subcommittee to Investigate the Administration of the Internal Security Act and Other Internal Security Laws. *Red Chinese Infiltration into Latin America*. Hearing, 89th Congress, 1st sess. (August 4, 1965). Washington, D.C.: U.S. GPO.

Varas, Augusto, ed. *Soviet-Latin American Relations in the 1980s*. Boulder, Colo.: Westview Press, 1987.

Veliz, Claudio. "Latin America's Opening to the Pacific." In *Latin America and World Economy: A Changing International Order*, ed. Joseph Grunwald, pp. 121–32. Beverly Hills: Sage Publications, 1978.

Vera, Luis Roberto. "Relaciones internacionales de China imperial," *Comunidad*, 10, no. 52 (May 1975), pp. 276–85.

Vicuña F., Carlos, and Luis Soto M. "Negociación y establecimiento de una joint venture en la República Popular China: la experiencia de Madeco y Codelco." In *Chile en la Cuenca del Pacífico: Experiencias y perspectivas comerciales en Asia y Oceania*, ed. Sergio Valdivieso Eguiguren and Eduardo Galvez Carvallo, Santiago, Chile: Editorial Andreés Bello, 1989.

Vicuña, Francisco Orrego. "Pacific Co-operation: The View from Latin America," *Pacific Review*, 2, no. 1 (1989), pp. 57–67.

Vidali Carbajal, Carlos. "El mercado de la República Popular China: perspectivas generals y posibilidades para México," *Comercio Exterior*, 21, no. 11 (1971), pp. 1000–1009.

Villannueva, Javier. "China: las reformas económicas de la última década," Techint: *Boletin Informativo* (Argentina), no. 252 (1986), pp. 3–44.

Wang, Chien-hsun. *Changes in Relations between Peiping and Latin American Countries*. Taipei: World Anti-Communist League, China Chapter, 1973.

——— . "Communist China's Relations with Latin America," *Issues and Studies*, 17, no. 3 (March 1981).

Wang, Lorenzo, Y. C. "Red China's Activities in Latin America," *Asian Outlook*, 8, no. 3 (March 1973).

Wang Xuewen and Chen Hong. "The Development of Chinese Joint Ventures in Latin American Region," *China's Foreign Trade*, October 1987, pp. 14–15.

Wang Yu San. "People's Republic of China in Latin America," *Asian Profile*, 6, no. 4 (August 1978), pp. 305–16.

——. *The China Question: Essays on Current Relations between Mainland China and Taiwan*. New York: Praeger, 1985.

——. "Peking's Latin American Policy: An Exercise in Pragmatism," *Issues and Studies*, 23, no. 5 (May 1987), pp. 122–45.

——. "The Republic of China's Relations with Latin America." In *Foreign Policy of the Republic of China on Taiwan: An Unorthodox Approach*, ed. Wang Yu San. New York: Praeger, 1990.

Wayne, A. Selcer. *Brazil's Multilateral Relations: between First and Third Worlds*. Boulder, Colo.: Westview Press, 1978.

Wei Yuming. "Boosting Sino-Latin American Trade Relations," *Beijing Review*, 28, no. 43 (October 28, 1985), pp. 15–17.

Weininger, Michael A. "People's Republic of China Latin American Trade Composition and Direction of Trade, 1965–1977." In *Change and Perspective in Latin America: Proceedings of the 1982 Meeting of the Rocky Mountain Council in Latin American Studies, 1982*, ed. Richard Bath, pp. 51–59. El Paso: University of Texas at El Paso, Center for Inter-American and Border Studies, 1982.

Wionczek, Miguel S. "The Pacific Market for Capital, Technology and Information and its Possible Opening in Latin America," *Journal of Common Market Studies*, 10, no. 1 (September 1971), pp. 78–95.

——. "Latin America and the Pacific Regions: Trade, Investment and Technology Issues." In *Latin America's New Internationalism: The End of Hemispheric Isolation*, eds. Roger W. Fontaine and James Theberge, pp. 56–72. New York: Praeger, 1976.

——. "Pacific Trade and Development Cooperation with Latin America," *Asia Pacific Community*, no. 9 (Spring 1980), pp. 21–41.

Woodward, Kim. *The International Energy Relations of China*. Stanford, Calif.: Stanford University Press, 1980.

Worden, Robert L. "China's Foreign Relations with Latin America." In *Dimensions of China's Foreign Relations*, ed. Chün-tu Hsüeh, pp. 191–231. New York: Praeger, 1977.

——. "China's Balancing Act: Cancun, the Third World, Latin America," *Asian Survey*, 23 (May 1983), pp. 619–36.

Worden, Robert L., et al., eds. *China: A Country Study*. 4th ed. Washington, D.C.: U.S. GPO, 1988.

World Bank. *World Development Report 1990*. New York: Oxford University Press, 1990.

Wu Guoping. "La apertura económica de China y el comercio exterior de América Latina." Master's thesis, Centro de Investigación y Docencia Económicas, México, 1986.

Xu Shicheng. "Las relaciones entre China y América Latina en el umbral de los noventa," *Cono Sur*, 8, no. 3 (May-June 1990), pp. 7–10.

Yeh, Hsiang-chih. *Chung Kung Tui Wai Kuan Hsi Lun Ts'ung* (On China's Foreign Relations). Taipei: Zheng Zhong She, 1977.

Zhang Husheng. "Broad Future of Unity and Cooperation between China and Latin America," *Latin meizhou chunkan* (Latin American Review), 1984, no. 4, pp. 11–19.

———. and Xu Shicheng. "Broad Prospects of South-South Cooperation between China and Latin America," *Latin meizhou chunkan* (Latin American Review), 1986, no. 3, pp. 1–8.

Zhang Sengen and Wang Ningkun. "Latin American Studies in the People's Republic of China: Current and Future Prospects." *Latin meizhou yanju* (Latin American Research Review), 23, no. 1 (1988), pp. 123–32.

Zhang Weimin. "China to Co-operate with Latin America in Food Industry," *Cooperation South*, 1989, no. 2, pp. 12–13.

Zhdánov-Lutsenko, Nikolái. "América Latina, parte del Pacífico," *América Latina* (USSR), no. 21 (January 1988), pp. 4–9, and no. 122, (February 1988), pp. 19–28.

Zhong He. "Development of Friendly Relations between China and Latin America," *International Studies* (China), 1984, no. 1, pp. 21–25.

Index

About the Author

HE LI is an Instructor of Economics at Austin Community College. He has worked as a Research Associate at the Institute of Latin American Studies of the Chinese Academy of Social Sciences, Beijing, and at the University of Texas at Austin. He holds an M.A. from the Chinese Academy of Social Sciences and a Ph.D. from the University of Texas at Austin.

Dr. Li's articles on Chinese foreign relations and on the Latin American economy have been published in numerous journals in both Chinese and English.